796.
334
FOST

RED

G000149085

Fighting for
HAKEEM

Fighting for
HAKEEM

How people power challenged two monarchies,
a military junta and football's
governing body FIFA ... and won.

CRAIG FOSTER

with Alex Engel-Mallon

hachette
AUSTRALIA

Some of the names of people in this book have been changed to protect their privacy.
Photos are from the collections of the authors and Hakeem al-Araibi unless otherwise noted.

hachette
AUSTRALIA

Published in Australia and New Zealand in 2019
by Hachette Australia
(an imprint of Hachette Australia Pty Limited)
Level 17, 207 Kent Street, Sydney NSW 2000
www.hachette.com.au

10 9 8 7 6 5 4 3 2 1

Copyright © Total Football Pty Ltd 2019

This book is copyright. Apart from any fair dealing for the purposes of private study, research, criticism
or review permitted under the *Copyright Act 1968*, no part may be stored or reproduced by any process
without prior written permission.
Enquiries should be made to the publisher.

A catalogue record for this
book is available from the
National Library of Australia

NATIONAL
LIBRARY
OF AUSTRALIA

ISBN: 978 0 7336 4316 3 (paperback)

Cover design by Luke Causby/Blue Cork
Cover images courtesy James van Leeuwen and AAP
Text design by Bookhouse, Sydney
Typeset in 12/18 pt Sabon LT Std by Bookhouse, Sydney
Printed and bound in Australia by McPherson's Printing Group

MIX
Paper from
responsible sources
FSC® C001695

The paper this book is printed on is certified against the
Forest Stewardship Council® Standards. McPherson's Printing
Group holds FSC® chain of custody certification SA-COC-005379.
FSC® promotes environmentally responsible, socially beneficial
and economically viable management of the world's forests.

For my amazing wife Lara, who held everything together.

*To my three beautiful children. Thanks for your
support of each other as Dad ran off around the world
to help a kid we didn't know. One day, I hope you
will do the same for vulnerable people everywhere.*

*For those whose names do not appear in
these pages who deserve to be acknowledged,
but whose identities I've had to protect.*

For all those seeking safety and refuge in our world.

And for my younger brother Hakeem, most of all.

FOREWORD
by Anthony LaPaglia

This book is a must-read for football fans and people interested in creating positive social change the world over. It redefines the way we think about sport and human rights, and reveals just how powerful communities, athletes and sports fans can be when they rally behind a positive cause.

I love football and have a deep appreciation for what it has to offer the communities and nations that celebrate it. From my time as a goalkeeper in Australia's National Soccer League in Adelaide back in the 1980s, through to my ownership of A-League club Sydney FC, I have been lucky enough to experience first-hand the dedication of the game's players, the passion of its fans, and the crucial responsibilities of its governance.

While my acting career has since taken me far from the country of my birth to the United States, Hollywood and beyond, my passion for and knowledge of the game has only deepened throughout my life. Similarly, my interest in what the game can do to strengthen communities and human rights has also grown. So when Craig Foster reconnected in early 2019 and asked me to support the campaign to free refugee footballer Hakeem al-Araibi, I was keen to engage. At the time, I was in the middle of shooting my latest feature film *Below* in Western Australia. The #SaveHakeem campaign had already hit the US news and my social media was lighting up with updates. Craig's request to me was simple – could I use my public profile to help raise awareness about this young man's case?

I've long respected Craig as both an ex-player and broadcaster and knew of his passion for social justice and human rights issues, so I was not surprised by his taking the lead in freeing Hakeem. It's one of many extensions of his passion for the World Game. When I saw the incredible drive and commitment Craig had concerning Hakeem's dire circumstances, it was unquestionable that I join his effort to rectify this pending atrocity in any way I could. I was able to use my football contacts from around the world to ask for support. The response was overwhelmingly positive.

As you will soon discover, mine was neither the first nor last door that Craig would knock on to get involved in this young man's fight for freedom. His efforts to connect and amplify the work of human rights organisations, the football community, political leaders and everyday individuals are nothing short of astounding. In this incredible, behind-the-scenes account, you will discover just how much was put on the line for this young man. Craig's actions, alongside the disparate but committed web of individuals who each played their crucial part, are an inspiration to us all – to do what we can, with whatever we have, for what is right. Craig Foster represents everything that is good about the global game and community. Solidarity. His tireless efforts will not be forgotten. I'm proud to be associated with not only Craig, but with the countless others who shared in his fight and vision.

Anthony LaPaglia

CONTENTS

Football is not a sport and it's more even than a religion. It's a culture. Like all cultures, football has its rituals, its customs, its deities, its language, its music, its respect for its history, its sense of identity and its urge to celebrate and demonstrate it. Football's ultimate source of strength is its fans, the global football nation, billions strong, who live and breathe the game every minute of their lives and express through it a sense of their belonging . . .

The mission was not to simply build or promote football, but rather to enrich Australia through the medium of football. To bring our country to being a true citizen of the world and converse with it in the only true universal language.

Laszlo Urge (Les Murray),
'Mr Football' Australia, 1945–2017[1]

THE WILL OF LIFE
If the people will to live
Providence is destined to favourably respond
And night is destined to fold
And the chains are certain to be broken
And he who has not embraced the love of life
Will evaporate in its atmosphere and disappear

Abu al-Qasim al-Shabbi, Tunisian poet, 1909–1934[2]

INTRODUCTION

Fighting for Hakeem is a story about how everyday people can change the world. At its heart is the ordeal faced by a courageous young man, Hakeem al-Araibi, which touched the hearts of tens of millions of people. Hakeem is the hero of this story, along with all those fighting against tyranny. It was Hakeem who bravely spoke out on behalf of the people of Bahrain for democracy and justice. It was Hakeem who, having survived detention and torture, made one of life's hardest decisions – to leave his home, his loved ones and all that he knew – to find refuge and secure his freedom.

While this book recounts the story of a momentous global campaign to help one young man regain his freedom, it also provides an opportunity to accentuate broader issues that his case exemplifies. The corrupting influence of money and power in sports governance, the audacity of monarchies and governments to disregard international law, the escalating plight of displaced people globally, Australia's mistreatment of people seeking refuge and the power of people coming together to confront injustice.

Capturing the full story of this campaign is important because this book also presents a vision for the world game, and sport more broadly, as a force for good in our world. It stands as evidence that football can serve as a great unifier and a champion of universal human rights, if its players and fans wish it to be so. I hope this story will inspire today's generation of sport stars to use their platform for social justice; for athletes everywhere to commit to making the world a better place. As #SaveHakeem demonstrated, sport has this unique power and possibility.

Ultimately, this story has a glorious ending, but that is too often not the case. In 2019, millions of human beings have no rights, are persecuted, sold as slaves, tortured and jailed for speaking up against injustice.

So, while we won an important victory and can take a moment to celebrate, we must also use the #SaveHakeem campaign as inspiration going forward. To ensure that sport, governments and all institutions are held accountable for improving access to human rights, and so that the next 'Hakeem' will not need a global campaign to realise their freedom.

This is also my thanks to all of you, no matter how large or small your contribution. It is the story of how we all did something special, together. I want you to know how powerful you are, that I couldn't have done it without you, and to introduce you to the team of brilliant practitioners behind the public face: those who fought so hard and took their own professional risks. No one could have done it alone, as you will see in these pages – the forces restraining Hakeem were too powerful, too influential and went right to the very top of the countries involved, and of sport.

The story is written from my perspective. Others may tell it differently. I hope that, one day, Hakeem will be free to tell his story in his own words, without fear of retribution for his loved ones in Bahrain. Thanks to millions of people around the world, he now has a chance to write many more wonderful chapters of his young life. This book is for him and his extraordinary wife, Nani, who was the strength of the movement that saved his life.

In the end, the question I still get asked most often is what, or who, made the decisive difference in the campaign? You did, I tell them. You created the conditions and pressure for organisations and governments to act. Without a coordin-ated, sustained public outcry, no one could have protected him, nor would they have gone to the extraordinary lengths required to do so.

People power is truly an unstoppable force, and together we *can* create a better world. One Hakeem at a time.

Chapter 1

A HONEYMOON ARRESTED

Most Australians would have been fast asleep in their beds at 1 am on Wednesday, 28 November 2018, when more than 10 Thai immigration officials arrested Hakeem al-Araibi as he disembarked Jetstar flight JQ29 in Bangkok. It was 8.50 pm local time, and Hakeem and his young wife, Nani, had just landed at Bangkok's Suvarnabhumi airport.

It had been a relatively uneventful flight from Melbourne on the Boeing 787. Nani had slept for most of the roughly nine-hour trip. Hakeem watched two American movies, and at some point ordered an overpriced salted caramel muffin and soft drink. They were ecstatic to be heading on holidays. It was their honeymoon, and the first time they had ever travelled overseas together. Hakeem recalls, a little sheepishly, that they were even wearing similar outfits on the plane. 'We both had black t-shirts and jeans on, you know, like the way parents sometimes dress children matching . . .

it sounds silly, I know, but we were just really excited to be travelling together.'

Nani and Hakeem were married in a small ceremony on 25 February 2017 in Melbourne's north. She wore a dress, he wore a suit. They had some close friends as witnesses and took photos outside in the front garden. Neither of them had any family members living in Australia, so it was a quiet affair. An overseas honeymoon wasn't possible back then, as Hakeem was still on a bridging visa that didn't allow him to re-enter Australia if he travelled anywhere.[1] In late 2017, the Australian Government granted him a permanent protection visa, which meant that Hakeem and Nani could apply for a United Nations Australian travel document and travel safely overseas. So they had started making plans and saving hard. At the time Hakeem was earning an income playing for National Premier League clubs in Victoria, including the Preston Lions and then Pascoe Vale, in Melbourne's north-west. Because they couldn't travel during the football season, they settled on November 2018 for the much-anticipated holiday.

This wasn't the first time Hakeem had been to Thailand. He had travelled there a few years prior to play in a tournament as a member of Bahrain's national football team. He visited again in 2014 while living briefly in Malaysia. He and some mates managed to get cheap, last-minute flights to Phuket where they enjoyed three relaxing days of delicious food, tropical temperatures and white-sand beaches. 'I have beautiful memories of Patong Beach,' he recalls. 'I went every day . . . walking and running in the morning time, swimming and playing football on the beach.' He had travelled there on his Bahraini passport, and experienced no problems whatsoever getting in or out of the country. This second visit is important to note because the next time Hakeem would travel to Thailand, his experience would be markedly different. 'I wanted Nani to see how beautiful it was,' he says. Which is why, just four years later, they had decided to head to Thailand for their honeymoon.

A professional footballer in Bahrain, Hakeem had spent years playing in Bahrain's top divisions and travelling with the country's national squads. In 2014 he was forced to flee the country as a political dissident and made his way to Australia. In 2018, Bahrain issued an international warrant for Hakeem's arrest, but by that time he had been granted refugee status by Australia and been issued his new United Nations travel document[2] that would allow him to travel safely without relying on his Bahraini passport.

Despite having this new document, which looks much like a regular Australian passport, Hakeem didn't qualify for the 30-day tourist visa that Australian citizens automatically receive upon arrival in Thailand. So instead he applied for a three-month tourist visa, which the Thai authorities granted him on his 25th birthday on 7 November 2018. This date and document are critical to note for reasons we'll get to later, but for now let's stick with Hakeem, Nani and their excitement about their impending honeymoon plans.

They were to have a seven-day trip, staying the first night in Bangkok before travelling down to Phuket, where they had a modest resort booked near Surin Beach. Their plan was to spend a few days relaxing on some of Thailand's most popular beaches, swimming and enjoying the famously good weather, then to head back to Bangkok on 1 December to enjoy the city until their flight home on 4 December. They thought they'd visit Bangkok's famous floating markets, Buddhist temples, and perhaps most exciting of all, the Vana Nava Water Jungle park. 'It had a four-star rating on TripAdvisor from 1327 reviews,' Hakeem says, 'and Nani, she really loves water slides!'

On Tuesday, 27 November 2018, they arrived at Melbourne's Tullamarine airport with their luggage and headed through immigration at 12.08 pm, in plenty of time for their 2.35 pm flight departure. Hakeem recalls that he was stopped when the automatic SmartGate scanner didn't accept his travel document. 'It was my first time travelling with it and the scanning machine didn't understand it, so I was asked to go to the counter. The man there called somewhere to ask for details, but I just thought everything was normal. I thought it made sense that the machine didn't understand the passport, because it was new.'

We now know that this phone call Hakeem remembers was from an Australian Border Force officer to the Australian Federal Police National Central Bureau, which is Australia's contact point for Interpol – the International Criminal Police Organisation. The officer made the call because the system had alerted him to the fact that Hakeem's name was on something called a Central Movements Alert List, administered by Border Force. They had added his name to this list after receiving an Interpol red notice, published by Bahrain on 8 November 2018.[3] The Border Force officer informed the Federal Police official on the other end of the phone about the alert and requested advice as to whether he should prevent Hakeem from boarding his flight. The official responded that Australia didn't have a warrant to detain or prevent Hakeem or his wife from travelling, so the officer was free to let him through. He put down the phone and handed the travel document back to Hakeem, completely oblivious to the 22 characters emblazoned on the front cover. Twenty-two critical letters and numbers that obligated Australia to protect Hakeem from Bahraini authorities, from Interpol red notices and from any other country who sought to harm him: 'Convention of 28 July 1951'.

Hakeem placed the document safely back into his bag and, after putting their carry-on through security, he and Nani walked off hand in hand to browse the duty-free shops. They had no idea that their planned holiday of beaches, temples and water parks in the self-professed Land of Smiles was about to turn into a 77-day nightmare. A few short hours later, as they boarded their flight, wrapped in the contented happiness of each other's company, they were completely unaware of the political maelstrom awaiting them. A battle that would see governments, monarchies, global sporting goliaths and millions of people around the world lock horns in what would become a fight for their very lives.

•

I had never heard of or met Hakeem al-Araibi prior to learning about his arrest and subsequent imprisonment in early December 2018. Many people have asked me why, then, did I come to care so much about him? The answer to this question lies partly in my fundamental beliefs about what football, its players and sport have to offer the world.

I was about to turn 50, exactly double Hakeem's age, and was acutely aware of the opportunities I'd been given in my life. Hakeem had spoken out for democracy for his people. And yet while I took that right for granted, he'd been tortured for it and forced into the disorienting, uncertain and too often harrowing world of those who must seek asylum in a country foreign to them. He had a young wife, a life of sports stardom ahead of him. He should have been training hard, learning, making his way in this great game that provides limitless opportunity. Instead, he was facing a return to a country where he had no rights, no hope, and a future without his wife; of torture or worse. Why did I, and countless other players around the world, have bountiful lives, careers to recall fondly and opportunities to transfer that goodwill into other fields of life while this young man faced these unjust challenges? What was the difference?

I have always believed that football players should support each other, give back to the community and advocate for social justice through sport. I used my time as CEO and Chairman of the players' union in Australia, Professional Footballers Australia (PFA), to this end through advocacy for gender equality, Indigenous rights, refugees and the homeless. I have spent decades assisting refugee and Indigenous kids through sporting and social programs, lending my platform and voice to do everything within my power to make a positive difference.

Australian football's journey reflects that of the nation from its British roots (after more than 60,000 years of cultural longevity from our First Nations peoples prior to dispossession) through immigration, including refugees and multiculturalism. This is why the contribution of immigrants and people seeking refuge is a natural focus for the football community, part of our DNA. Further, I also had the pleasure of working in broadcasting for fifteen years alongside one of the most prominent, celebrated and respected refugees in Australia's history, Les Murray.[4] I am also a Refugee Ambassador for Amnesty International Australia, using my profile and networks to try and improve the rights and protections afforded people in desperate need of refuge. So Hakeem was right in the epicentre of many causes that I believe in deeply.

I have also experienced first-hand the power of football to transform lives and bring people together. To me, there is just no denying that football truly is the 'world game'. It is played by more than 250 million people all over the globe, and adored by hundreds of millions more. From Brazil to Italy, from Indonesia to Senegal, it is a common language that binds people, no matter their gender, culture, race or religion. At a time when Australia, like many countries, appears at a critical juncture in relation to our immigration policies and perceptions of multiculturalism and diversity – and in the context of a deeply concerning rise of right-wing extremism, division and hate around the world – I believe that football can be a shining light. And I knew it would have to be, for Hakeem.

Chapter 2

HAKEEM'S STORY

To understand how and why Hakeem al-Araibi's name came to be on an Australian Border Force alert list, you need to understand Hakeem's personal story. A story which sits on the colourful and complex backdrop of Bahrain's political history. When I first became involved in the campaign, I knew little about the socio-political dimensions of Bahraini society. From my perspective, it was a Middle Eastern nation ruled by a royal elite that was growing in influence in international football alongside its regional allies, the UAE and Saudi Arabia, whether through rapidly expanding investment in clubs and commercial partnerships or through key people in influential positions in football's governing body, including the International Federation of Association Football (FIFA) and the Asian Football Confederation (AFC). I expect many people who became involved in the #SaveHakeem campaign, particularly in Australia, were in a similar position at the outset in terms of their knowledge about Hakeem's country of birth.

It is only in turning a looking-glass to some key events in Bahrain's recent history that we can get to the heart of Hakeem's 77-day detention in Thailand, and understand why a global campaign of such enormous size and scale was needed to set him free.

Bahrain is a small Gulf kingdom made up of over 30 islands. It has a total landmass smaller than Australia's capital city, Canberra, and its 1.4 million people are mostly Muslim. The country has been ruled by just one family – the Al Khalifas – since 1783 and members of this family hold the majority of senior positions in the government, security forces and public institutions, including national sporting bodies. While there is scarcely time here to skim the surface of Bahrain's long and turbulent history of civil uprisings and sectarian divisions, two things are plainly clear from even a rudimentary reading of its history books. Bahrain's people know violence, and they understand autocracy.

The Al Khalifa monarchy is Sunni, a branch of the religion of Islam. Most Muslims in the world are Sunnis and they form the majority in most Muslim countries, but in Bahrain they represent a minority. The majority of the population belong to a different branch of Islam – Shia. Hakeem and his family are Shia, along with many people in the neigh-bourhood of Jidhafs, where he grew up. Despite the wider rift that the Sunni and Shia divide has caused in the Middle East, these two branches of Islam have, historically, lived with each other in Bahrain in relative peace. This is not to understate the very real, systemic discrimination that Shia in Bahrain face, like not being able to work in the military or the police force, but many Bahraini activists are at pains to emphasise what the real causes of civil unrest in Bahrain are: dictatorship and nepotism.

Sayed Ahmed Alwadaei is the founding director of the Bahrain Institute for Rights and Democracy (BIRD), based in London. He was a successful engineer before being imprisoned and tortured for speaking out against Bahrain's regime. He fled to the UK in 2012, where he has worked as a pro-democracy advocate for the Bahraini people ever since. Sayed became an important ally throughout the campaign, with information about the specifics of Hakeem's case, but also the broader political and human rights context in Bahrain. At the time of writing, Sayed's three relatives, including his mother-in-law, are in Bahraini prisons, where he says they are being tortured as reprisal for his work.[1]

'We are known to be a very peaceful, easygoing and welcoming people. This issue of extremism or religious sectarianism wasn't in the country ... People are well educated. Women's empowerment is strong compared to any neighbouring state [and] we even had movements of trade unionists ... as a Bahraini, I don't see the split between Sunni and Shia to be a core problem. The issue is political not sectarian. Injustice could be random and affect anyone. To be frank, Sunni will be equally targeted if they criticise the government ... leaders who are Sunni are also imprisoned and remain in prison today, too.'

Bahrain's closest economic and political ally is Saudi Arabia, which it's connected to by a 25-kilometre causeway. Bahrain's strategic geographical location in the Persian Gulf has also long attracted attention from Western countries. The simple reality that much of the world's petroleum needs to transit through the Gulf to reach the open ocean goes some way to explaining Bahrain's longstanding historical ties with the United Kingdom, and its close alliance with the United States, which has a large naval fleet permanently stationed there.

Bahrain's geopolitical importance has cemented the ruling 'House of Khalifa's' wealth. The king's personal superyacht is almost 70 metres long, and the family's second one, gifted to the crown prince by Saudi Arabia, reportedly has 130,000 square feet of floor space, a garage, a hospital, a salon, and five kitchens. This tangled knot of wealth and powerful allies has secured the Al Khalifas' rule in Bahrain for centuries and made it extraordinarily difficult for either the Bahraini people or outside countries to effect international accountability or influence social change. This was a critical campaign factor. How does one pressure a country that is largely dismissive of and unresponsive to international opinion?

After Bahrain gained independence from Britain in 1971, two decades of civil unrest ensued. A British citizen called Colonel Ian Henderson led Bahrain's secret police during this time, stepping down in 1998 after earning himself the nickname 'the Butcher of Bahrain'.[2] It's a moniker which paints a vivid enough picture of what life must have been like for the Bahraini people in this period. By the mid-1990s, violent confrontations between protesters and government forces were commonplace. Between 1995 and 1996, escalating street demonstrations took place, led by organised political

11

opposition groups and networks, calling for social and political reform.[3] The Bahrain Government denied repeated requests by international human rights organisations to conduct formal missions and monitor these events.[4] So, without widespread mobile phone technology or internet use at this time, the reported human rights abuses, including the killing of civilians, that occurred during this crisis remained largely hidden from the outside world. In 1999, the ruling emir Isa bin Salman Al Khalifa died and a new leader, Hamad bin Isa Al Khalifa, came to power on a platform of political stability and economic growth. And for a brief period, democracy seemed attainable.

At this time, Bahrain also ramped up its investment in sports. Some say this was tantamount to 'sportswashing', a term to describe authoritarian regimes investing in mega-sports events to advance their reputation and influence, while distracting attention from the horrific human rights abuses they are committing.[5,6] Others contend it is because Bahrain, like many Middle Eastern countries, is trying to diversify its investment portfolios, recognising that the current source of its wealth – oil – will one day expire. Perhaps its rulers merely love sport and have the capacity to indulge their interest? Whatever the reality, many countries in the Middle East today have unprecedented investments in, and have acquired vast power through, global sports – foremost among them football.

The intertwined relationship between the royals and sport in Bahrain is striking, with strong evidence that the family invests in but also uses sport, from football, equestrian and

Formula One, to cycling and martial arts[7,8] as a vehicle to exert political control.[9,10] Family members not only occupy a majority of senior positions in sport governing bodies, but the domestic sports media also dutifully publicises their activities. Sheikh Nasser bin Hamad Al Khalifa, for example, was President of Bahrain's Olympic Committee, President of the Royal Equestrian and Endurance Federation and Chairman of the Supreme Council for Youth and Sports, while also holding military positions including Commander of the Royal Guard. An Ironman athlete himself, Nasser has less glowingly been dubbed by an independent news outlet the 'poster boy for regime whitewashing'.[11] Another member, Sheikh Salman bin Ibrahim Al Khalifa, previously president of the Bahrain Football Association (BFA), holds senior and influential positions in football globally, including President of the Asian Football Confederation (AFC) and Vice President of FIFA. Both of these men are paramount to Hakeem's story.

Despite all this and somewhat ironically, as you'll discover in this tale, Bahrain is held up as a progressive beacon of hope within the region and, as recently as October 2018, became a member of the United Nations Human Rights Council.[12] Back in the late 1990s and early 2000s, it was demonstrably a more democratic country than its nearest neighbours – a low threshold, it must be said.

By the late 2000s, King Hamad had ruled for a decade. The promised democratic reforms hadn't materialised and the hoped-for social harmony was elusive. It was in this context that Hakeem grew up. A divided country. A government willing to rule through the imposition of force. And a nation that loved, and was deeply politically and financially invested in, the game he excelled at.

•

Hakeem's family lived in a neighbourhood called Jidhafs, just over 10 kilometres from Bahrain's capital, Manama. His father married twice, so Hakeem was brought up in a blended family. 'We had two families living in one large, three-storey house,' he says. When asked if he would choose to marry twice, Hakeem laughs. 'That was common before, but not now . . . the thinking and culture is very different.' His own mother had nine children, four boys and five girls, and Hakeem was number seven. He had five half-brothers and sisters, one of whom was Emad, the second oldest, who plays a role later in this story. Hakeem has fond memories of his childhood. 'We would go on holidays as a family, I remember, to Syria and Lebanon . . . countries where my family would go for religious reasons to visit special sites and mosques, like in Damascus.

'I've been in the sea many times,' he says. 'When I was young my sister threw me in the swimming pool and I wanted to go out, but later, as [a] teenager, I really liked going to the sea and fishing in the night, like at midnight. I would go with friends [and] we would catch dinner and cook it on the fire,' he says nostalgically. He didn't have time for pets growing up, but his brother had a collection of over 15 birds that he cared for in a huge aviary on the rooftop. 'We have a view from up there, over the whole neighbourhood . . . Whenever something happens on the street, like if the police are coming, everyone goes up there to look and see what's happening . . . you could see everything.'

When Hakeem was just eight years old, tragedy struck his family. His father died suddenly of a heart attack. 'I was riding my bicycle [and] when I came home something was wrong. I asked a friend . . . my neighbour what had happened. Then I saw my mother crying. I thought he was just at the hospital, not dead. After that, many people came to the house. I heard what happened and when I heard the truth, I went upstairs onto the roof. For three hours I stayed up there by myself. It was a surprise and very sudden . . . he wasn't sick.'

After his father's death, the family struggled to make ends meet. 'We were living on a pension provided by the government, and my older brother supported us. We also received help from charities.' He doesn't think they would have survived if his mother wasn't so strong. 'I am very close with her and call her every two days . . . she is so kind, everyone loves her,' he says. 'She is a very trusting person and she doesn't make small things into big things . . . everyone who meets her knows what a good person she is.' He also misses her cooking a lot. 'My mum, she cooked *Machboos* for us many times – it is [a] famous dish – every Bahraini knows this food. It is brown rice with fish or sometimes chicken, [and] my mum, she makes it the best.' He pauses, and looks up at an invisible menu in the air. 'My sister also makes the best cheesecake, it is my favourite,' he recalls longingly.

Sport was an important outlet for Hakeem growing up: 'In Bahrain, football is a game that's played on the streets. It's the most popular sport for the people. When you walk around the streets, it is common to see kids playing football, in parks, everywhere. Saturday was family day and we would all play together. I started playing club-level when I was 10 years [old]. My favourite teacher at school was called Sadiq ... he was the sports teacher. Sadiq recommended me to a local club, al-Shabab, and I played there for four years. All my free time I spent just playing football, over the school holidays, everything was about football and training.

'In 2009, when I was 15 years [old], my club talked with a scout and I was asked to play for Bahrain's national team. There was another player the same age, and we were the youngest players on the Under-18 squad. I trained very hard with them,' he says. 'Sergio Ramos was my favourite player then ... he still is. Every day I watched his video and still now I do this. In the bus on the way to the game, every day in the morning, I watched videos of him playing on my phone.'

•

In late 2010, eight years before his arrest in Thailand, Hakeem was 16 years old. He was still living in Jidhafs and had already played in Bahrain's national youth squad for almost two years. He remembers that as early as 2009, there were clear signs that the temporary peace forged in Bahrain had begun to fall apart.

'The police started arresting people randomly, even if they were not involved in protests. I faced many difficulties and worries at the time [and] I was scared to go to training. I didn't have a car ... so I took the bus everywhere. I remember waiting at the bus stop in my village one day and I saw some police cars coming. I tried to hide from them, because they can just arrest people on the roads with no reason and they use force.'

He recounts one fateful night in early October 2010. 'I returned to my house after playing a match in Kuwait. I achieved best player in that game. I arrived in Bahrain around midnight . . . then police came to the house at 3 am looking for my older half-brother Emad. They used violence to enter the house, but he was not there. They looked for him because he was an activist, writing things about the government that they didn't like. I was the only male in the house, so they took me to the police station as [a] guarantee. The police told my family to tell Emad to go to the police station and they would keep me there until he did. They kept me in prison for five months without any charge. I was the youngest one among all the prisoners and worried about missing my study . . . I had no idea when I would be released and was worried about school and my future.' Hakeem was finally released at the end of February 2011. But he emerged into a very different social context from the one he had left back in October.

•

Lulu is the Arabic word for 'pearl' and has special significance in Bahrain. The country was once the centre of the global pearling industry, a history that has attracted a UNESCO World Heritage Listing.[13] Not surprising then that the country chose to erect a giant pearl-shaped monument in the heart of Manama in the early 1980s.

By the time Hakeem was released from prison, the 'Lulu roundabout', as it was known locally, had become the symbol of a nationwide uprising. On 14 February, while many in the world were celebrating Valentine's Day, the Arab Spring protests had kicked off in Bahrain, and the Lulu roundabout was ground zero. Peaceful pro-democracy demonstrations were also taking place all over the country, inspired by successful movements to topple authoritarian regimes in Tunisia and Egypt.

Sayed Ahmed Alwadaei participated in these protests. 'This was a popular uprising, an overwhelming majority of the public. Bahrain was unique in the Arab world on this . . . it was the most popular uprising in terms of public participation numbers . . . almost one third of entire population, this was something that has never been seen anywhere in the Arab world . . . the people were hungry for democracy and there was thirst for change.'

Protests for reform were not new in Bahrain. However, this movement was not orchestrated by institutionalised political opposition groups, but by networks of discontented, polit- ically unaffiliated people. Social media and mobile phones played a strong role in the protesters' ability to organise and communicate with the outside world,[14] unlike during the protests back in the mid-1990s. 'There were doctors, trade unionists, teachers, young people, athletes . . . both Sunni and Shia participated, and both were arrested and put on trial,' explains Sayed.

In a terrible response to the peaceful protests, the ruling Al Khalifa family authorised troops from Gulf countries, including Saudi Arabia, the United Arab Emirates (UAE) and Qatar,[15] to combine forces with Bahraini authorities to crush the uprising. Clashes between protesters and police resulted in many fatalities, arrests and the subsequent torture of many who had taken part. Sayed explains how the security forces now included paid mercenaries from countries like Syria, Pakistan and India. 'This was the grim reality . . . it's about a government that needs someone to do their dirty work. Bahrainis did not want to torture their own brothers, cousins . . . so they have to get someone who is a mercenary.'

If you want greater insight into the events of 2011, I highly recommend that you watch Al Jazeera's undercover documentary *Shouting in the Dark*.[16] For those who prefer detailed reports, an Independent Commission of Inquiry (BICI) with international experts was established by King Hamad in July 2011, to investigate and report on the events in February and March. In November 2011, it released a 500-page report detailing its findings, and concluded that the Ministry of Interior and National Security Agency 'followed a systematic practice of physical and psychological mistreatment, which in many cases amounted to torture, with respect to a large number of detainees in their custody'.[17] The report specified the most common techniques used on detainees were blind-folding, handcuffing, enforced standing for prolonged periods, beatings with rubber hoses, cables, whips, metal, wooden planks or other objects, electrocution, sleep-deprivation, exposure to extreme temperatures, verbal abuse, threats of rape to the detainee or family members, and insulting the detainee's religious background.

Hakeem remembers the Lulu roundabout protests well: 'I was studying every day in a school very near the round-about and went there maybe three or four different times to join. Some people were killed and the world was starting to see.'

He remembers one day in particular, 17 March 2011. 'On this day, we were peacefully protesting. Bahrainis now call it Black Thursday because so many people were killed. At this time, there was tear gas all the time. They were out-of-date cans, made in Israel . . . my friend still has some, you can see the expiry dates are old, from the 1970s, and the police were using it on the people. Many times I was coming home from training and could see the police firing tear gas . . . I would ask the driver to take me to another area and wait in the bus till I received a call from my family that the area is clear.'

Hakeem was not the only elite athlete who participated in the protests. Among the crowds had been representative handballers, wrestlers, table-tennis players, basketballers and many other prominent footballers, including Hakeem's teammates Sayed Mohamed Adnan and brothers A'ala and Mohamed Hubail.[18] A'ala is Bahrain's all-time top goal-scorer, with more than 60 caps. All three players were widely known and loved in Bahrain.

The day after Black Thursday, the authorities completely destroyed the Lulu roundabout monument in a symbolic repres-sion of the movement. And then, retributions commenced. Sayed recounts how athletes were specifically targeted by Prince Nasser bin Hamad, who was president of Bahrain's Olympic Committee at the time. 'Prince Nasser went on state TV and threatened the protesting athletes and said that "judgement day" had come for them,' he says.

Hakeem remembers watching the now infamous program live.[19] 'I was scared because [I] thought I would also be seen on the TV . . . most of this program was focusing on athletes, footballers, basketballers . . . more than [one] hundred of them putting circles on their face, with the word "treason" written below . . . I was afraid that people would recognise me . . . the royal family knew me, they are watching all the matches and know us.'

Hakeem goes on to explain the close interest that the royal family took in football. 'We knew many of them very well . . . they came to our training sessions often and watched us play. We met them many times. Sheikh Salman was a close friend of the president of my club. In 2011 we had a party and I spent time with him there.'

In April 2011, as president of Bahrain's Olympic Committee, Prince Nasser created a special investigation committee[20] to identify and punish members of the sporting community for demonstrating. He also reportedly made public statements, including on his Twitter account, calling for athletes who had protested to be imprisoned and punished.[21] This 'commission of inquiry' appointed Sheikh Salman bin Ibrahim Al Khalifa as its head, along with other senior sporting officials. As noted, Salman was also President of the Bahrain Football Association (BFA) at the time.

Nasser insists that, while announced, the commission was never formally established. This is despite the release of a public statement noting that its first meeting had occurred and 'legal advisers' had been requested 'to catalogue the breaches by some members of the sports associations . . . in preparation for a detailed report which will be submitted to the commission in order to take necessary measures against those who have offended the country'.[22] Further, Bahrain's news agency announced on 20 April that Hakeem's club, al-Shabab, among others, had been downgraded by the BFA to second division and fined, due to the club's involvement in the protests.[23]

In October 2014, in response to calls for accountability by Bahraini activists in the UK, including Sayed, Britain's High Court overturned a ruling that Prince Nasser, who graduated from Britain's elite Sandhurst Military Academy, was immune from prosecution over torture claims that were submitted to Britain's Crown Prosecution Service while the prince was in the UK enjoying the London Olympics in 2012.[24] Subsequent investigations were dropped, partially because key witnesses remained in Bahraini prisons and couldn't be interviewed. At the time of writing, the prince remains a frequent visitor to the UK, including attending the Royal Windsor Horse Show in December 2018 where he met Queen Elizabeth.[25]

In late 2011, US-based television sports channel ESPN produced *The Athletes of Bahrain*, a documentary that shone a spotlight on the six weeks of protests that had left 24 dead and hundreds missing.[26] It shows confronting footage of the protests and subsequent government crackdown, including an unarmed man being shot in the head at point-blank range. Through interviews with athletes and doctors, including

A'ala Hubail, it recounts how nearly 200 sportspeople were imprisoned by the regime for up to three months without hearings, and subjected to torturous interrogations.

In June 2011, prominent Bahraini human rights defender Nabeel Rajab called for sports governing institutions, including FIFA and the AFC, to get involved. 'The people who are in charge, they don't care about international image,' he told football commentator James Montague. 'They are military people [but] footballers have rights like any other human to be a citizen. It's time for FIFA to raise its voice. The people of Bahrain are looking at them and asking, "Where are you?"'[27] Rajab, the head of the Bahrain Center for Human Rights, is currently serving a five-year prison sentence for using Twitter to call for democracy in his country.[28]

Predictably, the Bahrain Government, along with the Olympic movement, FIFA and the AFC have, to this day, not investigated Prince Nasser, Sheikh Salman or the events of 2011. Nor has anyone been held to account.

•

From the end of 2011 into 2012, Hakeem continued to play football, progressing through different youth teams. But it was a difficult time. 'Especially closer to events of the Lulu roundabout, most of the clubs have stopped training,' he remembers. 'I wanted to keep qualifying for the national team, so I kept going to my local club, many times by myself, just to train. I played Under-20s that year and travelled many times ... I just wanted to play.' He was made captain of al-Shabab that year at just 18 years old.

On Saturday, 3 November 2012, Hakeem's al-Shabab team had a scheduled first-round match against Busaiteen Club at al-Muharraq Stadium. The game was shown live on Bahraini national television[29] and Hakeem can clearly be viewed at multiple points in the footage, including at the very end of the game. The official match sheet from the game also clearly lists his name and national identity number.[30] 'It was a normal game, we weren't very strong. I was angry because we lost the game 3–0. I went home afterwards and then went to meet a friend for dinner. That was it, it was not a special night.' Little did he realise how important the events of that night were soon to become.

The following Wednesday, 7 November, was Hakeem's birthday. Five of his friends surprised him by taking him to one of his favourite restaurants that showed sports and had billiard tables. They watched a football game, either Real Madrid or Barcelona, he can't remember, and they stayed playing billiards and drinking coffee until around midnight. His friends then offered him a lift home and they left together. On the way, their car was stopped at a checkpoint and they were asked to show their identification. Hakeem had forgotten his that night, so the police asked him to step out of the car. He was then taken to Isa Town police station.

'When they found [out] who I was, they took me from that police station to al-Khamis police station. There was complete silence in the car, no speaking . . . I thought they were taking me home . . . then the car stopped and they told me to get out. They started hitting me and one of them was singing . . . they were happy, taunting me. Then they took me into an office directly and blindfolded my eyes. They threw cold water on me without even asking me anything. This was just to welcome me . . .

'Then they started asking "What did you do?" . . . over and over. They took me to the floor, put me on my stomach, pulled my two legs behind . . . there were five people and they started hitting me on my legs. Two people were holding my legs and one jumped on my back to stop me from moving . . . one was holding me from my hair, and the other one was hitting me on my two legs . . . they were hitting me with two types of pipes or hoses. One of them was using this type of drainage pipe, it was rubber and flexible, like a drainage pipe for water . . . it was hollow. The other pipe, it was hard . . . I couldn't see it, but I could feel it. It might [have been] metal or wooden. From 1 am in the morning until 6 am they were beating me. While hitting, they kept asking what I did. I kept saying "Nothing" so they continued hitting me. After a short time, maybe 10 to 15 minutes, I couldn't feel my legs . . . they know the blood has run out and they asked me to go and walk in the room, and then come back . . . and then they started again. Because of the hard hitting, I could feel my legs are very hot, it was burning . . . and they were laughing at me, saying "You are football player", "Show us how you play", "Walk around". After around five hours, they started to say that I burned down a police station. I said I was playing football, and they said, "Don't say that, don't lie." All the time, I was blindfolded and I couldn't see them. Then, a very senior policeman came and asked me what I did . . . I said nothing, and he slapped me hard across my face. My head hit an electrical box on the wall . . . really hard. I fell down and was unconscious, but I don't know how long I was down. They took me back to another room and began to torture me another way. They had small metal balls . . . when I felt them start hitting my face I knew they were marbles. Afterwards, they took me to the hospital and I showed the doctor the marks on my legs. The doctor certified that I was in good health . . . they do this so that they can give it to the court later on. You could see the marks on my body for many days, but they make them mostly on [my] chest and legs, because they can be covered by clothes in a court.'

Hakeem was detained alongside Emad and another well-known activist, Yousef Al-Mahafdha.[31] 'They kept me for three months . . . they sent the riot police in often [and] they started hitting us with tear gas . . . all the people inside were political prisoners, around 120 people. They had arrested Emad while he was sick in hospital and had got a confession from him in the police station that I had committed the crime [but] it was clear that his confession was from torture by the police.'

Hakeem was released on bail in early February 2013. 'I remember because on 14th February a big event happened in Bahrain,' he says sadly. 'Across the whole country there were protests and I went along . . . I was in my village and when the riots came, everybody ran away. The police killed someone very young . . . from a one-metre distance they shot him. Hussain al-Jaziri was his name [and] he was just 16. They killed him on the second anniversary of the Lulu roundabout protests, about three kilometres from my home.'

Hakeem returned to playing football as soon as he was released. He had presented the judge with key evidence that he was playing in a televised football match on the date of the alleged event and had a rock-solid alibi. The case continued, but Hakeem could be forgiven for thinking he was in the clear.

He remembers that year being about travel and career success. He played with the Under-23 national team in Qatar and Turkey, and then he was finally called up for the senior team and travelled to Thailand, Malaysia and many other countries for matches. It is important to emphasise that Hakeem was consistently allowed to play in the national team during this period. 'I got many awards that year,' he says. 'I got runner-up in Under-23 squad and then first position in Bahrain.' In August of that year, he even visited King Hamad, who presented him and his national teammates each with a gift of 3000 Bahraini dinar (almost $8000 USD). If the royal family considered Hakeem to be a felon deserving of a significant prison sentence for his crimes, then they had a very strange way of showing it.

In late November 2013, he travelled with the senior national team to Qatar to prepare for the West Asian Football Federation Championship, scheduled for 25 December to 7 January 2016. At 10am on 6 January, the day before Bahrain and Kuwait would compete for third place, Hakeem received a phone call from home that changed his life forever. It was from a friend who had been in court attending a hearing for Emad and incidentally heard some news about Hakeem's case. A court had convicted him of attacking the police station and he'd been sentenced to 10 years in prison.

Amnesty International's Bahrain Researcher Devin Kenney has reviewed the court judgement closely: 'Any reading of the case documents quickly reveals the conviction to be a farce ... there are numerous fair trial and procedural violations, and an open and shut time-based alibi, so it is completely brazen that this proceeded all the way to a conviction.' He continues, 'It is not even clear to us that an attack on a police station had even occurred. We use several databases to conduct detailed research, and an event like this would have appeared in their data, but there was no sign of it.' And still more: 'The judgement was based largely on the confession of his co-defendant and half-brother, Emad Ali al-Araibi ... the court judgement plainly disregarded Emad's assertion that his "confession" was obtained under duress.'[32]

Most comical of all was the alleged timing of the incident that Hakeem supposedly participated in. Besides the live footage showing Hakeem playing a match, a letter from the al-Shabab Club[33] confirmed that the match began at 5.45 pm and concluded at 7.45 pm. This is consistent with what was reported in local sports media at the time. The match was also reported on by the official Bahrain News Agency. The club's letter adds that Hakeem was in the presence of the other players on the team from 4.45 pm until at least 8.40 pm, after which his whereabouts are further attested to by non-team members up to 9.10 pm. The Interpol red notice states that Hakeem 'met his accomplices at around 18:00 hours in order to execute their plan of attack' and 'at around 20:00 hours ... deliberately attacked a police station with improvised explosive devices'. According to Google, the stadium and site of the alleged incident are 20.1 kilometres apart, and the quickest route to drive there is 23 minutes – without factoring in any weekend traffic. Even if the court dismissed the club's letter, the recorded live footage of the game and the official match sheet the court was given prove that it was physically impossible for him to have been present at the scene of the alleged incidents.

Hakeem had to think fast. 'Many messages came to my phone from friends. My mind was running and I immediately wanted to leave Qatar because they are friendly with Bahrain . . . I was panicking. I called my mother and she was crying, telling me not to come back to Bahrain. I called Nani too . . . we had been texting for almost one year now and although we [had] never met in person, we were very close, talking every day. I wanted to keep my future and my family. I was very sad because I was in the Bahrain national team, that was my future. Now, I was worried about my life . . . there are many other cases like this where people are killed in Bahrain. I decided to travel to Iran because it is mostly Shia and I thought it would be difficult for Bahrain to get me from there. After that, I could go to Europe to play football. At 11 pm that night, I went to the airport to book myself a ticket . . . they said there's no flight [and] the earliest would be 6 am, so I booked that and waited.'

It was the beginning of a four-month nomadic escape. 'I only had a few clothes with me, so my mother, brother and sister came to visit me in Iran . . . they brought me clothes and money. I lived in a hotel for about three weeks in Mashhad, only two hours' flight from my home. I travelled to Iraq with my mum one time to visit a religious place in Karbala. After this, we said goodbye, and I travelled to Malaysia, which I thought would be my final destination. I stayed there for about three months and applied for admission at university. But it was different to what I expected . . . when a close friend in Australia contacted me and told me that it was possible to play football and have a good life there, I decided to go and see. I didn't put in my mind that I was seeking asylum but when I got there, I saw the people living in the democracy . . . I saw the safety and how people are respecting the human rights. After two months, in June 2014 I applied for asylum there. I sent my case to [a] lawyer and they said it was very strong.'

Hakeem received a bridging visa and started to set up a life for himself in Melbourne. 'The first six months were very hard . . . I stayed at home and used my time by studying, because my English was very weak. I went to the Asylum Seekers Resource Centre in Footscray every day and was relying on them for food. I was broke, but I didn't want to take from others. I was lucky my friends gave me accommodation. Because of my bridging visa it was hard to be secure in work, because they are worried that you won't be able to stay with them for sure. I was speaking to Nani every day by phone, and she was really motivating me to improve myself. She was the reason I kept going forward. After six months I got a contract with Green Gully premier league club. I struggled to communicate with my teammates so I was determined to improve my language.'

In January 2015, Bahrain's national team came to Melbourne to play in the Asian Cup. Hakeem was very excited to support his old teammates. 'I visited them in the hotel and slept with them there for three nights ... on 29 February, there was a match against Iran and I went to cheer for them. I also spoke to the president of the team, Sheikh Ali. I asked him, could he speak for my case back in Bahrain, thinking maybe he could arrange [for] me to go safely home. I hadn't heard anything about my case and was thinking maybe they don't care. He told me that nothing would happen to me back in Bahrain. I gave him my phone number and he said I should wait for a call from him when he got [back]. Weeks later, he still had not called.'

In October that year, then President of the Asian Football Confederation, Sheikh Salman bin Al Khalifa, announced that he was running for FIFA's presidency to succeed the corruption-mired incumbent Sepp Blatter. Members of human rights organisations, including Sayed Ahmed Alwadaei, were furious. 'If a member of Bahrain's royal family is the cleanest pair of hands that FIFA can find, then the organisation would appear to have the shallowest and least ethical pool of talent in world sport,' said Nicholas McGeehan, the Gulf researcher at Human Rights Watch.[34]

Sayed began desperately trying to piece together evidence of Salman's involvement in the oppression of athletes back in 2011 but he faced one critical challenge. He found many athletes with accounts of torture, but no one wanted to go on the record. 'Everyone was terrified to speak,' recalls Sayed. 'Many were in fear of reprisals and many of them were [still] in the country and wanted to get on with their lives ... some people also wanted to end that terrible chapter in their lives.' Sayed had contacted Hakeem via activist Yousef al-Mahafdha, who had met Hakeem in prison back in 2012. 'He was the only one willing to speak publicly to the media.'

Hakeem recalls, 'Sayed contacted the media and told them about my case. Suddenly I [received] many calls from the media and did many interviews.' He was careful not to make accusations but stuck to the factual truth. 'In 2011 [Salman] was the president of football association in Bahrain – all the media in 2011 showed how they were tortured ... and he did not do anything at that time. Hundreds of athletes and he took no actions to help.' Even without reference to the special investigations committee that Salman reportedly headed, Hakeem saw Salman's unwillingness to speak out and protect players as an abject failure and reason enough to disqualify him from FIFA's presidential race. Which, of course, to any reasonable mind and in a sporting industry that wasn't endemically politically riven, would have been uncontroversial.

Media and politicians globally responded to Hakeem's story. On 23 February 2016 a UK parliamentarian named Damian Collins even urged the UK House of Commons to confirm it would not support bids from the English Football Association to host FIFA tournaments, should Salman be elected. Salman did not win the FIFA presidency that year. Instead, the crown went to then Secretary-General of the Union of European Football Associations (UEFA), Gianni Infantino.

Almost another year passed and, at the end of 2016, Hakeem had exciting news. His girlfriend Nani was coming to meet him in Australia. For three and a half years they had communicated almost daily and now, finally, they would meet. 'As for a while . . . we knew each other very well, but we had never had the chance to be together, to enjoy each other's company without our families,' Nani reflects, a smile on her face. 'We were both prepared for this moment,' she offers, 'but I wanted more time to get to know him, and to see if I could make a life in Australia. It didn't take me long . . . I know him and I love him. He's very kind, more than usual. That's why I love him.'

He counters, 'I love her character . . . the way she thinks. We are sharing the same ideas together, and want the same things in our future,' he says, grinning.

Chapter 3

EARLY DAYS

There were two groups of Thai authorities waiting for Hakeem and Nani when they landed in Bangkok. One group waited just outside the plane's main door and the other stood further along the transit tunnel in plain clothes, filming them with a video camera. A uniformed official from the first group walked up to Hakeem and said his name out loud, confirming who he was. He then showed him some documents written in Thai. 'They were saying I was a criminal case . . . they showed me papers and another paper with an old photo of me, from my old Bahrain passport,' says Hakeem. He was then taken by the arm and led to an office in the airport, with Nani close by his side.

Despite panic starting to set in, Hakeem acted quickly in the precious time he had while they walked to the office. He recorded a short voice message on his phone and began firing it off to his friends, many of whom were members of the Bahraini community living in Australia. Yahya Alhadid from the Gulf Institute for Democracy and Human Rights (GIDHR) and Hakeem's migration agent Latifa al-Haouli were among this group.

When they arrived at the office, he was told he wasn't allowed to use his phone in there, and the Thai officials started asking him questions. They were stunned Hakeem openly admitted that he knew about his conviction in Bahrain. 'They were very surprised to see my Australian travel document and the treatment started to be very different then in the office after that . . . different from when we were at the plane in the beginning.' Hakeem sensed that they believed him when he explained that he had not committed the crime that the Bahraini authorities were accusing him of. 'I have visited Thailand before,' he told them. 'I love Thailand.'

'They took us to prison cells in the airport where I stayed for four nights. The first night I was separated from Nani and stayed in a cell with just men, but the second night I asked to pay for us to stay in the same room. They said yes, and the second room was a "family room" . . . that is where we shot the video that was in the first SBS news story.[1] The cell was very basic, just with rubber on wooden beds and bars on the door. There was one police standing behind the door at all times. We still were allowed phones, so we started calling everyone in the airport to say what was happening to us, even the media.' Nani has since calculated that they paid the officials around $150 AUD or more so that they could stay in this cell together.

The next morning, they called the Australian embassy in Thailand. 'I [spoke] with a woman, Emily. She asked me one time did I want to change my ticket to an earlier flight and I asked her, could she check that the Thais agreed, because we didn't have a decision they would let us go and we would bear the cost to change the ticket.'

On 29 November the Thai police told them to change their flights – they would be allowed to go back to Australia on Saturday. Hakeem checked with the Australian embassy and they confirmed he could leave. Hakeem and Nani's original flight home was on 4 December and they had non-transferable tickets, so they bought completely new flights, leaving at 9 pm on 1 December. 'We were four nights there in the cells and just wanted to go home to Australia.'

At this stage it was very unclear who was responsible for the arrest. As I would find out some weeks later, Australian officials spent these days frantically trying to amend the error they had made regarding the Interpol red notice. For now, the most important thing to note is that the red notice was cancelled late on 30 November by Interpol headquarters in Lyon, France, which was the morning of 1 December in Thailand. Meaning that Thailand was told that day that the red notice from Bahrain was no longer valid, and while they had a formal request from the Bahrain Government for Hakeem's arrest and extradition, they could've used their discretion at this point to release him.

Of course, Hakeem and Nani, still without a lawyer, had no idea any of this was happening. They had their tickets back to Australia and thought that their nightmare would soon be over.

27–30 NOVEMBER 2018 (AUSTRALIA)

It was 3 am on Wednesday, 28 November 2018 when Fatima Yazbek was woken up by her husband, Yahya, in their home in Melbourne. She was groggy with sleep and struggled to comprehend what Yahya was saying. 'You need to wake up, Hakeem was arrested.' Yahya's voice was urgent. He'd just discovered a voice message on his phone sent two hours earlier. Hakeem al-Araibi and his wife were in trouble in Thailand, and needed urgent help. Fatima was confused. 'Hakeem and Nani are in Australia, Yahya,' she remembers thinking to herself. 'They're married here, you must be making a mistake.' Within a split second, though, she recalled her husband mentioning the night before that the couple were travelling to Thailand for their honeymoon. She shot up in bed and told Yahya to play the message again. Now, both wide awake, they talked quickly about what they should do. They decided to contact DFAT and find out what was happening. The pair got out of bed and immediately set to work.

Fatima Yazbek is the Head of Reports and Studies at GIDHR, a small research organisation founded in 2016 that documents human rights violations in the Gulf. Her husband, Yahya Alhadid, is the organisation's president and a Bahraini national. He came to Australia in 2010 and has spoken out against the Bahraini authorities for years and helped Bahrainis fleeing persecution reach countries where they will be safe. 'Whenever any person leaves Bahrain, [they] try to find someone from Bahrain that can help them settle in their new life,' Fatima explains, 'so when Hakeem came to Australia, that's how he found Yahya. Yahya's name is so known in Bahrain, because since the beginning of the uprising in 2011, he was outside Bahrain so had the opportunity to speak up.'

Sayed had also received Hakeem's SOS message. At around 3 am Sayed, Yahya and Fatima started texting to coordinate a plan. Fatima phoned the DFAT hotline and Sayed drafted a media alert. They emailed DFAT confirming their phone conversation and the facts of Hakeem's case. They collated all their media contacts in Australia and abroad, and sent out the media alert. At some point, they received a call from Latifa Al-Haouli, Hakeem's migration agent, who offered to help in any way she could.

By late afternoon, they were panicking. They had received no response from the media, and they were questioning how seriously DFAT was taking the case. Fatima recalls with frustration the conversation she'd had on the hotline: 'I remember the woman, at the end of our conversation after explaining how much his life was in danger if he was sent back to Bahrain. She said, "Look, I understand what you're saying, but Hakeem is not an Australian citizen, there's not much we can do."'

Finally, a breakthrough. Someone in their Melbourne network knew an SBS journalist who agreed to conduct interviews with Latifa, Fatima, one of Hakeem's friends and, critically, with Hakeem himself from inside the police cell in Bangkok airport. The story was published along with video that Hakeem had taken on his mobile phone, showing the inside of his bare cell, with a few metal-framed bunks with wooden slats and basic black foam mattresses.

Fatima emphasises how important this first story was. 'Nobody in media was interested in the case or published anything. We needed to make pressure and change public opinion, in order to get the government to do something. When the SBS story went public this was a key moment.' While SBS pulled their story together, Fatima sent the media alert to the inboxes of dozens of other news desks, hoping for a response. The following day, Helen Davidson from *The Guardian* published an article including details about Hakeem's back story and the Interpol red notice used to arrest him. Helen is one of the many outstanding Australian journalists who would cover the case and would quickly become a key media ally. A few other news outlets also ran stories, including the *Herald Sun*, *Free Malaysia Today* and *The New Arab*. By late Friday, the story had hit Reuters and the *South China Morning Post*. It was painstaking but, gradually, media outlets were taking notice.

Human rights organisations were also becoming active. BIRD and Human Rights Watch had issued press releases and were trying to gain visibility on social media. News was moving quickly, but too quietly, when the Bahrain embassy in Thailand tweeted that Hakeem was wanted for security reasons and that it was 'following up with the relevant security authorities in this regard'. Phil Robertson, Deputy

Director of Human Rights Watch in Asia, hit back with a blistering reply on Twitter, noting that Interpol red notices don't apply to recognised refugees:

> INTERPOL Red Notices do NOT apply to recognized #refugees like Hakeem al-Araibi. @MFAThai should coordinate with @dfat& @Refugees to ensure that he is not forced back to #Bahrain to face imprisonment, & torture.[2]

The fight for truth, control and supremacy on social media had begun. In those first few days, no one could possibly have had any inkling of the ferocity, scale or stakes this fight would encapsulate.

Meanwhile, in north-west Melbourne, Lou Tona and Athena Babo had been following the news closely. Lou is the charismatic chairman of the Pascoe Vale Football Club, a volunteer position that he's held for more than 20 years. 'He's the backbone of the club,' says Athena, 'a really selfless and driven person who's put the club on the map where it is today.' Athena is the club's official secretary, which she also does voluntarily. Her parents were both founding members back in 1966. The club was founded by immigrants as a place for people to gather socially. 'I was pretty much born into the club. I'm not really all that interested in the game, it's more about being passionate for the club and the community.'

Pascoe Vale, whose home ground is in Coburg North, has remained true to its multicultural immigrant roots with most players being second generation Australian with parentage as diverse as Italian, Greek, Brazilian and from many Arabic countries. In Lou's time, the club has risen from the lowest

Victorian state league division to the highest, now holding a valued place as a semi-professional club in the second tier of Australia's National Premier League. It is the prototypical football institution in Australia, truly and proudly multicultural. Lou and his staff feel close to their players, respect different backgrounds, and consider the club one big family.

Hakeem joined the club in early 2018, after stints in a number of other Melbourne-based clubs. Lou and Athena had been broadly aware of his background when he joined, as his story had been covered in football news media several years prior during the FIFA presidential race involving Salman. 'None of the players really knew his story though,' recalls Athena, 'and he never spoke at all about his past.' Both Lou and Athena had seen the SBS report and contacted Latifa al-Haouli to find out what was going on. On Friday, they were relieved to hear that Hakeem had booked a ticket back to Australia and was to be leaving Bangkok on Saturday night. Their relief was palpable. It should all be over very soon, they thought.

1–11 DECEMBER 2018 (THAILAND)

'Only a few hours before our flight, they took us from the cells and I thought they would take us from here to our airplane, but instead they took me to an office about 40 minutes away from the airport in the IDC.' Bangkok's Suan Plu Immigration Detention Centre (IDC) is where you end up if you're a visa overstayer or considered to be an 'illegal immigrant'. As Thailand has not signed the 1951 Refugee Convention, these 'illegal immigrants' include asylum seekers and refugees. The centre was originally designed for people to stay for weeks, but many people end up there for months, even years.[3] The centre is right in the middle of town next to the financial district, tucked far down the end of a side street.

'In IDC they kept us in [a] room like an office, with computers and desks with chairs. It was very strange and there was no real bed. After two nights I was taken to court and they told me I had 12 more days in detention. Officials come and told me, "You don't need a lawyer," and they made me sign something in Thai language. They told me, "After the court you will go back to Australia, don't worry, just wait two hours."'

Hakeem's situation was confirmed on 4 December by Thailand's Immigration Bureau Chief Police Lt-General Surachate Hakparn, who told the media that the Interpol red notice had been lifted but Bahrain still had an opportunity to submit an arrest warrant. Despite the fact that they had given Bahrain extra time to submit this paperwork and could already have sent Hakeem home, Surachate expressed optimism, at least publicly, that this would be the outcome. 'When the period runs out and an arrest warrant from Bahrain hasn't shown up, we will send him back to Australia,' Mr Surachate said.[4]

Nadthasiri 'Nat' Bergman, who would soon be Hakeem's lawyer, commented of this time: 'In the IDC, they kept him in the office because they did not want to put him "on the books" . . . he had no status in Thailand, so they could not enter him into the system. He was not detained by book but by action at this time. It was illegal detention. They already had enough grounds to reject him but they kept him in Thailand.'

The day after Hakparn's comments to the media, Bahrain submitted the necessary legal documents required to begin an extradition hearing to Thailand's Foreign Affairs department. Hakeem and Nani had been in the IDC for four nights at this point when they should already have been preparing for the return journey to Melbourne to share honeymoon stories with friends. By 6 December, they were near breaking point. 'We had no idea what was happening,' says Hakeem. 'We are in the same clothes and Nani is in the hijab, but we are unable to wash for days now. She is very uncomfortable. We were sleeping on the floor with just a blanket and were not allowed to go out . . . just to the toilet and back, that's all. We were just eating and thinking too much. I was talking to the Australian embassy but all they said was "I have no update, we work hard" . . . they did ask for the police to bring us Halal food, which we were very thankful for . . . Halal Kentucky and Pizza Hut, we ate only these things.

'On Thursday night, I was cc'd on an email from local human rights people that said I would be deported to Bahrain the next day. I didn't sleep that night. I was crying and saying goodbye to Nani. I asked her to forgive me . . . it was out of my hands. I told her all that's happening is just about revenge against me, and I cannot do anything about it. Nani had more faith, though. She believed that they would not return me back. She was making me feel better because she believed this inside.'

Meanwhile, Nat Bergman had been rushing around Bangkok frantically trying to locate Hakeem. 'I went to many places, police stations . . . in central Bangkok . . . when I did not find him, I called a journalist friend who had spoken with him on the phone. She told me that he was at the IDC. Sayed also spoke to Hakeem that day and told him to call me. We spoke on 6th December and I explained I was a lawyer and would try to help him. I went to the IDC that day and submitted a request to meet with him, but they told me he wasn't there, because he wasn't "on the books" you know . . . so I wrote a report based on the information I'd received from the Thai journalist with the BBC and went back next day, demanding to meet with him. I told them, if they denied me to meet him I would fight for habeas corpus,[5] because someone had confirmed he was at IDC. I only got in because, by then, the prosecutor already had the warrant to arrest him and then they needed a lawyer. You see, from this moment, Hakeem's detention was then legal,' explains Nat. 'The attorney-general had confirmed Thailand's endorsement for a provisional arrest warrant to be issued to the court, who approved it that day. The attorney-general then had 60 days to file an application with the court for his extradition to Bahrain, as per Thailand's extradition act.'

When Nat came to meet Hakeem on 7 December, it was the first time he'd been given the chance to speak to a lawyer. 'I remember it was Friday because that day my wife Nani left the IDC. After they left, I was put in a different room and

Nani went to stay at a hotel nearby. She was bringing food from 7-Eleven and giving it to the guards for me . . . I wasn't sure I would ever see her again. The Australian embassy also visited me during this time. Nat told me I would be going to court next week and that I was likely to be held in a prison for 60 days more in Thailand.'

The next day, Saturday, 8 December, the Thai Government issued a press statement confirming the details of Hakeem's arrest and the court's approval of the arrest warrant.[6] Monday, 10 December, was a public holiday in Thailand, so the court hearing didn't happen until Tuesday, 11 December.

Hakeem was in the same Puma t-shirt he'd been wearing for the past two weeks. 'I was really terrified in this court. They asked me if I agreed to be extradited and I said "No, no, no" . . . but I didn't know if this would happen or not. After the court I was taken to prison straight away. For a second time, I said goodbye to my wife, maybe forever.'

The 60-day window for the preparation and submission of court documents commenced that day, when Hakeem was sent to Bangkok's Klong Prem remand prison.

1–11 DECEMBER 2018 (AUSTRALIA)

On Sunday, 2 December, Athena received a message on Pascoe Vale's Facebook page at 1.15 am. It was from Fatima. Athena grabbed her phone and replied straight away. Fatima was soon on the phone, frantically informing her the situation had changed. News had leaked out that Thailand had prevented Hakeem and Nani from boarding their flight and had instead taken them to a detention facility somewhere in the city. Lou and Athena knew the main facts of the case and had expected the Australian Government to be able to resolve it quickly. Hakeem was supposed to be on the way home by now. So, what had gone wrong? Anxious, fumbling, they hurriedly rang their football contacts to see if anyone had information or might be able to help.

Lou knew Peter Filopoulos, CEO of the state governing body, Football Victoria (FV), who was the obvious point of contact. Unfortunately, Peter was away, so Lou spoke to other officials to impress on them the matter's urgency. 'At that point, I got on the phone and I said, "You need to support his case." We thought it was important to get the message out there.' Several days later, running out of options and working on a volunteer schedule, his frustration was rising. 'We said you've got to get onto the Football Federation Australia [FFA]. The response we got was, "We're working in the background." For us, that wasn't enough.' Lou and Athena were doing all they could in a situation no community or semi-professional club could prepare for or should ever be thrust into, and they were fast running out of ideas.

At the global Fédération Internationale des Associations de Footballeurs Professionnels (FIFPro) conference in Rome, the Chief Executive of Professional Footballers Australia (PFA), John Didulica, woke to two new emails in his inbox. One from Lou, and the other from the PFA Chairman, Brendan Schwab. Both emails, from different ends of the globe, had the same subject matter.

Brendan's, in particular, caught his attention. It said 'Please urgently and carefully read the email chain below,' and underneath lay correspondence from Human Rights Watch's Director of Global Initiatives, Minky Worden, with a news article attached. John recalls, 'After reading Brendan's email and the article closely, I thought to myself, this is going to be interesting.'

Soon, Lou received the call that he'd hoped for. 'FV were in contact with us but then we got a phone call from John Didulica of PFA. He said, "Do you mind if we take the lead on this?" It was what we needed. It was failing. I don't think they [the FFA] were taking enough of a leadership role in it.'

The PFA is the national representative and collective bargaining agent of Australia's elite professional footballers, including national teams. It is a member of FIFPro, which represents professional footballers worldwide. The PFA is also a congress member of the FFA, the governing body of football in Australia and a member of FIFA.

Lou and Athena knew John 'JD' Didulica very well, and they thought he could perhaps exert the influence needed to get things moving. Later, when Peter Filopoulos returned from holidays, he would prove a worthy ally too. But for now, John was the great hope.

Lou was in luck. John is a former player and lawyer, highly respected in the game in Australia as someone who cares about and represents the players very well. As PFA chairman, I had headhunted him to become chief executive of the PFA a few years before because I knew he was not only capable but deeply committed to the profession and we've shared a very strong working and personal relationship in recent years. He has the game at heart and is completely trustworthy. For players, as much as for we grey-haired former players, trust and integrity are everything.

John's current chairman, Brendan Schwab, is a legendary figure in players' rights within Australian football. He co-founded the union back in 1993, was its first legal counsel, has undertaken a variety of roles for the organisation over the past two and a half decades and we've spent many years working together in different capacities. When I agreed to return to the PFA as CEO in 2005 at the request of the Australian National Team (Socceroos) to secure a Collective Bargaining Agreement for the 2006 FIFA World Cup, I called him and said, you need to come back as chairman. And just a few years ago, after I'd run an independent review into governance as PFA chairman, I made sure he replaced me in the chair to ensure the organisation was in the best possible hands.

Brendan has been leading the efforts to reform global sports law so that it embeds human rights. This notably included drafting the Universal Declaration of Player Rights,[7] which was signed by all player unions throughout the world in December 2017 and is the global benchmark for the human rights of athletes. He works at an exceptional intellectual and practical level out of the limelight to make the world a better place through sport. He's also a 25-year colleague and very dear friend of mine.

Schwabby, as he's known, is also executive director of the world players association, based in Switzerland. World

Players United (WPU) is an autonomous sector of UNI Global Union, a federation representing 85,000 athletes through more than 100 player associations in over 60 countries, which has grown considerably in size and influence in recent years. A conversation with Schwabby always includes the latest game of his adopted team, Young Boys of Berne, or Australia's national teams. He knows and loves the game and is an expert in its culture, history and, of course, legal and regulatory frameworks. Like John, Brendan deeply respects the players and has never spoken a bad word about a player in all the decades I've known him. This respect and affection is reciprocated by generations of players, and he has literally saved hundreds of careers.

More importantly though for Hakeem, Brendan had been a central part of a movement which, over the last half decade in particular, had worked to integrate international human rights standards into sport. He was involved in setting up the Sports and Rights Alliance (SRA) in 2015 that brought human rights organisations, unions, non-government groups, sporting governance bodies, and the United Nations together to embed human rights into the world's largest sporting organisations. Representatives from FIFA's major corporate sponsors, Coca-Cola and Adidas, are also members.

After the first few years, it became clear that SRA's work highlighting abuses was not changing behaviour quickly enough so, in 2016, their strategy shifted to applying pressure to codify a set of legal standards within sporting institutions, such as the International Olympic Committee (IOC) and FIFA. Continued human rights abuse in connection with mega sporting events including the granting of FIFA World Cups to both Russia and Qatar and the global outrage this engendered, especially following revelations of the abuse of migrant workers in Qatar, resulted in FIFA committing to respecting and upholding internationally recognised human rights. This enabled the SRC to apply leverage on the IOC to embed human rights requirements in its host city contract in late 2016, and the establishment of a landmark human rights policy by FIFA in May 2017. From that moment, all of FIFA's bodies, officials and employees became bound by the highest internationally recognised human rights standards.

FIFA also launched an independent Human Rights Advisory Board (HRAB) in March 2017 and charged it to provide expert advice to strengthen delivery of FIFA's human rights responsibilities. Its chair is another Australian lawyer, Rachel Davis.

A third sport and human rights organ would also become involved in Hakeem's case: the Centre for Sport and Human Rights. Launched in June 2018 in Geneva, the centre is an unprecedented coalition of around 40 intergovernmental organisations, governments, corporate sponsors, human rights organisations and trade unions. Its formation was the result of many years' work by people like Brendan and others in the Sports and Rights Alliance, including Human Rights Watch, Amnesty International and Football Supporters Europe, who serve on its advisory council. Mary Harvey, a former goalkeeper for the US Women's national team, is the CEO. When Thai authorities arrested Hakeem in November 2018, all of these entities and policies were relatively new, and they were about to face their first real litmus test. Of the most extreme kind.

Back in 2016, during Sheikh Salman's candidacy for the FIFA presidency, Brendan and others involved in the alliance knew about the allegations against the sheikh and were very concerned about his bid for FIFA's most senior role. 'I was aware of the media surrounding Hakeem's case back in 2016, and [the allegations of] Sheikh Salman's complicity in the arrest and torture of athletes. In fact, I presented the ESPN documentary to the FIFPro Asia Congress in 2012 in India,' Brendan says. 'At the time, we were starting to realise that, as a players' union movement, we possessed very little ability to protect the most fundamental rights of players. We called on all FIFA presidential candidates to make public commitments on the protection and implementation of human rights, and Sheikh Salman, at the time, made only a very conditional one.'

So, when Hakeem's case came to light, Brendan immediately contacted the human rights and player union network globally, including his PFA CEO, John Didulica. In his role, John's accustomed to helping players navigate the commercial world of football, contracts, lost salaries, agents, and negotiating the collective bargaining agreements for Australia's players. This case, though, was extremely disturbing and he spent those first few days wondering what he could do about it. 'Looking at Hakeem's case, there wasn't an immediate way out for him. He was in prison, he'd spoken out against a high-profile Bahraini, and there was some sort of extradition process activated against him . . . I'd never had to deal with anything like that before.' John was far from alone in this respect.

•

After everything that occurred over the ensuing months, I don't remember exactly how I first heard about Hakeem's case, but I do know it was before the end of the first week of his detention. Perhaps the PFA had reached out. Or I saw it on social media. Or someone told me about it. It hardly matters now, of course, but thanks to whoever got in touch.

When I read about it, I thought, what the hell is going on here? As football fans well know, we have a very high threshold for scandal in the global game. With so many countries and characters, something scandalous is always breaking somewhere in the world. But this kid was from Bahrain, living in Australia, and jailed in Bangkok. Even for the global game, that's quite something.

After doing the usual sharing and retweeting of articles to help, I quickly devoured every article I could find, going back to 2016 when Hakeem had burst into notoriety during FIFA's elections to understand exactly who he was. It didn't take long to realise that Hakeem's case was squarely within my field of life experience and interests.

I first tweeted about Hakeem's case on 3 December 2018 but at this early stage I assumed others were in control of the situation. I could see that his club was active and was impressed by public protestations from Lou and Athena. Good people, I thought, heart and soul of football by the looks, but who else was involved? What might the government do, or more importantly not do, here? I had played a number of roles on government councils and diplomatic missions over the years, so I had insight into their likely line of thought.

It was clear Hakeem was a protected refugee but what did this mean for the level of diplomatic assistance the Australian Government would provide, especially given Australia's problematic record on asylum seekers, which has become an intractable political issue over several decades? Throw in the relationship with Salman, the AFC president, and the fact that Hakeem was a member of the Muslim community of Australia, which I was well aware, through my membership of the Australian Multicultural Council, was experiencing feelings of marginalisation, and this kid was starting to look in a very tenuous position. To put it mildly.

Like everyone else, I grappled with what an Interpol red notice was, how it worked, and why it was placed and later lifted. There were clearly larger agendas at play. Bahrain must want him badly to reach out halfway around the world, it seemed. But the articles said he'd been in Australia for some years and had almost qualified for citizenship. Why hadn't Bahrain sought his extradition from Australia in the past four years? And why now in Thailand?

I tried to piece together who was involved, where the pieces lay, what the key influences and issues were, who could help and what I could possibly do, or say, and to whom. After decades as a player and player rights activist, I know football governance culture as well as any. Given the protests and subsequent reported targeting and torture of Bahraini athletes in 2011, and with Hakeem speaking out in 2015 against Salman's bid for the FIFA presidency,

I thought: there is absolutely no way the AFC is going to help. It was extremely brave to speak up as he did; very few players would be capable of that. I liked this kid already. He'd also spoken up while in Australia, where he'd clearly felt safe and I felt a certain responsibility that speaking out in our media had apparently contributed to the dire situation he was now in. As yet, I didn't know quite how much.

I knew it was an election year in both Asian and global football, and wondered if the FFA would step up. The new FFA chairman, Chris Nikou, would be up for election to Salman's AFC board. That was a worry. Infantino was seeking re-election as FIFA president, and Salman, his vice president, was one of the most powerful football officials on the planet. Help from Infantino? Forget it. And Thailand? Would their football community help? Oh, no. The president of the Thai Football Association was also running for the AFC board. How was this kid's timing? Couldn't have come at a worse moment if he tried. All round, there was no way that anyone would be prepared to do anything that might put votes at risk. We can forget about governing bodies making anything more than token gestures, I decided. He will need his fellow players. And with so much money coming out of the Gulf, how many of them could he rely on? I wondered.

Amnesty International, for whom I was an ambassador, had just launched a public petition calling on the Thai authorities to release Hakeem, so I got in touch with the Head of Campaigns, Tim O'Connor, to find out what was going on. Tim is a highly experienced operator who has been working in this field for decades. He sent me recent reports on Bahrain and the latest on the case. The brief only worsened what was fast becoming a dismal assessment. It was difficult to know exactly what was going on with the Thai Government. It was chaotic and the situation fluid to say the least. Everyone was struggling to get accurate information out of Bangkok, which exacerbated the problem.

Much worse though, Tim's material included reference to a 21-year-old youth activist, Ali Haroon, who had participated in the same protests as Hakeem back in 2011. Evidently Hakeem's was not an isolated case. Ali was jailed and tortured in Bahrain and, after receiving a life sentence, escaped from prison and fled to Thailand via Turkey and Hong Kong. In December 2014, he was arrested by Thai authorities in Bangkok, also on the basis of an Interpol arrest warrant from Bahrain, despite UNHCR confirming he had a valid visa at the time. He was handed over to Bahraini officials at Suvarnabhumi International Airport, the same airport where Hakeem and Nani were kept in police cells for four nights. Same story, almost identical. What had happened to him?

Ali was reportedly severely beaten, shackled and put into a wheelchair, before being forced onto a flight to Bahrain. UNHCR later confirmed that an initial attempt to board him had failed but a second 'reportedly succeeded after the individual was sedated and beaten'.[8] Subsequent reports by human rights groups and media reported that Ali had received some pretty severe injuries prior to arriving in Bahrain and was transferred to a hospital upon arrival. Bahrain's authorities didn't try to hide their knowledge of Ali's injuries, but stated that they had occurred because he resisted boarding the flight which 'made him fall and caused minor injuries'. Quite a fall, it seems. Was it from the top of the boarding steps, perhaps?

Ali's family visited him in prison two weeks after his return. He told them that he had been tortured and officials had shown him a document withdrawing his nationality. His family said that his hands and feet were shackled during the visit, and that there were bruises on his eyes. The last anyone heard of Ali Haroon was in March 2017. Amnesty received reliable reports that the situation was 'getting worse' for him and other detainees at the prison. After that, there's no record of what has happened to him. Ali's story made it clear that Thailand and Bahrain had a history, one that put Hakeem in extreme jeopardy. I needed to do something, but what, exactly?

•

By now, Brendan and John were sending me email updates often, and I had connected with Fatima and Yahya. They had seen my posts on social media and sent me messages of support. Unhelpfully, I was in the middle of the final year of a law degree on top of my other roles, constantly switching from textbooks and assignments back to Twitter, posting, sharing and trying to stay abreast of whether anything had shifted. There was a real sense of immediacy and urgency, as news changed by the hour. People were messaging and calling directly by this point, wanting to know what was going on. I told them I was still trying to work it out but provided the elementary knowledge I had about the 2011 protests and Hakeem's connection to Salman. Above all, one thing was abundantly clear. He was caught in a complex political web and the consequences for him of a forced return to Bahrain were nothing but grave.

I needed to understand Hakeem's case in more detail. If I was going to get louder, I wanted to know more than others and be in a position of authority. I had the perfect resource for this task. Brendan sent through a host of documents that he'd authored that framed the issue of sport and human rights. 'Send a copy of the FIFA Human Rights Policy as well, mate, I'll need to review it too.'

I'd also by now seen the name Sayed Ahmed Alwadaei in articles online which were thorough, detailed and knowledgeable. Some background research showed his experience as a former Bahraini detainee and expertise in the area, so I reached out to him over Twitter. We scheduled a Skype call so that I could see him face to face and get a sense of who he was and what his motivations were. He clearly understood the need for public proponents and was forthcoming with documents about the decision in 2014 when Hakeem was convicted of an alleged act of vandalism, as well as submissions to the UN Human Rights Council Special Procedures. We agreed to maintain open communication and collaborate where possible.

Fatima asked for a phone conference with John at the PFA, who were trying to assist where they were able, and me. We listened, as I tried to get a clearer sense of who she was and what help she could provide. Like Sayed, she had quickly identified me as a worthwhile advocate who had a public platform that could be utilised. She didn't say as much, but she pushed hard, kept in frequent touch, and asked me to share social media posts and provide advice and government connections. I could see that she and Yahya were trying to establish a working relationship, but I was wary and kept some distance. I knew too little about their history or motivations yet.

Confirming for myself that Hakeem was innocent was important. Whilst in any event he deserved my assistance as his rights as a refugee were being breached, I was acutely conscious that others would place their trust in my judgement. I would need to lend my reputation, firstly, and to get as many people onboard as possible. They'd place their trust in my judgement. I couldn't let them down. Discovering the highly dubious facts of his court case, and learning about the other athletes who had been tortured back in 2011, also provided powerful protection from online trolls and detractors. This was, after all, an immigration and refugee case, and Australia has been arguing in this space for a very long time. Anticipated backlash would need to be carefully managed.

In the end, everything that I read and all discussions with informed parties pointed to one conclusion: Bahrain wanted him back as punishment for speaking out against a member of the royal family, and they were somehow working with Thailand to this end. It was highly credible, and also terrifying to think that the hand of royal retribution could extend right around the world. He was in very, very deep trouble.

•

As the days ticked by, I was in a unique position as I was talking to a range of people and organisations involved from Amnesty, PFA, World Players United, GIDHR and no one seemed to have a clear picture of the precise chronology of events, who was at fault and how Hakeem was going to be freed. I could see that all the various organisations were working in silos, doing their best, all trying to reach Hakeem's lawyer for information, different people talking publicly, with little coordination or sharing of resources or intelligence and for all the greatest intentions, it was becoming a mess. I shared content and lent my voice to help, but when I had seen the video where he was led into court for the first time, in handcuffs, shouting 'Don't let me go back to Bahrain,' it really struck me to the core. I couldn't get it out of my mind and went back and looked at photos of Hakeem in his cell. He said he had been tortured in Bahrain, and that Australia had granted him refugee status. In a country where entry as a refugee is not a simple matter, I knew he had exceeded a very high threshold of evidence. Further, he told the cameras, 'If I'm sent back to Bahrain, don't believe anything that I say.' I thought to myself, this young man is just 25 years old and he's having to prepare the world for the false testimony he anticipates having to give as the consequence of impending torture. Frightening. I also realised that he was only about 18 when he was tortured. Eighteen! And when he spoke out against Salman, he was still only 23. My daughter was 19, my son 21 at that time, and I'd be mortified if they were placed in harm's way of any sort, let alone torture or worse. How must Hakeem's mother feel? And his wife was in Thailand as well; she had been sleeping in the original detention facility. I remember talking it through endlessly with Lara, my wife, and wondering how difficult it must be for the young couple to cope. Our hearts went out to both of them. To their whole family.

He's been granted Australia's protection, for Christ's sake, I thought. Where is everyone? Where's the government? He's one of us, a footballer – where's our community? So much of modern sport is about commercial value, corporate part-nerships, broadcast and digital revenue, politics, yet this was far more important: a player's life. I have to do something here. I have to get the community engaged. We need to start writing to the key stakeholders, putting pressure on them. Who are they? I started compiling a list and Lara pulled the details off the internet: Thai foreign minister, Australian foreign minister, members of parliament in Australia, both prime ministers, FIFA and the AFC of course.

The FIFA human rights policy was an important reference point against which to measure the obligations these officials were bound by and to be able to specify with accuracy the actions they should be taking. Without it, we would have been simply shouting and pleading, which is futile where vast power and money are involved. Certainly in football, in any event. And I knew well that the preponderance of money, and rapidly growing political influence, was coming from the Gulf region, including Bahrain which had hosted the FIFA Congress as recently as 2017. Not only was Salman therefore central to football geopolitics, but Infantino had a direct personal relationship with Prince Nasser and his father; more bad news for Hakeem.

I published open letters to the Thai Government and more detailed correspondence to FIFA's President, Gianni Infantino, and Secretary-General, Fatma Samoura, who were the first ports of call. In them I outlined the basic facts of the case and their corresponding responsibilities under the policy. It was a good start, to show the community that there are measurable, objective responsibilities here and to encourage others to do likewise.

Meanwhile, Fatima urged communication with the Australian Government, and it turned out that Hakeem had left Australia just four days before being eligible for his citizenship. Four days! Apparently, he and Nani had realised the application process would take weeks and they only had a small window for their honeymoon. I wrote to Australia's Minister for Immigration and Citizenship, David Coleman, with whom I was familiar as a member of the Australian Multicultural Council, to request that Hakeem be granted Australian citizenship. This seemed an obvious way for the government to provide greater consular support to him, to publicly show Thailand that he was important to us and quite possibly give the Thais a diplomatic exit point while preserving the bilateral relationship. In other words, a way out.

There were differing legal opinions on whether citizenship could be granted in absentia, but I sent the letter and shared it publicly anyway to let Minister David Coleman know I was invested in the case and willing to act. David advised that, unfortunately, Hakeem didn't meet the requirements for citizenship and that neither he, nor the Department of Home Affairs, could action anything on that front. Couldn't or wouldn't? It was the first of countless times we would ask that question.

The silence of the AFC was no surprise given Salman was its president, but came into sharper focus after FIFA issued a statement on 6 December that was then widely commented on in the media:

> FIFA has become aware of the urgent situation with regard to Mr. Al-Araibi, a football player in Australia who is currently being held in Thailand, facing possible extradition to Bahrain, where it is alleged his safety may be seriously at risk.
>
> In view of the potential gravity of the situation, FIFA has written to the Australian FA requesting that they take the matter up with their government, as a matter of urgency.
>
> FIFA is committed to the respect of internationally recognized human rights, in particular, as these rights relate to the safety and wellbeing of all individuals involved in football.
>
> FIFA expects the situation of Mr. Al-Araibi to be solved in accordance with well-established international standards. In that respect, FIFA supports the calls for the Thai authorities to allow Mr. Al-Araibi to return to Australia where he currently enjoys refugee status, at the earliest possible moment.[9]

Under FIFA statutes, their human rights policy and human rights defenders statement, FIFA and all its confederations, member associations, bodies and officials were duty-bound to apply their maximum leverage to ensure Hakeem was allowed to return safely to Australia. This public statement was one such step, and it demonstrated the efficacy of the sport and human rights movement, as this would never have happened as quickly in the past, if at all. It was very welcome.

However, it was typically weak. The statement said it was 'alleged' that Hakeem's safety was at risk. How much more unsafe can one be than being jailed on an erroneous red notice by the country from which you fled? I wondered. It was 'potentially' a grave situation. The kid was already a torture victim and Bahrain wanted him back; pretty damn grave in my view. It also called on the FFA to do something, when it was FIFA that had global leverage, and was a bland statement without the support of the president. FIFA was also not yet 'calling' for Thai authorities to let the kid go, merely 'supporting' those calls. I thought to myself, it's calculated not to offend Salman, likely passed by him or his office too, as FIFA would never issue a release on the matter without letting their vice president know when it directly pertained to his own country, and Confederation.

The FFA was coming under increased pressure to do or say something. I thought it was a powerful opportunity for them to make a public commitment to the rights of players and the concept of human rights in the game, in fact all sport, and demonstrate Australian football's and Australia's leadership on the issue. They even had FIFA policy as a reference point and protection. But it was not to be. Four days after FIFA, on December 10, the FFA issued their own statement outlining concerns.[10] Overdue, but welcome. That phrase would become well worn by the end of the campaign to free Hakeem.

We continued looking for any chance to magnify Hakeem's case and World Human Rights Day on 11 December was one such opportunity. SBS's The World Game is Australia's most popular football website and represents a 40-year legacy of covering football. A player in peril was unusual subject matter but nevertheless highly relevant, so I penned a piece on 'Football's duty to protect the rights of every Australian', and emphasised that, as Australia's largest participation sport, football has a lot to offer to the country in terms of the universal values of respect, inclusion and equality. I believe this passionately. Hakeem was only mentioned briefly. The primary purpose was to highlight the positive contributions that former refugees like Les Murray, my former colleague and highly respected Australian broadcaster, and young national team star, Awer Mabil, have made to the Australian community and to shape the narrative so that, by standing up for Hakeem, we would demonstrate the power of the game to make a difference.

And yet privately, we were still wondering – what would make the difference in Hakeem's case?

Chapter 4
A DEAFENING SILENCE

By mid-December, the sport and human rights movement was becoming vocal about Hakeem's case. Brendan had been lobbying hard behind the scenes, relaying an avalanche of emails that kept me abreast of the politics, thinking and people involved. And he was making headway. The Centre for Sport and Human Rights 'Sporting Chance Forum' on 12 December was perfectly timed. It brought together nearly 300 leaders and advocates in Paris to coincide with the 70th anniversary of the Universal Declaration of Human Rights. The centre's chair, Mary Robinson, the former Irish President and UN High Commissioner for Human Rights, released a statement just prior to the forum saying that 'No one in sport should be exposed to such intimidation and threats', and calling on 'all those responsible and those who could exercise their influence' to protect Hakeem and return him safely to Australia.

She mentioned Hakeem again in her welcoming address, followed by Brendan who reinforced her message. He called on FIFA's Senior Vice President and Asian Football Confederation President, Sheikh Salman, 'to uphold the duties of his offices and use his leverage to have Bahrain's request for extradition withdrawn'.[1] It was time to put the blowtorch to the AFC and its president, who had provided no public support to Hakeem in the preceding three weeks. Let's raise the temperature. Brendan had mentioned Hakeem in a respected international forum on behalf of 85,000 professional athletes, I would use the masses of social media as well as more traditional outlets and John at the PFA would speak on behalf of Australia's players. It was a multi-tiered approach that we would leverage to full effect.

I can't recall ever writing open letters before, certainly not to governing bodies or prime ministers, but these next few months would be full of new experiences and would test the capabilities of all involved. The letters served to let these people and institutions know that we weren't going to manage this issue quietly, behind closed doors with private letters and off-the-record conversations. I already had taken the view that this would not be enough. They were going to be held to account publicly and things were going to get uncomfortable for them unless they fulfilled their responsibilities and helped Hakeem. Very uncomfortable, as it would turn out. The letters also ensured the issues were publicly ventilated, created a court of public opinion and kept people informed. They would prove invaluable precisely because they operated outside the political system, and opened the game to scrutiny it is neither accustomed to nor adapts to well. Exactly what was required, in other words.

We requested Salman issue an immediate statement and indicate whether he supported the earlier statement of FIFA, in his capacity as a FIFA Vice President. It was also an opportunity to question whether he would ever publicly contradict his own government. This conflict between family, nationality and duty was one that might have been uncomfortable for him. But that is the very point of high office. He was required to put a player's life before personal or political relationships, or self-interest, and this principle, which should have been immutable, was guaranteed to provide a high level of discomfort for him. And I wanted him as discomforted as possible.

It worried me that someone implicated in alleged human rights abuses when president of his own national association, and who was associated with several AFC officials indicted by the FBI in 2017 was so critical to saving Hakeem.[2] No one had independently investigated the Arab Spring athlete abuse allegations; football had carried on while looking the other way and no reparations had been made to the athletes tortured during this period. Football's, and the IOC's, unwillingness to investigate those events and all involved is a stain on our game and the integrity of sport itself.

Meanwhile, more and more everyday people globally were becoming emotionally involved in Hakeem's plight. It was impossible not to, when the kid was on television in cuffs, so obviously terrified for his life. So the #SaveHakeem hashtag was created to bring everyone together. It would become a phenomenally powerful symbol of people power but the beginning was, well, inauspicious.

It was chosen by Hakeem's Bahraini friends in Melbourne and not long after we started to use it, someone pointed out that the word 'Save' was disempowering and insensitive. Others quickly clambered aboard this line of argument and the line of reasoning started to take on a life of its own. Since it had been created by Hakeem's friends, I felt I was on safe ground, but still a group of Twitterati went off on a tangent, quibbling over semantics. It was keeping them engaged, I thought, and better to be discussing Hakeem than not, but I was wary of those raising oblique concerns on social media as the motives are often not what we think. It was a timely reminder to maintain precision and particular care in our messaging, because this was a very delicate case in many respects.

The captain of Australia's national women's team, Sam Kerr, one of the finest footballers in the world, shared the hashtag. It's not easy for athletes to jump aboard such an issue, especially one with numerous legal dimensions, and Sam's input at this early stage was critical. Other players soon followed suit and provided much-needed visibility. Social media presented a huge challenge timewise though, and as I spent hours and hours monitoring it through the day and night I could see the issue growing, but sporadically and in a disjointed way.

In early December I had felt, or assumed, that I was adding my voice and whatever public platform I had to an existing campaign and an organised effort by human rights organisations that would take the lead. This suited me as I was extremely busy with SBS commitments, study, family and various charity programs. But over the following weeks it became obvious that it wasn't going to be enough. We were a disparate bunch across many fields of sport, unions, player unions, NGOs, refugee advocates and global human rights bodies. Information was coming in from all angles, there was little coordination of message and Hakeem needed scale, and effect. I was being asked by human rights organisations to act as a spokesperson, and I had a decision to make. Someone needed to step forward and take leadership.

This case was in the intersection of law, sport and international diplomacy where I knew that a single wrong step could potentially be fatal for Hakeem. I turned it every which way in my mind. Can I? Should I? Am I even capable of committing to a campaign with all of my existing commitments? And the answer was always the same: if not me, then who? I thought about the issues involved: refugees, sport governance, social justice, the power of sport to make a difference, all of which I cared about very deeply. I had been politically active as a player, speaking for the Republic movement in Australia as a national team player at roughly the same age as Hakeem was now. He'd been tortured for standing up for democracy. The difference between our experiences couldn't have been greater. Why should this kid suffer for things that I took for granted simply by virtue of being born in a different country?

Lara had become accustomed to my racing off trying to help the players or fight causes. She always said that I had trouble saying no to people asking for help, a 'broken wing syndrome' she called it. So she knew what was coming but was extremely worried about the risks. 'You don't know what you're getting yourself into,' she said. Years before, the Socceroos had asked me to come back to the PFA as CEO to secure a collective bargaining agreement, and I'd honoured my commitment despite being stood down by SBS because I'd given the players my word. Lara could see it happening again. While I'd work with the legal and communications department of SBS, a government broadcaster, to try to manage any potential conflicts as far as I possibly could, there is always risk and we knew that I might not be able to reconcile the two.

'You're going to put the broadcast career you love at risk again for a boy you don't know?' she asked. 'You don't know where it's going to lead and you'll have to put your whole reputation out there for him.'

'I can't stand by,' I told her, 'I love all my roles, my darling, but some things are more important than reputations, talking football and going to World Cups. How can I sit on air having a fabulous time, taking advantage of what I've been given and then look away when a kid needs my help? It's not right. He needs me, I'm responsible as a former player and if I don't help him, he's gone. We've had a wonderful life and have a beautiful family. I have to give this young family the same chance.' Lara is my voice of reason and balance, but she also knows sometimes there's no use trying. If I feel strongly enough, there's no stopping. We both knew very well this was different to other causes, though. A mountain of concerning information about Bahrain's deadly crackdown on protesters in 2011 and ongoing human rights abuses was emerging, and there was clearly something between Thailand and Bahrain. It was a deeply uncertain time and we could not possibly anticipate where it would lead. I was far from a seasoned campaigner and would have to learn extremely quickly but, for all the worries, and a few tears shed at what might lie ahead, we agreed. I would give Hakeem everything I had. Come what may.

From that moment, time spent on the case exploded. There is nothing like a young man's life being in danger to make one squeeze much, much more into a busy schedule. People clearly needed coordination, direction, information so every morning, bleary-eyed and as Lara ferried a fresh flood of coffee up and down the stairs from the kitchen to the bedroom, I'd write a hastily prepared update, share the actions for people to take, give credit to as many as possible and publish tweets of any influential or famous people who had come onboard, thanking them. Three rules – share, act and rope someone else in – would be the new directives. The overriding imperative was to make enough noise to stop Hakeem being forcibly returned to Bahrain. As long as he remains in Thailand, we're a chance.

I needed to bring everyone along for the ride or we could not possibly hope to succeed. Supporters would want, and need, to hear from me so I spent countless hours responding to people, thanking them and reaching out. I felt very strongly that we all needed to share the issue, to own it, to feel part of a greater whole. I also well knew from almost two decades in the media that moving people to act in a mass collective is not only about injustice, refugee law, conventions and protection visas. It's about an outcry. It's not only logic, but emotion. That's what moves us to tears or anger and is the fuel that drives the necessary action. We would all experience several lifetimes of both in the next few months.

At the beginning, I felt uneasy reaching out to people on Twitter who I'd never met – government ministers, athletes, singers, superstar footballers, you name it. I had no idea at that stage if it would work and can tell you that I was well out of my comfort zone in an entirely new field of activism but we needed high-profile supporters so I pushed through and, before long, started to gain traction. Mind you, I was very well aware that it could have been a catastrophic fail but, then, I'd lost any fear of that long ago. In sport and the media alike you learn to improvise, to deal with the imperfect, adapt on the run, give the very best you have at that time with the information to hand and move on. I could live with failing, but not with failing to act.

Of course I could have simply picked up the phone in many instances, but it was critically important to put politicians under public scrutiny, to let the football community know that I'd contacted them. This is the real power of social media: visibility and accountability. There'd be no hiding here and many would respond privately, if not publicly. I would later use this to good effect with other athletes, and even footballers once the campaign grew sufficiently in size, calling them out publicly. As the US women's 2019 FIFA World Cup winning co-captain and brave social rights activist, Megan Rapinoe, would later quip in relation to Gianni Infantino's poor record on gender equality and the growing disparity in prizemoney, a little public shaming never hurt anyone.

Later, when the campaign grew in acceptability and people were drawn to get onboard, to be a part of something inspiring, Twitter would become an incredible tool of advocacy. I was truly staggered by the reach we would achieve. For now, though, where to start? Close to home. Everyone I knew from thirty years in football, sport, government and broadcasting would be called upon. Publicly. My broadcast colleague on Australian television who has a very caring heart, Lucy Zelic, felt strongly about the case and agreed to a photo for social media. But I hadn't prepared anything. What should we do? I grabbed a piece of A4 from the sports department printer, scribbled the hashtag, and we took a shot on the set of our English Premier League (EPL) broadcast that night. Planning was, clearly, at a premium in these early stages. It was chaotic as I was covering matches on air for SBS for which I'd need to be on top of the tactics and pre-match information, all of which was mixed up with the latest campaign information for Hakeem coming through on the phone by the minute. I'd have one eye on the match, the other reading an endless stream of texts, emails, Whatsapp messages, Twitter messages and tweets, Facebook messages, Instagram messages, Signal messages, LinkedIn messages. You name it.

Elsewhere, the public campaign was ticking over, with activists trying to make some noise. This included a public demonstration and hunger strike organised by human rights groups and the Bahraini community outside the Thai consulate in Melbourne. This, along with the two public petitions launched by Amnesty International and GIDHR, had received some media traction, but nowhere near enough.

As players, when we need help we can always count on our teammates, and I needed them now. I hit the phone. The former men's national team captain, Alex Tobin, one of the most respected people in Australian football, is also a former president of the PFA. 'Of course,' he said when I approached him, 'whatever you need, Fozz.' Alex roped in another great of the Australian game, former captain Paul Wade. They shared an open letter.

I approached Robbie Slater, another ex-teammate and playing legend, who won an EPL title with Blackburn and is a big voice in the Australian game. 'You're a big personality at Fox Sports,' I told him, 'and this needs to be across all sectors, all networks.' Rob shared the hashtag. Frank Farina is another legendary former player, former coach of the national team and PFA life member. 'Fozz, I trust you, if you say the kid is innocent and needs my help, send a letter and I'll sign, no questions asked.' I was humbled and heartened. The greater challenge would be to move the issue outside of the playing profession, then the sport, but these legends' fame would assist greatly towards early momentum and credibility.

A final call to another teammate from both the national team and Crystal Palace Football Club in England – Socceroos and World Cup star Craig Moore, also a Glasgow Rangers legend. Craig was happy to share the hashtag and, again, invested an enormous amount of trust. 'If you say so, Fozz. This is not my area, international law, but I'm happy to get onboard if you're sure it's up front.' The kid's innocent, I've read the case, Moorey, if we don't stand up, no one will. He was in. We now had four captains, an EPL champion and a former national team coach. Plus John at the PFA was pushing players everywhere to help out, and more were getting onboard by the minute.

SBS being the multicultural network, I knew that I could rely on its amazing staff and presenters. Well-known Tour de France presenter Michael Tomalaris: reach out to your cycling contacts, mate. Get those world champions you work with onboard. Three-time Tour de France green jersey winner Robbie McEwen was soon onside and he'd bring along the community. Bravo, we had cycling.

Broadcast personality Liz Deep-Jones, a champion of social causes; Indian Super League commentator Andy Paschalidis; former Leeds United star Michael Bridges; football comment-ator David Basheer; luminaries across all networks in Australia and beyond – they'd all soon be roped in to help. And, so we grew. One person at a time.

In Thailand, human rights organisations had been on the phones leaning on every contact possible for information. It was heartening to see respected Thais become involved. Former foreign minister of Thailand, Kasit Piromya, lent his voice. 'The task falls to Thailand's Foreign Affairs Minister to determine justice,' he said. 'The ministry has to keep in mind that Bahrain is an absolute monarchy and it has to look whether there will be a fair trial.' Did he know something that we didn't? 'Bahrain will surely pursue the extradition,' he said, 'but the Thai ministry has to weigh the relationship of Thai–Bahrain and the consequences [for the Australia–Thailand relationship].' Indeed. It was that relationship we aimed to put to the most severe test.

Despite all these developments, however, nothing changed. I was conscious that every day was a new realm of torture for Hakeem. The feeling of urgency and dread, that something awful could happen at any moment, was unlike anything I had experienced before. And I wasn't sitting in a Thai prison. How could this young man possibly be coping? And what about his poor wife, how petrified must she be?

I called in every favour and contact, and all responded brilliantly, using their visibility to amplify the messages. One such former SBS colleague, and beloved friend, is journalist and presenter Andrew Orsatti. 'Orsat', as his friends know him, is now head of communications at FIFPro, having worked at ESPN in the US, and was pushing hard in the background, hugely invested in the case. We had been conversing daily by call or message for weeks. Orsat knew the world's football media intimately. He had a direct line and access to the world's top players through the 65 member unions of FIFPro. He was offered a contract by Italian club Pescara as a young man but, after injury forced his early retirement, he moved on to forge a brilliant career as a journalist and media professional. All of these highly polished skills were now put at Hakeem's disposal and he couldn't have been in better hands.

Privately, FIFPro's Secretary-General, Theo van Seggelen, had sent a letter drafted by Brendan to Salman requesting that he take action. Theo let Salman know that as a member of Bahrain's ruling family, he was uniquely positioned to uphold the duties of his offices as AFC President and FIFA Senior Vice President, and must transparently take the action needed for Hakeem's safe return:

> The game cannot see any refugee footballer suffer harm under its watch. No issue is more important to football as a global and universal game than protecting vulnerable people such as refugee players from detention and torture.

The sheikh did not bother to reply, leaving it to the AFC's General Secretary, Dato' Windsor John, to respond a week later in a letter copied to FIFA and Sheikh Salman:

> We thank you for your letter dated 17 December 2018, the contents of which are duly noted. Kindly be informed that the AFC is monitoring the situation closely and is in close contact with FIFA and the respective Member Associations involved. Please rest assured that the AFC takes this matter very seriously.[3]

'Very seriously'? There had been no public statement, not even to say the AFC was behind FIFA's efforts. They had not visited Hakeem in prison. I'd reached out to Fatima to check with Hakeem's wife whether the AFC had contacted her, his Melbourne lawyers or GIDHR, had offered any assistance or legal support. Nothing. This boy was languishing in detention just a six-hour flight from the AFC office in Kuala Lumpur, and no one had taken the time to even go and offer assistance. They were ghosts. In contrast, though, we were becoming louder by the hour.

In my mind, there was considerable uncertainty as to how much influence Salman had within the Bahraini royal family and government. Our intelligence was mixed on this point. In any view that I formed, though, he was front and centre. Opinions from a range of sources vacillated between him being most able to solve the issue, to his being on the outer with his extended family and useless to an outcome. Irrespective, he was in the firing line. His role as President of the AFC and Vice President of FIFA was to advocate for Hakeem, as far as I was concerned. We could also use him as the symbol of entitlement and disregard for basic values that Hakeem was up against. Knowing that he would do nothing substantive, merely tokenistic if at all, I felt it was actually preferable if he maintained his silence. It would feed the narrative and drive the public agenda.

So, we applied more pressure from all sectors, with rising calls for him to vacate the position as president by John at the PFA, Brendan and me, when he received a ringing endorsement. Despite the forthcoming election being in April the following year, over four months away, the President of the Bahrain Football Association (BFA), Sheikh Ali bin Khalifa bin Ahmed Al Khalifa, fellow member of the royal family, issued a glowing statement fully endorsing Salman for a further four-year term.[4] A clear signal of where his priorities lay and that Hakeem's case would have no bearing on their political ambitions. Two things were abundantly clear: if the kid was to be freed, it wouldn't be due to the

AFC and, secondly, the BFA could be utterly disregarded. Interestingly though, Salman could evidently call on favours from Bahraini football when needed. But, could we force him to call on his own government and royal family? That would be the real test.

•

Beyond the paltry response from within football boardrooms, Australians were waking up to the injustice, including athletes from other sports, I'm delighted to say.

There are some incredible examples of Australian sportspeople who have relished their power and responsibility as athletes and willingly used their public platforms to shed light on social injustices. Who could forget when Cathy Freeman carried both the Australian and Aboriginal flags after winning the 200 metres at the 1994 Commonwealth Games? Her simple act of defiance and pride became a true symbol of reconciliation and pride for all Australians. Or Peter Norman, silver medallist in the men's 200-metre final at the 1968 Olympics in Mexico City, who bravely supported American sprinters Tommie Smith and John Carlos on the podium when they raised their fists in support of the black civil rights movement in the US. It became one of the most iconic photographs of the twentieth century. Globally, tennis great Billie Jean King's threat to boycott the US Open led to more equal pay in the tennis world, and NFL player Colin Kaepernick sent shockwaves through the US for 'taking a knee' rather than standing for the American national anthem, to draw attention to police brutality and the #BlackLivesMatter movement.

In a world where sport governing bodies continue to openly oppress athletes' rights and where humanity is facing vast existential challenges like climate change, the international, inclusive and apolitical currency of sport is more important now than ever. Athletes have a role to play in helping people see what is right and just. To do this, though, I knew that they'd have to be prepared to risk themselves. I was trying to find out, quickly, which ones were willing to do so.

By late December, our minds were partly on the looming Asian Cup and how the national team, the Socceroos, might get involved in the campaign. My anger was boiling and Brendan and I talked at length about a national team boycott unless we saw action from the AFC. How can our country play in good conscience in a tournament managed by an organisation that was not doing everything in its power to investigate the torture of athletes and which refuses to help our own player, and a recognised refugee, for heaven's sake?

Both Brendan and I had been heavily involved in one of the most important player rights' cases in Australian football history, a threatened strike by the national team in 1997, when I was still playing, so a boycott was always going to be a strong possibility. The Socceroos had experienced a generational change, however, and Timmy Cahill and skipper Mile Jedinak, whom I had a trusting relationship with and who were strong voices, had gone and new coach, Graham Arnold, another former teammate of mine, had taken the opportunity to regenerate the squad. Was it fair or even achievable to ask this young group to pull out? John raised the valid question as to why our players, and our game, should suffer when it was the AFC and FIFA who were bound to act. And what about Thailand and Bahrain, shouldn't they be banned rather than us pull out? Both countries were responsible for a grievous breach of human rights, after all, when Australia had done nothing wrong. Yes, and it was open to us to stress that action must be taken against both federations as part of any considered and threatened boycott.

We all knew, though, that a proposed withdrawal would be fraught. Some, if not most, fans would find it difficult to support, but then, some things are far more important than international success. If a national team does not stand for the values of the game, who the hell will? What the shirt represents is far more important than when or where it's worn. So a potential boycott was on the table but, for now, there were more pressing issues.

The GIDHR were pushing for a press conference and John and I sat on a call with Fatima and talked it through. Fatima stressed that my profile would be necessary to draw media to the event and I made time in my schedule to be there at the PFA offices. We needed to get in the face of our national media and get this issue moving. Hakeem had been detained in Thailand for a month already. There'd been more stories coming out of the prison as journalists found their way in, and they all spoke of a young man crying for help, terrified of what might become of him.

We also inquired about how Nani, who was now back in Australia, was coping. John offered for the PFA to provide financial support. Did she need anything? Rent? Car payments? Her husband was in prison, overseas, we didn't even know whether he worked outside of playing. What were her outgoings? We tried to get a picture as to the family and their needs; the players wanted to help out as much as possible. Fatima agreed to approach the issue with sensitivity and the PFA would subsequently provide financial support at an incredibly difficult time for Nani. One weight off everyone's minds, and another demonstration of values in action. No questions asked. Of course, the players would help.

The day before the press conference, Sam Kerr had led her W-League team, Perth Glory, and opposing Sydney FC players to wear orange armbands in the W-League match. The PFA's player-advocacy efforts were starting to come to life.

Fatima had reached out to Amnesty, and Rodrigo Vargas, a champion of Australia's professional competition, the A-League, had also agreed to attend the press conference on 22 December. John was worried, though, about whether anyone would turn up. This was a new experience for him. 'We put a great deal of energy into getting the right people there but I was uneasy to say the least. I was telling people that this was not our core business, saving players from torture.'

When I entered the PFA's inner-city Melbourne offices on the morning of 22 December, a throng was building and staff were tense. Everyone was on edge, smiles strained. They'd been working weeks on a case no one had been trained for with deep emotional fluctuations, getting nowhere, feeling the pressure, always with the spectre of failure and the ramifications of what that might mean for Hakeem hanging over their heads. The office wall formed the perfect back-drop, with a large image of Hakeem projected behind the press conference desk. The rest of the wall was covered with stencilled black outlines of footballers as well as the five PFA organisational values writ large. Courage. Intelligence. Respect. World Class. Trust. It read to me like the perfect wish list of how to free Hakeem.

The conference gave us a welcome public boost with the #SaveHakeem hashtag trending for the first time. I had been trying to form a clear sense of what we needed the Australian Government to do and, on the advice of a range of human rights and government contacts, focused on a call to action for Australia's Foreign Minister, Marise Payne, asking her to engage in person with her counterpart in Thailand as soon as possible. Rodrigo Vargas' words, though, were incredibly powerful that day. As a former teammate of Hakeem's at Green Gully, he spoke from the heart, his voice cracking. 'Hakeem is an incredible young man and I have seen his bravery first-hand . . . The entire football community, from top to bottom, must come together to support him. It is what a real community does.' I didn't know Hakeem personally, so it was good to pull Roddy aside and quiz him on who Hakeem really was, what type of person and teammate. As he answered, Roddy's eyes welled up with tears, which told me all I needed to know.

Vitale Ferrante, Hakeem's coach at Pascoe Vale, and Lou Tona were emotional and passionate on camera, giving personal perspectives. This was important to show the human side of the issue, that not just Hakeem, but also his friends, colleagues, teammates and family were deeply affected. Peter Filopoulos of Football Victoria also spoke and would shortly urge all of the state's clubs and participants to share a photo with the #SaveHakeem hashtag, which was tremendous to see. Peter would prove himself a model of official advocacy, forthright and unafraid in contrast to the general reticence of other officials and states to act, and later we would need to give them the Rapinoe treatment to step up.

Several days later, on Christmas Eve, as I spent welcome family time, my phone buzzed in my jacket pocket. It was a text from Australia's Foreign Minister, Marise Payne. 'Can I give you a call?' Progress, I thought. We had reached an important stage. The campaign was loud enough to gain the government's attention.

For the past few weeks, the issue of how to manage the government had been percolating in my mind. I would either have to publicly attack them to force action, work with them, or a combination of the two. It wasn't yet clear which option would be most appropriate and I needed to know more about the people involved, so I had reached out to personal connections in Parliament for a detailed brief. I needed to know more about the relevant people involved on a personal level. Were they good people? Did they have a reputation as trustworthy? I also wanted some ideas on what was going to make this government move.

Marise Payne had released a brief media statement on 9 December saying that she had raised the matter with her Thai counterpart, Foreign Minister of Thailand Mr Don Pramudwinai, but I was aware through human rights channels that progress with the Australian Government was slow. Is Marise really committed or paying lip service? What is going on inside Home Affairs? What's the real agenda here?

The advice I received on Marise was positive. Irrespective of any Australian Government position or policy, she was fundamentally a good person, which was important to me. I would form my own view along the way and keep an open mind on everyone involved, but if I knew from the outset that she would try to do the right thing, I could extend the benefit of the doubt and possibly support her publicly through what was undoubtedly going to be a difficult issue publicly for the government. That was a risk and would require a lot more comfort on my end and the extension of trust, both ways.

I was advised to avoid any ministers with a record of being particularly anti asylum seeker so as not to put the government in a position from which they couldn't resile and that the Prime Minister, Scott Morrison, would move when it was in his political interest. No surprise there, my job would be to make it so. Marise was doing all she could within her power but needed more support from above. Morrison would need to be pushed but getting him to fight for a refugee in the current environment when he'd been one of the architects of Australia's punitive immigration and border policy as a minister? That would be an almighty challenge, I thought.

On this point, the Interpol red notice had the potential to put the government in an uncomfortable position. The media and general public, particularly in Australia, were starting to ask questions about Australia's role in tipping Thailand off prior to Hakeem's arrival in Bangkok. Like me, most people probably didn't really even know what an Interpol red notice was prior to Hakeem's case, let alone all the intricacies involved with it. But some advocates, organisations and journalists had started to become very vocal on the issue, and for very good reason.

An organisation called Fair Trials, an independent criminal justice watchdog, had published a letter in early December to the Minister for Home Affairs, Peter Dutton, expressing serious concerns about Hakeem's arrest.[5] I noticed other names popping up online, like Radha Stirling, who was also very vocal on this point. Radha is founder and CEO of Detained in Dubai and has been a leading voice against the abuse of Interpol systems for more than a decade. I came across some of her writing online and connected to her via Twitter, and she was extremely helpful in explaining what had likely happened with Hakeem's case. She outlined to me the evidence showing how Interpol's red notice system had been used by authoritarian regimes to secure the return of refugees and asylum seekers who had escaped from them. She told me about her longstanding work calling for greater Interpol transparency and regulatory reforms to end this abuse of the system. She was also clearly dissatisfied, as were many others, with the Australian Government's response to the role they had played in warning Thailand (and as we would find out later, Bahrain) of Hakeem's arrival. She stayed hot on the government and Interpol's heels throughout the campaign,[6] which assisted in maintaining the pressure on Australia and also Thailand. I needed this to continue to keep the public heat on high.

But by late December, only a few things were really clear about the red notice. Firstly, despite the fact we knew Australia had, at some point, alerted Thailand to Hakeem's arrival, it also appeared that Bahrain had actively colluded with Thailand to ensure Hakeem was arrested. Thailand's Immigration chief, Surachate Hakparn, had in fact openly revealed this in an interview with the BBC ten days after Hakeem's detention, stating, 'The Bahraini government knew that he would be arriving in Thailand [on 27 November], so they coordinated with Thailand's permanent secretary of foreign affairs to detain him, pending documents sent from Bahrain.'[7] How had Bahrain known when Hakeem would be arriving?

Secondly, it was clear that Interpol's involvement up to this point required serious scrutiny. The red notice from Bahrain should never have been issued, because of Hakeem's refugee status and his Australian protection visa. It went against Interpol's own policies and, according to one source who used to be very high up in Australian Border Force, the red notice request from Bahrain itself was 'light enough on detail' and 'probably only needed a quick Google search' for Interpol's headquarters to put its validity into question. Both Bahrain's human rights record and Hakeem's personal experience of torture would've popped up within seconds on the internet, which meant that no kind of reasonable due diligence had occurred. The same ex-Border Force official was also not surprised at this, essentially revealing that Interpol's headquarters had very few staff or capacity to do thorough analyses of red notices. It was probably a junior officer somewhere behind a desk who had processed it. Thirdly, it was clear that the Australian Border Force and the Australian Federal Police were involved in Hakeem's situation, and this was emerging as an important point of leverage.

Finally, and perhaps most significantly, the Australian Government's unwillingness to clarify the specifics created great confusion regarding responsibilities and timelines. This enabled the red notice issue to be used as a red herring by the Thai Government to deflect responsibility for Hakeem's ongoing detention to Australia. It allowed them to point the finger at Australia, regardless of who was truly at fault. You put him in this mess, they were saying, and this was damaging to our prospects of holding them to account and raising pressure for his release.

So, when Marise Payne phoned on Christmas Eve, all of these things were running through my head. How candid would she be? The press conference had attracted the government's attention, all right. She had heard my request and assured me of her commitment to the case and her intention to travel to Thailand in several weeks. I sought information about the campaign's tone and value, whether getting people lobbying the Thai PM directly – writing letters or on social media – would be effective. I was candid and honest with her about my intentions, letting her know that, while I would maintain pressure on our government where appropriate, it would be done respectfully. I also impressed upon her that I would be doing whatever was needed to free Hakeem, but that it had nothing to do with politics. Human rights are universal; this issue crossed all political lines. Importantly, she mentioned that a highly experienced and capable diplomat had just taken over the Bangkok post only a month prior. Though I didn't know it then, this timing would prove immensely fortuitous. Our phone call was a warm but cautious start, naturally; however, trust was shown and reciprocated, and I had a sense that she was a genuinely nice person.

By then, I had contacted members of parliament across almost every party, including Greens Senators Sarah Hanson-Young and Nick McKim, who would be tremendously helpful given their strong public support for humane treatment of refugees, as well as Labor MP Peter Khalil (who formerly worked at SBS, is a fellow football lover and whose constituency included the Pascoe Vale club) to ensure that pressure could be applied from all sides of politics. The strategy would be to work directly with the government as far as was appropriate but keep the blowtorch on them through other channels.

Very often during the campaign, it was difficult to separate fact from fiction. One of the issues gaining prominence on social media was that Hakeem had asked the Australian Government whether it was safe for him to travel. It was being reported that he had been given assurances by Home Affairs. Obviously, this was a point of weakness for the government and these aspects give people a sense of indignation and outrage, which we know social media feeds and drives. The government was acting too slowly and days were ticking by. I would alternate between sharing direct challenges to them or posting my own, or staying arms-length and encouraging others to do so. On this occasion, I posted about Hakeem receiving erroneous government advice. It was our fault, I said in substance, and our government needs to right their wrong.

Marise called. It had touched a nerve, a good sign. Social media was starting to become a threat. Marise explained that, had Hakeem in fact asked for that information from the Department of Home Affairs, they would not have provided an answer in any event. The department does not provide individually tailored advice to travellers based on their visa type and circumstances. Whatever the case, I was pleased she'd reached out again. It indicated she was aware of the campaign, sensitive to its tone and direction and likely wanted to keep me on side. This suited me, and I respected her willingness to keep me informed. I wouldn't go hard on the point from then on, but nor would I discourage others from maintaining that line of attack; it was a point of leverage that would be useful.

My family spent Christmas at home that year. Lara's brother and family visited from out of town and we hosted lunch. Whenever I get intensely involved with something, I get obssessive and just can't switch off. My family know the signs and allow me the space to work. By that stage, #SaveHakeem had already taken over our family life and our lunch may as well have been a Human Rights Watch or Amnesty meeting. This young man named Hakeem al-Araibi and the deep injustice of the world were the entree, main course and dessert.

Chapter 5
KLONG PREM PRISON

'From the moment I entered Bangkok's Klong Prem remand prison on 11 December,' Hakeem remembers, a pained expression on his face, 'I tried to isolate myself from the other prisoners. I had no idea what crimes they had committed and I didn't want to stand out or get into any trouble. They tried to communicate with me; but I always turned my face and didn't speak to them. I was afraid and there were also obvious language barriers. As a result, most of the time in those early days in the prison, I spent alone. For the first week I was there, Nani remained in Bangkok and visited me every day.'

If a prisoner at Klong Prem prison was lucky enough to have a visitor coming to see them, their name would be called over a loudspeaker that could be heard from anywhere in the prison. They would then go to a reception area and, after going through a screening process, would get to see and talk to visitors through bars and perspex for 20 minutes.

Lawyers were only allowed to visit their clients on weekdays; however, they were allowed to visit prisoners for much longer timeslots than family or friends. So on her first visit, the day after Hakeem's appearance in court on 11 December, Nat Bergman showed, not for the first time, her incredible resourcefulness. She saw how important seeing Nani was to Hakeem, and she knew that Nani would soon be going back to Australia leaving her client without any immediate family or friends in Thailand. So, she told the guards at the prison that Nani was her Arabic translator. This meant that their visit was technically a lawyer's visit, and they were able to spend a few hours with Hakeem without interruption.

'On Friday [14 December], Nani came to visit me for the last time before heading to the airport. Both of us had decided she had to go back to Australia. We didn't know how much longer I was going to be in there, she was fast running out of money, and we thought that she would be able to do more for my case if she went back to Melbourne. She told me to be strong and that she would work with the Australian Government to get me citizenship.'

After she left, Hakeem returned alone into the depths of the prison. 'I felt very alone. I was crying inside . . . she was back to Australia. Will she stay with hope?'

Despite mostly keeping to himself, Hakeem did get to know some of the other prisoners. One character whom Hakeem remembers meeting in those early weeks went by the name of 'Mr Big'. 'He was very rich,' Hakeem explains. 'They had charged him for some money-related issues, like stealing millions from a Thai club or something, and he was getting special attentions from the police in the jail, they are treating him very differently . . . but he was very kind to me.' Mr Big was a short man in his early forties. He had Chinese–Thai heritage and told Hakeem that he was the owner of two football clubs in Thailand.

'He was also one of the few prisoners in the jail who had a television in his room with a remote control, meaning that he had access to the news and the outside world. Two weeks after I entered the prison, there was a small football tournament organised between the inmates. I played in Mr Big's team and we won. After that, we got to know each other and sat together many times in the prison. In the prison there were also many other rich people there [and] when they saw I was walking with Mr Big, they felt jealousy towards [me]. I felt that my connection with him protected me from the other prisoners.' But Mr Big was also a vital way for Hakeem to get the news that he craved from the outside world.

'Days in the prison was very tough. For 15 hours of every day we spent in a small room that I shared with about 45 other men,' Hakeem says. 'The floor was hard concrete, and the heat was very bad.' Despite being in the middle of Thailand's winter, January in Bangkok can reach stifling temperatures of up to 31 degrees Celsius. 'There was only a small fan in the prison cell, and we were only allowed one bottle of water in the room with us. I sweated from the heat, even when sleeping. Each [prisoner] had three thin blankets. I put one down on the hard ground, one under my head as a pillow and pulled the third one over my body.'

Hakeem continues, 'There was a small television mounted up on the wall at one end of the room, which was switched onto the same one or two channels most of the time and controlled by the guards. Directly under the television was a communal squat toilet, a single hole in the ground, with a small tap to wash your hands. There was a low door in front of the toilet hole that [came] up to your waist, but everybody could see me when I [was] going to the toilet. Also, everyone is looking in this direction, because of the TV.'

There was a hierarchy among the prisoners that determined where everyone slept based predominantly on how long they'd been there. 'I tried to position myself on the wall in the centre of the room, so that I was away from the stench of the toilet and the constant noise of the television. Because of my height, my feet sometimes touched one of the men who were laid down in the centre of the room. There were about 18 or 19 men against each wall, maybe five along the back wall, and then three in a line down [the] centre of the room.

'We could choose to shower at either 6.30 am or 2 pm, but soap and shampoo had to be brought with our own money at the prison shop. The shower rooms were large areas with no walls, where more than 50 men would stand at one time while water sprayed from long tubes along the ceiling. We were allowed out of the cell from 6.30 am to 3.30 pm each day. My day would be to get up and walk around for 15 minutes in the common area to stretch my muscles, especially my back, because of the hard floor. At 7 am, I ate a breakfast of plain bread and bitter coffee. Lunch was at 10.30, then dinner at 1.30 pm, which means we [went] for 15 hours without food every day. Most meals consisted of rice and watery soups, and the only people who ate it were [those] without money or visitors from outside. I ate as little as possible.

'After stretching, I would spend the first three to 3.5 hours of the day just walking around the edge of [the] room we were in, which was about 10 metres by 50 metres in size. About 300 people were put into this room, but I felt lucky because another building in the prison had a common area like this with 700 to 800 people in it, with no room to walk around. On Saturdays and Sundays only, we were allowed outside to use the small dirt football pitch.'

Beyond visitors, there were some other brief moments of reprieve. One prisoner – a singer – became quite attached to Hakeem. 'I think he felt that his case is similar to mine. He was a Thai national . . . he told me that he had spoken out critically of the royal family and was sentenced to 15 years in jail for it.' Hakeem has a fond look on his face when he talks about him. 'He sung for everybody, the old man, maybe sixty years old from Thai . . . he was a good singer. I couldn't understand [the songs] but they made me happy.

'Christmas and New Year's in the prison were the hardest days of my life. New Year's Eve was 35 nights in a row behind bars, and it had been already weeks since I had said goodbye to my wife.' There was a celebration organised by the prison guards, but he didn't feel like celebrating at all. 'I felt there but not there at the same time my mind was somewhere else.' Most nights he was asleep by 9 pm, but on New Year's Eve the guards came and woke all the prisoners at around 11.30 pm. They let everyone come out of the cell and watch TV for a while, before forcing them all to say Buddhist prayers. 'Even if your religion was Muslim or Christian, you had to pray with them. I remember I was just hurting on the inside that evening, wondering how my wife was going to spend her night. Wondering, why is this happening to me?'

That same night, many thousands of kilometres away in his home country of Bahrain, another human rights defender was no doubt asking himself the same question. Bahrain's Court of Cassation had, that same day, upheld Nabeel Rajab's five-year prison sentence for posting tweets expressing his opinions about Bahrain's justice system. Hakeem remained in constant fear that his extradition to Bahrain could occur any day, and that he would end up in a situation like Nabeel's. Indefinite detention, or worse.

•

Lying in his cell on Wednesday 9 January, Hakeem had no idea that Australia's Foreign Minister Marise Payne was on her way to Thailand to advocate for his release. Or that, for the past 48 hours, his remarkable wife Nani had been knocking on the doors of human rights organisations and government bodies all over Sydney, demanding they do more for her husband.

I met Nani for the first time on Monday 7 January in a small hotel room in Mascot. Fatima and Yahya had asked me to advise on their campaign strategy and, while Yahya outlined what he hoped to achieve and how I might assist,

I had one eye firmly fixed on Nani, a quiet, withdrawn woman on the corner of the couch, listening intently. Petite, polite hellos, big searching eyes, watching. I was trying to get both a sense of whether GIDHR had a broader agenda and if there were any pitfalls I needed to avoid. How much should I bring them along, work with them? The campaign had to be absolutely secular: the Bahraini protests in 2011 were political not religious, and I was extremely sensitive to any signals that any other agendas were at play.

And I also wanted to understand what Nani wanted and, moreover, what she was capable of. As yet, she had not spoken out publicly and had declined our invitation to be present at the recent press conference. We knew that a more personal message from Hakeem's wife would be extremely powerful, but all of us and particularly human rights organisations were very sensitive to her grief, wellbeing and security. It was a delicate matter to even ask, with potential concerns for other family members, but I thought that it would very likely be necessary at some point. Would she consider it?

For the first half-hour, indications were hard to read. Then, all of a sudden, as Yahya spoke, Nani turned directly to me. 'Can I say something?' Of course. 'Will you help my husband? Can you speak to the Australian Government to do that?' A soft voice, but direct. There was strength there. No tears – I imagine she'd shed enough already – but emotion radiated from her whole body as she sat forward and got straight to the point. She wanted action, now. 'Are you going to help my husband?' I was doing the best I knew how at that point but didn't want to overcommit to them either.

'Can you talk to the Australian Government to get him citizenship?' she asked. I replied, politely, that I had already written to them. But she persisted, 'Can we have a meeting with the Australian Government?' It became clear that she would not let me out of this room with just lip service. I was very pleased to see this side of her. We would need her personal experience – having been in the detention centre and lived the nightmare – to bring a range of stakeholders along and if public comments were not possible, private advocacy was critical. Later that night, I told Lara, 'She reminded me of you.' Fiercely protective of her family and strong-willed, resilient. I was convinced, said I'd give her everything that I could and agreed to attend meetings with them the next day.

We met Tim O'Connor, Alex Engel-Mallon, Dr Graham Thom and several of their colleagues at Amnesty International's Sydney office. I'd worked with them over the previous year and knew they were incredible human rights advocates and had networks all over the world that they could mobilise at a moment's notice to support cases like Hakeem's. They had been active since early December but now we needed their scale, campaign expertise and brand to really ramp things up. GIDHR was a husband and wife team, they'd juggle baby duties with their young child during meetings, and Hakeem's campaign was quickly becoming something well beyond their experience. They wanted to join a larger coalition and Amnesty was a vital component with a global reach in the millions.

Yahya talked and Tim responded professionally, 'We're aware of the case and feel strongly about it. We'd like to let

Nani know that we respect her suffering, know how difficult this is for her and acknowledge her pain.' Beautifully handled, I thought. Caring, sensitive, passionate about injustice.

Alex provided a briefing on government relations and ongoing discussions regarding consular support in Bangkok. She was very thorough, measured and calm. We'd only met briefly at various promotional events but I was very impressed with what I now saw. Highly professional and well researched, she would quickly become a key ally providing sound advice. The meeting was meandering through information of one sort or another, when Nani spoke up. 'I would like to say something.' Of course Nani, please, said Tim. 'Will you help my husband? Can you help with the Australian Government, they are too slow, they should make him a citizen.' This time, emotion was in her voice. The room stopped, transfixed. As we listened to her explain what happened in Bangkok, Tim would later say, the highly experienced campaigners in the room were deeply touched, and became personally invested in the case.

An hour later, we met with Elaine Pearson, Australia Director at Human Rights Watch. I had asked for a briefing on Elaine from Brendan who worked closely with Minky Worden, HRW's global expert and an important component in the global sport and rights movement including with SRA. Minky was active on social media about the case and clearly passionate about the impact of sport around the world. She had been in touch from very early on, providing information and reports and lobbying privately, and I'd taken the opportunity to Skype with Minky to speak directly. That simple video conference medium would be so beneficial in quickly getting a sense of who people were on a personal level rather than just tweets, direct messages and emails.

Human Rights Watch was also a hugely impressive organisation; less campaign- and activist-focused than Amnesty, but very much research and policy driven. Together, the two organisations would be extremely powerful if we could get them both working on the campaign. Elaine was focused, sensitive but strategic, wanting to know details, and I could see her thinking it through, planning. Nani made an emotional impact again, and Elaine committed the organisation to the case. She'd just arrived back from abroad and it was a high priority. They were happy to collaborate with GIDHR and Amnesty. As the issue grew in complexity, the coalition tasked with solving it was fast expanding too.

The Racial Discrimination Commissioner at the Australian Human Rights Commission, Chin Tan, had issued a statement on Hakeem's case and expressed a strong interest, to the point of perhaps even travelling to Bangkok to meet with Hakeem. Fatima was a powerful advocate in our meeting later that day with Chin Tan while Yahya remained downstairs to mind their child. I respected this greatly and grew to like them more.

Finally, we met with Paul Power and staff at the Refugee Council of Australia, late in the day. Paul offered all his support, though he wasn't sure exactly where he could make an impact. 'Have your people get involved on social media, and connect everyone in,' we said, 'the more the merrier.' Nani was quicker at asking for help this time and didn't hold back, going straight for the jugular. I told her afterwards, when all this is over and your husband is free, you should work in human rights, you're a ferocious advocate. She smiled. She knew perfectly well what she was doing. Hakeem's most important ally, it turned out, was the one he'd married.

Amnesty were already in contact with Evan Jones, a colleague they trusted in Bangkok, and we scheduled a video conference with him days later to see what more could be done on the ground. Evan is Program Coordinator at the Asia Pacific Refugee Rights Network (APRRN), an umbrella body for over 350 organisations and individuals. They run on a shoestring budget with just six staff in a tiny Bangkok office responsible for an enormous stretch of 28 countries, from Iran to New Zealand. Evan is an Australian citizen, born in Western Sydney, and spent his early career working for the public service in Canberra. After a stint living in Hong Kong, he became interested in refugee and migration issues in the region.

He moved to Bangkok in late 2013, met his wife, Poy, a Thai national, in 2016, and they were expecting their first baby at the time of the campaign. Evan says he feels more at home in Asia than Australia, which might seem strange given his physical appearance – he has bushy locks of ginger-red hair, a matching beard and a pale white complexion. But his mannerisms are very much attuned to Thai culture and he is semi-fluent in the language.

Evan had been following Hakeem's case since his detention and, seven days later, a friend called him out of the blue, having seen Evan post something about Hakeem's case on social media. His friend, of Syrian-Palestinian background, had recently found himself in visa troubles that had landed him in Bangkok's IDC for a few days. While there, he'd shared a room with a 'guy from Bahrain and his wife', whom he'd helped to communicate with the guards because he spoke both Arabic and Thai. He told Evan that Hakeem was a really nice guy and that Nani was very kind – he specifically remembered her bringing food and supplies from a local 7-Eleven store after she left the IDC. He told Evan that, at that time, they were being kept in an office, not a cell with the other prisoners.

That's irregular, Evan thought to himself, something is not right.

From mid-December to early January, Evan travelled for work and Christmas holidays. APRRN had issued a few press releases about Hakeem's case, and fronted the media in December, but they had thought, like many others, that the case would be resolved quickly between the Australian and Thai governments. By the time he received a call from Amnesty in early January, Evan had already been thinking about what more APRRN could do to help, and the conversation with Amnesty confirmed to him that he was overdue to visit Hakeem in person.

As part of his job, Evan spends a lot of time visiting Bangkok's immigration detention facilities and prisons. He knew Bangkok's Suan Plu Immigration Detention Centre where Hakeem had first been held, but not which prison facility he'd been moved to. He had no idea who he could ask to find out where a prisoner was being kept, so he jumped onto the internet and googled 'prison Bangkok remand' and chose the one that he thought it was most likely to be.

When he turned up at Klong Prem remand prison in north-east Bangkok, not far from Bangkok's famous Museum of Contemporary Art and only 10 minutes' drive from the famous Chatuchak weekend market, Evan was not sure he would be allowed in, or if Hakeem was even there. He asked at reception for Hakeem al-Araibi, and was told that there wasn't anyone with that name there. 'They said there's a Hakeem with a different surname, but there's no Hakeem al-Araibi, and I thought, that's weird, as I'm sure there are not too many other people of Hakeem's nationality in here . . . then they said, "Come round to the office and you can have a look at the mugshots in the computer system and tell me if it's your friend."

'So I did, and he brought up a photo of Hakeem on the screen. He was listed with his full name Hakeem Ali Mohammed al-Araibi, which is why they hadn't clicked it was the same person. So I saw the picture and I said, "Look, I'm pretty sure that's him" . . . at this stage, I'd only seen snippets on the TV and so, I was thinking to myself, surely that's got to be the guy.

'So I said to the officials, "Yeah, that's my mate." And then, of course, they wanted to know who I was and how I knew him. So I just said, "Oh I'm from Australia, Hakeem lives in Melbourne, and we're really good friends from way back – look, I've got an Australian passport." They said, "All right, yeah, no problem, that seems fair enough." Then they just assisted me with the sign-in, got my little visitor's slip, and I was visiting him 20 minutes later. It was actually an incredibly smooth process.'

Hakeem was surprised when his name was called over the prison loudspeaker that morning. By late December and into the early New Year, he was only receiving visits from his lawyer, Nat, some Australian embassy officials and the occasional journalist. So, when he walked into the small visiting area and a foreigner with pale skin and a bushy red beard was sitting on the other side of the perspex, he was confused and wary.

Evan remembers it well: 'It was good to see him and good to see that he didn't look like he was malnourished, not like he'd been beaten up or anything, so it was good to physically see him, to see, okay, he's looking okay. But he definitely had no idea who I was, I think he honestly thought it really bizarre . . . I tried to explain who I was, that I worked for a refugee organisation, but I hadn't thought to bring any ID with me, thinking that security wouldn't let me take anything in anyway.'

Hakeem suspected that Evan had been sent by the Bahraini authorities to check on or get information from him, so he was very reluctant to say much. It was only when Evan returned the next day and slipped his Australian passport and a business card in with him, that Hakeem knew he could trust him.

Evan would quickly become a regular visitor to the prison and take on an important role, seeing Hakeem more than 15 times over the course of his detention, helping to facilitate communications from Nani in writing as well as visits from myself and journalists. Hakeem describes how Evan became a strong support, both physically and mentally. 'Every day after they take us out in the morning, I wait for Evan to come and visit me. I love him. Every day I was waiting for him. He always come in the morning, and when he didn't come I really [missed] him.'

Shortly after that first visit, Evan published a Letter to the Editor in the *Bangkok Post* to raise the profile of Hakeem's case. That's when he became a person of interest. To Bahrain. Bahrain's National Communication Centre rang the APRRN office asking to speak with him. An email followed, detailing what they saw as inaccuracies in the piece, and the *Bangkok Post* published a response. Evan was shocked. 'It told me that Bahrain was taking this very seriously. Not only were they closely monitoring the media on Hakeem's case, but they were actively pushing back and trying to control the narrative around it.'

Back in Sydney, I saw the response from the Bahrainis and thought it extraordinary that a government would be so concerned as to respond to someone working in a refugee organisation, and who it was unlikely too many people knew in Thailand. I recalled that the Bahrain embassy in Bangkok had also tweeted something out shortly after Hakeem's detention in early December.

I tried to step outside the commotion for a brief respite and sat down in a favoured local café to clear my head, contemplating what this meant, putting the pieces together. Bahrain was evidently extremely sensitive to criticism of any sort, very quick to react and highly vulnerable in the international diplomatic arena given the case facts and, worryingly, obviously wanted Hakeem very badly. I knew that Bahrain would have a misinformation machine operating around the world, but I wasn't yet sure how agile or capable they could be. In an authoritarian country that criminalises dissent and arbitrarily arrests activists and incarcerates them, how experienced could they be in responding to attacks and manoeuvring publicly? The responses were coming directly from the communications ministry, not an external public relations company, which also surprised me. They seemed open to being engaged in a public battle and it occurred to me that that would be a very interesting fight. That's my territory. The media.

They'd obviously calculated that the whole affair would be straightforward. No one knew this kid, so they'd lean on the Thais, submit an extradition order and get him back, quickly and quietly. They'd succeeded with Ali Haroon a few years ago, so this shouldn't be an issue, really. Now, however, it was becoming an increasingly public battle and Bahrain was reacting quickly, with little apparent strategy. More like they expected to be able to impose their dictates abroad as at home. In order to defeat them we would need to draw them out, expand on their human rights record, and place their abuse on the global agenda. If they were prepared to issue statements and write responses to Evan's and our provocations then, for me, that was the perfect place to be.

Chapter 6

THE ASIAN CUP OF HUMAN RIGHTS

In early January, we had to decide what to do about Australia's impending participation in the Asian Cup in the UAE, which started on 5 January. The AFC still had not made a comment, after almost six weeks. What could we do? I wanted the team out of the tournament and Brendan felt very strongly as well. But we respected other views and were very concerned about the future of the players. Middle Eastern football has become a huge force in the global game and some of our players either played in the Gulf region or would in future, including with the national team. Might we put their professional prospects at risk or expose them to possible security issues at a later point?

John was to speak to FFA's security team to assess what could be done in the UAE. What risks were there if the players protested during games? I was planning to present to the players in camp, in the team hotel. To get in front of the group, fire them up. The advice we received was that any form of protest in the UAE, like in Bahrain, was a very serious risk and that it was strongly ill advised. But I was undeterred and ready to take the risk. Lara was frantic. 'No way, you can't go there, if you protest you'll be jailed,' I remember her saying. As usual, as it turned out, she was right.

On 31 December, a prominent human rights activist, Ahmed Mansoor, had a 10-year prison sentence upheld by the Federal Supreme Court in the UAE. His 'crime' was to express his opinions on social media about the UAE Government. This purportedly caused damage to the country's 'social harmony and unity'.

Later, an Arsenal supporter and Brit, Ali Issa Ahmad, who'd travelled to the UAE on holiday, got a ticket for the Asian Cup match between Qatar and Iraq. Unfortunately for Ali, he wore a Qatar shirt to the match, completely unaware of the strict laws in the UAE that make it an offence to do anything that could be interpreted as promoting Qatar. He was detained by UAE officials, who later told media that, no, he hadn't been arrested for wearing a Qatar football shirt and that his injuries were a result of, er, beating himself up.

In mid-February, after arriving back in Britain, Ali told the media that he had been 'arrested, beaten, interrogated and detained following an initial stop by security officials for wearing the Qatar shirt'.[1] He reportedly had knife wounds on his arm and side, injuries to his chest, and had a tooth knocked out after a security official had punched him in the face. And this was the 'Year of Tolerance' in the UAE?

At one point, so powerful was the #SaveHakeem campaign becoming, it looked like we might have our own diplomatic incident. During one Australian game, watching and tweeting away madly, sharing graphics made specially for the match and trying to use the tournament to amplify Hakeem's plight, I received a direct message from Pablo Bateson, head of the Australian professional league fan clubs. It showed several Aussie fans in Socceroos gear inside the stadium singing, 'Hakeem, he's one of our own', to the tune of a well-known football song adapted to the occasion. It looked funny, and at first glance I reacted as such. Incredible how far the campaign has travelled, I thought.

Then I remembered the security advice we'd received, and froze. If these guys get arrested, here, they're in serious trouble. We love the support, but be careful, please. Ballsy. But bordering on downright dangerous. Thankfully nothing came of it, as we would have felt, if not been, largely responsible.

Once withdrawal was off the table, the focus turned to using the tournament to make maximum noise, hijacking it as far as possible for Hakeem. Given all that was occurring, we termed the tournament the 'Asian Cup of Human Rights' to capture a sense of complete disregard for what was happening to Hakeem through the lens of other human rights defenders who were being equally mistreated. Not in the other half of Asia like Hakeem, but smack bang in front of tournament officials and the global sporting world. Key games where we thought we could create maximum noise were identified, including the Bahrain versus Thailand match and the final on 1 February. Much of the world's football media would be at the continental showpiece and we needed them to put Salman under scrutiny. So far, he had not publicly answered any questions on the issue despite having worked his way through many interviews during the 2016 FIFA presidential elections when these issues first came to the fore.

I sent a message to the international media suggesting a number of questions they might put to Salman as soon as the opportunity presented itself. That was as close as we could get to him, for now. I also called journalist friends and asked them to be ready to put him on the spot at any opportunity, public or private, and be sure to capture it on their phones if they did. And get it out to the world.

Well before this time, Brendan and John were working from their own strategic plan. True to form, methodical and meticulous, Brendan had developed seven campaign pillars to ensure the organisation could focus resources and measure progress. Government, human rights, sport, grass roots, activism, legal, family support. This allowed them to maintain some control over a constantly changing set of dynamics in the case. I asked them to keep the inform-ation flow open but was in a very different space. By now, I was in the centre of what felt like an almighty storm with NGOs, human rights organisations, refugee bodies, govern-ment, player rights advocates like the PFA, Hakeem's wife, the media all swirling around, wanting, needing, demanding attention. I was focused on broadening the reach of the public campaign, on managing the message, responding to threats, and also understanding where the opportunities for a speedy resolution might lie. I was both pushing stakeholders to act and maintaining good relations with them to stay abreast of the latest information. While Brendan and JD would work inside the institutional system, I would have to strike a difficult balance between working with every stakeholder and sharing information but remaining in the centre, independent and unrestrained.

Meanwhile, I was leaning on John to manage as much of the local logistics as possible so that, as people reached out to me, I'd refer them on. It was simply too much to deal with, and having the PFA available eased an unmanageable load. I was also starting to concentrate more heavily on the international media and therefore could be comfortable that management of domestic organisations would be well looked after. The PFA staff are highly dedicated to serving the best interests of players, and you could easily imagine the level of commitment they were applying to this young man. 'Please look at the legal team', 'We need the players onboard', 'How is the A-League and W-League campaign going?' 'What is planned for the Asian Cup coming up in a few days?' 'Any news from Lou and Athena?' 'FFA?' I'd already decided at this stage to leave the domestic governing body, FFA, entirely to John. With a new board in its first months and a new chairman seeking election to the AFC executive committee, their most effective contribution would likely be to sanction a league-wide protest in the domestic professional competitions, the A-League and W-League. That was John's task.

The PFA is an athletes' union and member of the Australian Council of Trade Unions (ACTU). John put in a call to ACTU Secretary, Sally McManus, who is a huge football fan. Meanwhile I was struggling badly to keep up with social media, my university studies were falling behind and we were already five weeks into the campaign. Energy was hard to find, sleep fitful and food taken on the run, if at all. Lara was worried.

Michele O'Neill, the President of the ACTU, called. 'We're here to help, anything you need?'

Please, if you can put some staff on social media to help out that would be fantastic. Very timely, thank you.

'But who are the targets?' she asked.

Well, at this stage, Michele, pretty much everyone. We are constantly trying to ascertain who will be able to make the decisive difference and targets change quickly. Check my Twitter account, the instructions are updated every day.

GIDHR had been talking about a protest at the Sydney Opera House on 10 January, the day of the Bahrain versus Thailand Asian Cup match. But John had taken off to the UAE on a holiday to watch the Asian Cup as a spectator. On one hand it shows the commitment he has to the game, which I loved to see; nevertheless, the practical reality meant that, at the time when everything was escalating, available support had disappeared, raising the difficulty and stress considerably.

Yahya and Fatima were on the phone. 'We need to do it tomorrow.'

But the planning is so late, guys, are you sure you can make it happen effectively? I asked. It was the day that Australia's Foreign Minister was meeting with her Thai counterparts in Bangkok, so visibility would be beneficial. They needed Amnesty and Human Rights Watch onboard, and so did I for the credibility of the event so I followed up with Tim, Graham, Alex and Elaine, and was relieved to hear they'd be in attendance. I'd seen the modest scale of Yahya and Fatima's protests in recent weeks and was apprehensive as to whether they would be able to organise a professional, effective event on the necessary scale. We wouldn't get too many chances to hit the mark with key messages, so the presence of the major partners was comforting.

En route to the Opera House, we had no idea how many people were going to show up. This was my first protest in the campaign and I hadn't been to many in any forum. I need to be fully prepared and briefed to feel comfortable, particularly when fronting the nation asking for support, and in the rush, detail was scant. Non-existent might be more accurate. I was extending a lot of trust to GIDHR and was very anxious that morning. Where is the run sheet, the process, is there any guidance as to outcomes, messages? Would we hold placards, march around in circles, shouting and chanting? Thankfully, all we had to do was stand in one spot and talk to media. That, I can do. The public turnout was disappointing, much fewer than I'd hoped but understandable with less than twenty-four hours of notice and enough to create an impression of size on television. By the time we lined everyone up in formation, we could just about cover the TV lens width! And, most crucially, there was media. Most of the major networks were there. We were starting to gather momentum.

Messages that day were about the need for the Thai PM to release Hakeem, and particularly about Bahrain backing off as, by now, we believed that getting Bahrain to withdraw the extradition order would be the most expedient way to let Thailand off the hook. Fatima, Graham, Elaine and I took turns to speak. It was a very strong line-up: the largest and most respected human rights organisations in the country and the little battler from the Gulf who was punching well above its weight. They were holding on for dear life in what was a major case for them, and pulling it off with bravado and sheer guts. I'd grown to really like them and was pleased for them.

While on the surface everything looked positive, though, privately there was devastating news. In the preceding days, we'd heard through Human Rights Watch contacts in Bangkok that there could be a resolution. This was more than six weeks after detention and things had seemed to be building well. With Marise going over to Bangkok and meeting her counterparts that day, a very strong indication that the Australian Government were taking the case seriously, news filtered through that Hakeem might even be released. Only a few of us knew and I was excited and nervous, thinking that Marise might be able to achieve a breakthrough. All the time throughout the protest and press conference, and into the evening, the thought that he might be getting out was swirling in my head and playing havoc with emotions. Then came the gut-wrenching news. Marise's meeting had not secured Hakeem's release. I was devastated for Nani and was surprised by how hard it hit me. I had really thought we might have got the job done and was very worried about how long we could all carry on with this level of energy and focus. From that point forward, I'd be careful not to get the hopes too high again.

I spoke to Marise a few days later and she shared what she was able to. Classified information was off limits throughout, naturally, but she provided some insights, high-level outcomes, and divulged where the case was generally headed. Although her meeting had been beneficial in opening dialogue on the issue and communicating to the Thais the gravity of the situation from Australia's perspective – and she was at pains to emphasise the very strong diplomatic language being employed – it was clear that much work would be required.

There were other problems to worry about, too. Seven weeks in and a growing number of people on social media were starting to point to an area that could quickly become a problem for the campaign, and for me. The volume was starting to have serious impact and it was thought by many that this might push the Thais into a corner. Millions of Australians have been to Thailand, of course; I myself had been there with my two eldest children only the previous September, just a month before they detained Hakeem. A lot of Aussies have some understanding of Thai cultural norms. Of course in large part it's on a somewhat superficial level, born largely from time spent on the tourist trail for most of us; nevertheless it was real, and a factor.

A discussion was quickly fermenting about the loudness of the campaign potentially forcing Thailand to react negatively and that, because of their culture, Hakeem's interests might be better served through quiet diplomacy to allow the Thais to 'save face'. I had my eye on it because, if we were unsuccessful and he was removed to Bahrain, not only would it be incredibly hard for us to get him back, a truly terrifying thought for him and his wife Nani, but it was evident that I would have to answer questions about how the entire campaign was managed both to her and the Australian public. I had accepted that risk as part of what I'd signed up to and took my responsibility to Nani extremely seriously. But it was worrying.

Then, out of the blue, we had a stroke of good fortune. A woman from Saudi Arabia, Rahaf al-Qunun, made global headlines when she barricaded herself in a hotel room in Bangkok airport and live-tweeted the standoff to an international audience. She had been on her way to Australia, where she planned to seek asylum from an abusive domestic situation in Saudi Arabia, and, fortunately for Rahaf, she had amazing help to hand.

Australian journalist Sophie McNeill, an absolute warrior for human rights who had spent time in the Middle East and seen the horrors of Syria and Yemen, had travelled to Bangkok to directly document what was going on from inside the hotel room. Sophie sent me a message about the case and, even as we climbed aboard and lent our voices to Rahaf's campaign, cheering for a positive outcome for her, we had to consider the potential effects on Hakeem's case. Would it help, or hinder?

The other person who came to Rahaf's aid was a lawyer by the name of Nadthasiri Bergman. The very same. While working on Hakeem's case, Nat was contacted by a human rights organisation in the Middle East to say Rahaf was in the hotel. She said she'd try and help. She called the immigration police and nobody knew who she was. 'Then I just called the hotel,' she stated simply. 'Rahaf and I spoke on the phone . . . she was terrified and crying. I asked her if she wanted me to represent her on this case [and] she said yes, and then I told her to make a big scene if she could, which is when she locked herself in the hotel room. I think this helped to stop her being put on the plane. Then I got power of attorney to represent her by telling her to post a tweet online stating that she wanted me to be her lawyer. It was a bit tricky but worked! I had drafted up all the documents to present her case to court in Thailand, but by the time everything was ready, she was already safe. It was a great outcome.'

The lightning-fast processing of Rahaf's case was unprecedented for Thailand. Having landed in Bangkok on 5 January, she boarded a plane to Canada, which had granted her protection, on 11 January. In just six days, a global social media storm had propelled her to safety. The hashtag #SaveRahaf was tweeted over 370,000 times in the space of just a few days, putting incredible pressure on Thailand. A Saudi diplomat, reportedly caught on video speaking with a Thai counterpart, summed up the impact of social media in this case: 'I wish you had taken her phone, it would have been better than [taking] her passport.'[2]

A precedent was set, one that we could use to our advantage. We knew that if enough pressure was applied publicly on Thai authorities, including through the power of social media, then they could be forced to take the right action. This was a huge lift in spirits to all involved and allowed friendly media to write about why Rahaf was granted freedom, and not Hakeem. Credit to the people at the *Bangkok Post*, who were particularly vocal on this point. With a junta in charge? Impressive journalism.

Rahaf's case also told us that key actors in the Thai Government, particularly Immigration chief Surachate Hakparn, were very active on social media and responsive to the attention. Having been forced into a corner on Rahaf's case, officials like the straight-talking Hakparn, nicknamed 'Big Joke' in Thailand, turned to Twitter in an attempt to soothe the global community about Thailand's refugee policy. In fact, Hakparn vowed Thailand would not force any refugees to return home 'involuntarily'. My perspective on this was that social media had become fundamental to Hakeem's chances in two respects, both in running our campaign and because others involved on the opposing side were willing to open themselves to scrutiny and pressure on its platforms. Like with Bahrain, we had another key actor responding and reacting publicly and we grabbed on to that quote for all it was worth. How could they send Hakeem back to Bahrain, where he clearly feared for his life, when they had just made this public promise?

Back home, as convinced as I was about Marise's intentions and efforts, we needed much stronger action from Prime Minister Morrison. How do we get him moving, put him under pressure publicly in a way that would be difficult to disregard? Athletes. Lots of them. Rugby league players, especially. Morrison is an avowed rugby league fan and the #1 ticketholder of the Cronulla Sharks. Australian politicians love to borrow sport's authenticity and, while Scott evidently genuinely loves the Sharks, in Australia just like almost everywhere else on the planet, sport is used to burnish reputations and provide a powerful connection to what we call in Australia the 'average punter', who also votes. So be it, I thought. Let's turn it around and place an obligation on him from sport, then. You use us, we use you. Quid pro quo.

It was time to branch out from football and to get other sports formally involved. I asked John to get in touch with the Australian Athletes Alliance (AAA), the peak athlete body, to get their presidents and former members onboard, but we needed Olympians as well. The National Olympic Committee of Bahrain through its president, Prince Nasser, was a fundamentally important part of this sordid tale and we would need the International Olympic Committee's (IOC) support in this regard. Australian Olympic athletes would be an important lobbying conduit to the Australian Olympic Committee (AOC) and, of course, many are legendary and socially influential names. Fortuitously, I was contacted by Nikki Dryden, a two-time Canadian Olympic swimmer turned immigration lawyer with a strong background in human rights law, through our mutual friend, long-time colleague of mine and highly respected sports journalist Tracey Holmes of the ABC. Nikki is a hugely passionate and immensely capable human rights campaigner who has been working in refugee and sports rights within the Olympic movement for decades and was perfectly placed to get Australia's Olympians behind Hakeem. Natalie Galea, an Australian judo champion and athlete rights activist who represented the country in the 1996 Summer Olympics in Atlanta, also became involved and they joined the fight with great vigour. It was welcome support.

For me, getting someone onboard from the Sharks was non-negotiable. I didn't care how it was done, but we needed to get a legend from Cronulla. We could then hopefully engage their fanbase, and the PM, in one go.

Nikki put Alex at Amnesty in touch with Australian Olympic swimming great Ian Thorpe, who shared some tweets. It may not have been another Olympic gold medal, but a noteworthy and meritorious performance just the same, I thought. Ian is a champion of environmental and particularly oceanic protection, and was vocal during Australia's marriage equality debate but this was a very different case. So many in his position would not have acted, so I greatly appreciated his stance.

Nikki also agreed to write some op-eds and had the acumen and experience to weigh in on the Olympic movement's obligation to get involved and to stress the need for an investigation into Prince Nasser, head of the National Olympic Committee of Bahrain, who'd been actively involved in the 2011/12 crackdown on athletes. By this time, some advice had indicated that Nasser may have been directly involved in Hakeem's current case since it was, after all, Nasser who'd promised that the world would come crashing down on the heads of the athletes involved in the Arab Spring protests. For this reason, I'd targeted Nasser during the Bahrain Merida[3] Tour Down Under in South Australia from 15 to 20 January and got others to do likewise. Prince Nasser founded the team in 2017, and it is financed by Bahrain as part of their sport diplomacy and marketing strategy, and he remains their number one supporter. By starting to engage with Bahraini royals directly and vociferously on Twitter, one thing was clear. A holiday in sunny Bahrain any time soon was out.

By this time, we had a whole team who were publishing opinion pieces whenever, and wherever possible: Minky Worden and Brendan in Europe and the US, Elaine, Nikki and others back home in *The Australian* and *The Guardian*. Football fans in Australia were by now fully activated, with #SaveHakeem banners appearing at games all over the country. In these social issues there's a critical threshold where the campaign crosses over from facing barriers of inclusion, to the point where loss aversion or the need to be involved, to demonstrate one's participation in a community takes over. When it becomes fully accepted, and acceptable to join. Whereas in earlier weeks people may have been uncertain, afraid of being on the wrong 'side' so to speak, we had clearly exceeded the threshold of public acceptability where our football community felt comfortable lending their support, as kids' teams, as well as professionals, were tweeting all over the place. John was working with the players, clubs and FFA to arrange a round of A-League matches in protest and was thinking through the most appropriate timing. When would the greatest impact likely be? Perhaps close to the hearing, thought JD, although there was no sign yet as to when that might be.

One night, as I trawled through tonnes of social media posts searching for something to seize on to make a noise,

I saw that someone had suggested that the fans might stand and clap at the fifth minute of the coming weekend's A-League round to signify Hakeem's shirt number and I jumped on it straight away. What a fabulous idea, guys, make it happen, you have my full support. Campaigns are one thing, but organic movements are the most powerful, especially when our extraordinarily passionate fans create their own initiatives. It showed that our community had now taken ownership of the campaign, they felt responsible and emotionally involved in Hakeem's wellbeing, and that is the ideal scenario, an inflection point.

A few days later, I watched it live on television with a tear in the eye, not for the first or last time over those three months. Sometimes, a host of strands converge in our mind and are manifested by a single event. That moment was about our game standing up to protect this kid, about fan solidarity, about demonstrating values of sport which had gone missing when Hakeem needed them most desperately. Everything I believed in, and was now fighting tooth and nail for, was represented in those 60 seconds. I'll remember that for a very long time. It wasn't the loudest moment of the campaign by any stretch, but it was one of the most treasured.

Inevitably though, politics interfered as if the forces of darkness were striking back. At one A-League match at Melbourne City's home ground, supporters were told by security that they had to remove a #SaveHakeem banner and pictures of the confrontation went viral among the fans. By this time, we had banners appearing around the world as we'd reached out to fan groups everywhere, in the

Bundesliga (Germany), UK and even Bengaluru FC in India, where Australian Erik Paartalu was a star, displayed banners at their games. And yet, in Australia of all places, and in Hakeem's home city, a fan protest was suppressed. Absolutely disgraceful. I could scarcely believe it could happen. City are part of the group of clubs owned by the royal family of Abu Dhabi, an ally of Bahrain. No one could be sure this was the reason behind it; nevertheless, it felt emblematic of what we were up against. The influence of money stretches right around the world into our own backyard.

It was suggested by some sympathisers that the club was bound not to allow political statements at the ground under FFA and FIFA regulations until Brendan, as good an authority on FIFA regulations as any, came in with a two-footed tackle that would have made any defender from the 1970s proud. 'FIFA is legally committed to promoting all internationally recognised human rights which include freedom of political opinion and the right to seek asylum,' he tweeted. Enough said, and now other fans could feel comfortable they were in the right. It was a small statement, only 140 characters, but so powerful to head off blind alleys of discussion and keep people focused on the important issues. It also reminded me of the importance of having people at all levels actively involved, taking ownership as their contributions were vital, even in small ways that seemed insignificant to onlookers. I saw my job as helping them all give the very best of their capabilities and feel part of the cause and redoubled efforts to make all feel welcome and encouraged to be involved.

While fans and players were concerning themselves with a player's life, though, the AFC was terribly aggrieved by a far more important and urgent matter. Money. A statement was issued about the pirate broadcaster beoutQ, from Saudi Arabia, which was illegally streaming the Asian Cup matches in breach of the commercial agreement of BeInSports, a Qatari division of Al Jazeera. It was concise, demanding and aggressive, threatening immediate legal action for this grievous breach of commercial rights. Human rights, though, were further down the list of priorities. Somewhere in the appendices, apparently.

Officials were hiding, but players continued to stand up. Gary Lineker, with over 7.2 million followers on Twitter, shared a tweet. Well, in truth, all he provided was an emoji, a 'thumbs up', but that was all we needed to celebrate his support from that moment forward, telling all and sundry, including Hakeem in fact, that Lineker was a big supporter of his case. Even this gesture, as small as it was, cannot be underestimated. The global football community knew who he was and it meant at a minimum that Hakeem's name had reached the very top echelon of world football. Thanks went to Orsat, who'd been working hard to raise awareness among superstars of football. He was straight onto Lineker when he displayed an interest and let me know immediately.

Longtime friend, Bonita Mersiades, who has played a variety of roles withing Australian football for decades, reached out to Rabieh Krayem, Chairman of the Association of Australian Football Clubs, who asked his former player from the North Queensland Fury, former English striker and

Liverpool legend Robbie Fowler to lend his support. To his eternal credit, Robbie did so immediately and with considerable enthusiasm. Later, Rabieh had Fowler donate a retro jersey that he'd personally signed to the auction winner to raise legal funds. According to the Anfield crowd, Hakeem now had 'God' on his side . . .

While great players created much-needed publicity, Bahrain's authorities kept up their habit of responding to it, particularly to articles that cast them in a negative light. Which we were making sure by now, of course, was an avalanche. After Evan's experience, Bahrain had also responded immediately to Nikki's opinion piece, describing the acts for which Hakeem had been convicted in Bahrain as 'terrorism related', and reassuring *Guardian* readers that all Bahraini citizens are entitled to legitimate legal representation and appeals, and convictions in Bahrain's criminal court relate to the penal code and 'do not in any way relate to political views or the right to expression'. Interestingly, despite a number of journalists saying they'd been personally contacted, Bahrain never responded to one of my articles or were in contact in any way.

While Bahrain clearly didn't know it, these statements were a valuable fillip. We had wedged them into a difficult public position. Every time we raised another issue, applied pressure, they had a decision to make. If they stayed quiet, we controlled the narrative, we were growing in volume and knew how to shape and fasten messages in the public mind. On the other hand, every time they spoke it was an opening to counterattack, hard.

Amnesty and Human Rights Watch were particularly brilliant at this. In regard to the *Guardian* piece, journalist Helen Davidson had reached out to Amnesty for some comments after they received Bahrain's criticisms of Nikki's piece. They turned around responses within hours. This agility was a major competitive advantage. The article published the next day about Bahrain's letter then also included Amnesty's cutting response, revealing Bahrain's assertions of legitimacy to be a complete sham. Elaine Pearson, Minky Worden and Phil Robertson at HRW, all superb practitioners, would tweet facts and statistics on Bahrain's legal system, history of abuse, number of incarcerated activists and the like. It was an entire library of work that would have been impossible to collate otherwise, years of advocacy and legions of cases distilled into hardcore knowledge, weaponised. By this time, we had an entire battalion lined up ready for these opportunities to talk about how the judge who had ruled against Hakeem in absentia was a member of the royal family, and how many Bahraini citizens he had made stateless, for example, stripping them of citizenship. The number seemed impressive. He was a very busy and committed man, it seemed.

I knew they were snookered, and they obviously could not have anticipated what they were up against. They'd say their court system is fair. Elaine would smash them about their history of unfair trials. The Minister of the Interior of Bahrain would say that Hakeem would be treated well. A list of demonstrators who were tortured would pop up in a flash. Any mention of the red notice and Radha Stirling was on the offensive. At every stage, Bahrain's appalling human rights record was being brought to light, rehashed, and we were showing the world the abuse they preferred to remain hidden. Our message was, the longer you want to keep Hakeem, the greater the damage we are going to cause to your international standing. That was the strategy, and they were very effectively, though inadvertently, helping us to deliver it.

Speaking of the red notice, after it had become clear that there was no immediate outcome from Marise Payne's visit to Thailand in early January, the public and political debate in Australia about who was to blame for Hakeem's predicament really started to heat up. We needed to agitate from all sides and I was speaking with a range of political parties, all of whom had a role to play. Within about a week of her visit, the Greens party and the ACTU had begun calls for a parliamentary inquiry, rightly asking key questions about the actions of the Australian Federal Police and Border Force. This was fertile political ground for other parties and an important lever to keep alive, but not to overshadow the immediate targets, Thailand and Bahrain. We didn't need Australia turning on itself. The targets had to remain mostly external.

Also, I knew that, given Hakeem's Thai visa was issued on the same day as the red notice, well before the Australian Federal Police had any idea, there was more going on than a blunder by the Aussies. It was important and maybe even sinister, I wasn't sure, but it was only useful as a tool to keep the pressure on and put the Australian Government in a position where, if they didn't step up in an election year and Hakeem was lost, they'd be damaged. That appeared the most likely way we'd get real action.

During the Asian Cup in the UAE, we knew that Hakeem would be raised in a meeting between new FFA Chairman, Chris Nikou, and Salman. It had taken 40 days to occur; Australia should have been pressing the AFC to respond publicly a month ago. I had left it to John to liaise with Australian football's local head office throughout and their response following the meeting left more questions than answers. FIFA's human rights policy mandated that officials must actively use their maximum leverage with all relevant stakeholders, including governments. It didn't seem this was occurring – and there was nothing to indicate it would happen.

Following this meeting and acknowledging urging by the FFA, FIFA issued another release on 9 January calling 'for a humane and speedy resolution of the case concerning the player Hakeem Al-Araibi' and 'on all the relevant authorities (in Bahrain, Thailand and Australia) to take the necessary steps to ensure that Mr Hakeem Al-Araibi is allowed to return safely to Australia where he can resume his career as a professional footballer'. It was another welcome step; nevertheless, it indicated to me that the AFC wouldn't be held to account. Everyone was dancing around the matter, playing politics with this kid's life. FFA hoped that FIFA could resolve it without having to confront the elephant in the room called Salman.

Nani was on email constantly wanting to know what was happening, asking questions, making suggestions. Lara and

I felt heartbroken for her and also personally responsible, as the campaign was gaining momentum but having no discernible effect. Nani was now at the point of giving up on the Australian Government and talking about trying to move to Canada, to get them to take responsibility for Hakeem as they'd done with Rahaf. This wasn't feasible as he was on an Australian protection visa, but I could understand her all-consuming desperation, clutching at anything that remotely resembled hope, every fleeting glimpse. We couldn't get good intel on Hakeem's case, Natalie the lawyer was difficult to get in touch with and Scott Morrison was silent despite our calls for greater support. We were loud, but stuck. I didn't know this kid personally, was feeling extremely upset each time Nani got in touch by email, wanted to blow up a media storm and to do so needed to know what was happening on the ground, so I thought about travelling to Bangkok. Without speaking to Lara, yet, in the third week of January I met with Tim and Alex at Amnesty's offices.

'You should go,' they said. 'We can support you with contacts, arrange the trip from here with Evan as point on the ground.' But should I go alone, or take some big guns along? I wondered. Anthony LaPaglia, who prior to becoming a well-known Australian actor and film star was a goalkeeper in the National Soccer League in the 1980s, playing for famous South Australian clubs Adelaide City and West Adelaide, had reached out to me by then to offer support. Anthony was vocal, and strong in his comments, getting stuck into the Australian Government for putting commercial and political interests, meaning Thailand and

Bahrain, ahead of the kid's life. I respected his forthrightness and independence.

I thought it might be better to take a high-profile, influential team over to Bangkok, and so I got in touch with Anthony through my old SBS colleague and national teammate, David Zdrilic. I thanked Anthony for his support, asked him to consider accompanying me and asked him to reach out to another famous Australian actor, Cate Blanchett, who is also a UN refugee ambassador. This should be absolutely on point for Cate.

If I can take these two over, I thought, we could create an international incident and really get this case moving! Though interested, Anthony was filming over in Western Australia, so wouldn't have been able to go for at least another week or two. Should I wait without any guarantees that he could find the time, or get over there and just get stuck into it?

I mulled it over in a planning meeting with Alex and Tim. 'We advised that it would be a more difficult trip with one, let alone two movie stars with teams of people looking after them,' says Tim. 'Particularly because of visa issues and with trying to keep his arrival under wraps ... plus, we were confident that Fozz had the profile to be able to make enough noise on his own, and we had the resources and connections to back him up. We didn't actually know Craig that well at the time. He'd been an ambassador for less than a year and was obviously passionate about refugee issues, but how far would he go? He'd lent his name, and talked about human rights breaches in Russia the year before during the World Cup, but would he put himself at possible risk?'

As we talked about the plans for the trip, it became very real, very fast. While I was pumped, full of bravado after weeks of frustration and a thousand roadblocks, these guys were professionals and highly experienced. When Alex and Tim started talking me through what the experience of visiting the jail would be like, letting me know that I had access to a psychologist on return if I needed it, I thought, it can't be that bad, surely? Then they explained the potential risks of travelling on a tourist visa and advocating noisily in a country ruled by a military junta and a monarchy that cracked down heavily on any hint of criticism with prison sentences under their 'lese-majeste' laws. Which laws, again?

'We'll keep in touch with you via an encrypted text messaging app, and you should keep your passport and wallet on your body at all times so that you can leave quickly, if necessary,' said Alex. Jesus, what was I walking into? They told me they could plan overland escape routes out of the country by train south to Malaysia or east to Cambodia, if my access to airports became blocked. 'The passport control on the borders isn't very tight when travelling by train,' explained Tim. How comforting.

In hindsight, they were preparing me for the worst. Still, it was deeply worrying and, for the first time, I started to think about whether my family would be okay if something went badly wrong. Is everything secured, could Lara manage everything on her own, are the finances all in order, insurances? Will the kids be okay? Nevertheless, I was fully committed to doing whatever it took to get Hakeem out. It was on. I'll be there and back in a week and we can all go back to our lives, right?

Oh, except I still needed to explain to my wife, and mother, that I'd be going. Lara and I sat down. 'I need to go this weekend, my darling,' I told her, 'and I will be working with Amnesty on security procedures so there is nothing to be worried about.' I didn't tell her about escape routes, Thai prisons, or that Amnesty thought I may already be on a black list by the Thai Government for my outspoken comments in recent weeks. That could wait till later. Afterwards. Er, maybe never.

As for my mother, she'd sensed what I'd been thinking and had been saying, 'Don't you dare go to Thailand.' 'You're not going, are you?' 'Promise me you're not going to go. It's not safe.' Not sure, Mum, we'll have to see what happens. I decided I'd tell her when I arrived over there, about a minute before she'd see it on the evening news. The less worry, the better.

There were only a few days between the decision to go, and the flight. While I sorted my work schedule and home life out, the Amnesty crew had connected with Evan, who started populating a schedule of meetings for the week, including a visit to the remand prison where Hakeem was being detained.

A few days before I left, I appeared on *The Project*, a popular current affairs show on Australia's Channel 10, to talk about the case. They later asked if I'd travel to Hakeem's club, Pascoe Vale, in Melbourne, to do a story with the coach and team and I jumped at the opportunity. It was a chance to drive up interest on a show with a very large following both on air and on social media, and an opportunity to meet Lou and Athena, Vitale the coach and all Hakeem's teammates personally.

I listened to stories of what he was like, for the camera, yes, but also for my purposes, as I knew I'd be meeting him soon and wanted to be as prepared as possible. Who was this young man we'd been fighting so hard for, anyway? Which teammates are closest to him who I can mention to create a personal connection quickly, establish trust when I meet him in person? We filmed a tonne of videos of the players and club staff asking Australia to step up and help, really valuable for social media, which is a voracious platform, news moving faster than ever, and we were constantly trying to keep up, to stay relevant.

To this point, I had been trying to get FIFPro to implement a global campaign. Amnesty and Human Rights Watch were running their own and the PFA was taking up the fight, but the world representative body should have been committing their massive resources to the case since, if Hakeem's rights were not upheld, the whole FIFA Human Rights Policy was in serious doubt and that affected over 60,000 professional players worldwide. The PFA, through life member, former teammate of mine and FIFPro Vice President, Francis Awaritefe, had applied for an emergency grant to cover costs for Nani, staff and the campaign and this would be appreciated but leadership was so far lacking.

It was extremely pleasing then to see FIFPro issue a statement on 16 January which indicated the organisation was 'deeply concerned about the manner in which Asian football authorities, including AFC's Bahraini President, Sheikh Salman bin Ibrahim Al Khalifa, have remained silent' and also, for the first time, called on the FIFA Human Rights Advisory Board (HRAB) to institute an immediate investigation into Salman's inaction:

> FIFPro wrote to FIFA in early December seeking assistance, before approaching the AFC President, who is also a FIFA Vice President, asking him to intervene.
>
> Furthermore, today we are asking FIFA's independent Human Rights Advisory Board to investigate if a breach in the football ruling body's human rights policy has occurred.
>
> We believe the policy, adopted in 2017, establishes clear grounds and obligations for FIFA, the AFC, member associations, officials, and other relevant parties, to exercise maximum possible leverage, including close cooperation with the governments of Bahrain, Australia and Thailand.
>
> We applaud the efforts to help Hakeem by the Australian football community, human rights activists, notably former international player Craig Foster, Professional Footballers Australia (PFA), and the World Players' Association.
>
> The clock is ticking and we ask all footballers to do what they can to help #SaveHakeem.[4]

Spontaneous combustion. Through Secretary-General Theo van Seggelen, FIFPro were a member of HRAB and were calling for it to act. So they should. Their role was to protect the players and to advocate for the board to fulfil its duty to this end. Some HRAB members apparently considered this inappropriate, which only highlighted to me that the voices of political constraint and compromise were everywhere, even inside the system supposed to save Hakeem. It certainly got their attention, and drove action.

Meanwhile, I had been reaching out publicly to the Australian chair of the HRAB, Rachel Davis. She is the Managing Director of the SHIFT project in New York, an NGO working with businesses to implement the work of John Ruggie, author of the UN Guiding Principles on Business and Human Rights, with whom she'd helped write the FIFA Human Rights Policy. I pointed out that the HRAB had so far issued retrospective reports and recommendations for future action. While I accepted that they had not intervened in such an urgent case before, and were very new as a body in any event, I emphasised that if they didn't step up now, a report on how Hakeem was being tortured in Bahrain, or worse, in six months' time, was of no use. I implored her to act and to urge FIFA to step up. If they didn't, all the work in implementing human rights policies in sport, FIFA or otherwise, was worth nothing. A mirage.

We were driving this message hard publicly, to pressure all sport and human rights chambers to act and there was considerable angst in that community about what failure for Hakeem might mean to the movement. Brendan had worked with Rachel as part of the SRA and broader movement and would provide the HRAB with the necessary tools to be proactive.

His lengthy formal submission to the HRAB the day following Orsat's statement, an 'Urgent Request for Special

Procedure Into The Severe Violation of The Human Rights of Football Player Hakeem Mohamed Ali Al-Araibi'[5] on behalf of WPU, FIFPro and the PFA provided the legal rationale for action and explicitly called on both the HRAB and FIFA to taken decisive action. Conference calls were scheduled, in haste.

The HRAB was split and uncertain, which is when Rachel, as chair, really stepped up. Just three days later, on 20 January, the HRAB sent a letter to FIFA outlining seven recommendations for action. I was elated. If FIFA wouldn't move, they needed to be pushed and the HRAB had urged them to do so in the strongest possible terms. HRAB's letter directed FIFA to 'use all available leverage' to ensure that Hakeem was released and, critically, recommended that FIFA communicate clear expectations to the AFC and its president that there was an institutional responsibility to make a clear public statement on the case. It had been almost two months by now, and still nothing from the AFC.

The HRAB called on FIFA to seek a high-level meeting with the Thai Government and communicate similar expectations to Bahrain and to be in court for Hakeem's next hearing. It also put paid to the excuse used by Salman that he couldn't interfere in government affairs:

> FIFA should clarify to the AFC that taking such a position is not in violation of the prohibition on political interference given FIFA's own human rights policy commitments, the gravity of potential harm to Mr Alaraibi, and the fact of his refugee status.

The pièce de résistance, however, was in recommendation seven:

> The Review Committee of FIFA's Governance Committee
> should use its mandate in reviewing candidates for relevant
> FIFA elections to ask all candidates for their views on how
> they intend to meet their obligation to comply with Art 3 of
> FIFA's Statutes should they be elected. This should include
> the upcoming AFC Presidential elections.[6]

In other words, step up, or your eligibility is in doubt. Or
should be, at least. At last, what I considered real action.

A few days before I was to leave for Bangkok, the serious-
ness of the security risk hit home to our whole family, quite
literally. On three separate occasions, unknown men appeared
and sat parked in cars directly opposite or in front of our
house. We live in a relatively quiet, close-knit neighbourhood.
We know all of our neighbours and they weren't among them.
This was not normal, at all. Each time, there were two in the
car with the window down, watching the house.

The first time, I was in Melbourne filming at Pascoe
Vale with *The Project*. Lara was walking home with our
daughter, who was still on school holidays. 'My first thought
was that maybe they were casing out our house to rob it
or something!' she laughs. 'I felt a bit silly, but I walked
on past the house to do a loop of the block, and we wrote
down the number plate. When we got back to the house
though, the car was gone. So we went inside and I didn't
think about it again.'

The following day, a different car was in the same place. It seemed too much of a coincidence to have happened two days in a row. This time, Lara called as I was travelling back from Melbourne and you can easily imagine the feeling of terror, not being there and with strange people watching the house. Two days later, we came out together and there was a third car, across the street. Window down. Two men staring. I grabbed the phone and started walking across the road taking photos. They didn't hurry, no panic, the car was already in idle. They just turned it around slowly, staring eye to eye all the way, and drove off, slowly. Their point had been made.

I had called a friend of mine, a former detective, for advice, who suggested they were likely wanting to let me know they were aware of where I lived. My friend gave us an action plan in the event it occurred again. Lara and I spoke to the kids about sticking together, not going out alone, sitting with groups in trains and buses, and staying with Mum as much as possible while I was away. Everyone stick together, until I get back. It'll only be a week at most. The next-door neighbours were notified and everyone was on the lookout in the street. I was torn between leaving my family to help Hakeem and my protective instinct as a husband and father.

We had no idea what these people's intentions were, or what might happen. I spent the next few days accompanying the kids everywhere, seeing shadows. Is that man following us? I knew that if something happened to the kids, it was my responsibility. I obsessed over whether to stay or go. Could we send the kids away until I'm back? Hire a security guard for the house? We were emotionally torn but, in the end, we put in place as many security protections as possible and I resolved to go. It was the hardest decision of my life. If anything had happened, I don't know what I would have done but while we might have been worried, Hakeem was in severe danger and Nani was alone, no money, no husband and no one else to rely on. I was absolutely convinced by now that, if extradited, he would never be seen again.

Amnesty coordinated with journalists from the ABC and *The Project*, who both wanted to come with me to Bangkok. SBS were also in, travelling with me on the plane. Channel 10 would be there the night I arrived and the ABC would have Liam Cochrane covering the story. I didn't know him, but it would soon be clear that he is a respected and highly knowledgeable journalist in the region.

Evan Jones would manage on-ground media, especially Thai-speaking, and would book meetings with embassies. I wanted to meet as many people as possible, find out what the hell was going on, why it was taking so long and particularly whether the Australian Government was doing enough.

The PFA would fund the trip out of campaign costs. By now, Brendan and John had put the issue to the executive, consisting mainly of current professional players. The players resolved to support Hakeem through the players' own funds as much as necessary. This decision can't be overstated.

Hakeem was an amateur player, none of us knew him. He was not even a member of our union, which principally represents Australia's national teams and top-tier professionals. And yet, here were A-League, W-League, Matildas and Socceroos players saying that the overriding principle of helping a fellow player was most important, whatever it took. They'd commit the full organisational resources to the case. Incredible. Especially if you contrast this with the outlook and actions of football officials in the vast majority of cases. This gap between player and football official has become chronic worldwide and in this case would prove cavernous.

The overriding concern was getting too loud, too soon in Bangkok. I needed to avoid getting thrown out of the country, which was possible, or thrown in jail, which was less likely but, er, something I'd prefer to avoid. We weren't sure how long it would take to see Hakeem in prison, or if I'd even be able to as Evan was not at all sure about getting in, but the risk had to be taken. We would visit the Australian embassy and other governments in the first few days, then Hakeem late in the week. That was the plan. We'd be in stealth mode until leaving the prison, as that was the most important part – to meet him, give him my support and that of everyone back home – then use the media to blow the story up worldwide. The final day I would speak at the Foreign Correspondents' Club and get the hell out of the country as quickly as possible. If I made it that far.

It was a struggle to concentrate but the international flight was the first chance I had to study for some weeks.

I was weeks behind in equity and property law and had to hit the books, or surely fail. While preferably avoided, that would be the only form of failure that could possibly be contemplated.

Chapter 7

BANGKOK

21–26 JANUARY 2019

When you first visit Thailand's capital as a foreigner, you'd be forgiven for thinking it is an impersonal city. With a population of more than 8 million people crammed into an area roughly 1500 square kilometres, it's one of the densest cities in the world and also one of the most popular. Every year, Thailand lures a whopping 38 million-plus tourists, the vast majority of whom pass through Bangkok. The city itself promises everything from mega-mall shopping to Buddhist temples, streets crammed with food carts selling fresh fruit and noodles to mobile phone covers and underwear, and of course sins of the flesh in its numerous red-light districts.

Many tourists, however, use the mega-city as a brief transit stop, before heading south to its white-sand beaches and tropical islands, or up north to its jungle-covered mountains as Hakeem and Nani had planned to do two months ago.

I had no idea what to expect in customs on landing on the afternoon of 21 January and had kept radio silence back home so that no one knew I was going or coming. I'd told a small group of social media activists to keep tweeting, keep the pace up while I was on the flight. The thought of being out of circulation and not able to interact while flying made me uneasy. I was in a hurry to get there, get back online, keep things moving along, without mentioning where I was, of course. Make sure the location tool on Twitter is off! It was a constant concern over those months that we'd lose momentum in a world where news moves faster than ever. One major scandal, I thought, and people might move on. We had to keep the issue alive.

I was nervous about going through immigration in Bangkok, but fortunately I had met a couple of Aussies on the plane who travelled to Thailand often and offered an express pass. Fortune was smiling, I thought, a good omen, maybe I can sneak through undetected. 'You on holiday in Thailand, Fozz?' Yes, just taking a break, guys. Liar. Thanks for the pass, gents. I owe you one.

On arriving in Bangkok, I set up a WhatsApp group chat with Lara and our three kids, my parents and two brothers, explaining that I was there, not to worry, I loved them and would keep them informed. I had never done that before. My mother sent three words back, 'I knew it.' And I knew that would be the end of her sleep until my return. It would be a much longer wait than anticipated.

Evan and Liam Cochrane were waiting for me at the arrival gate. While we waited for the SBS crew, I did a short interview with Liam and the usual shots talking, walking, leaving the airport and so on. I knew this meant they were serious about the story, preparing a longer piece, not only news coverage. Excellent.

We all clambered into a van together to the hotel. Oblivious to the city of Bangkok whizzing past, I grilled them the whole way – what was Hakeem's morale like? What were all the embassies saying? Had there been any recent developments on the case? What other meetings had been confirmed since I'd last seen the schedule? When can we go to the jail? I was emotionally shredded by this time, tired, my head swirling with law study deadlines, unknown men outside my house, politics, an upcoming prison visit, escape routes . . .

Channel 10 were staying at the Hyatt Hotel, in central Bangkok, and I needed to be near them. Like the week before, I'd agreed to put together a story for them which meant I could shape the narrative and not leave it to others. Meeting in the lobby that night, Evan gave me the best news I had received for weeks: I could see Hakeem the next morning. 'Nat the lawyer was scheduled to go, however she can go later in the day if necessary, we can be there at 8.30 in the morning if you'd like.' Wow, that is unbelievable, I was so elated. It would change the whole schedule, however, and Amnesty were very concerned about my getting thrown out of the country on day one without speaking to international media or embassies. But the chance to see Hakeem the next day was too important. It would give us an entire week of media and social media coverage, if we were really lucky. A risk that I viewed as well worth taking.

Evan went through the details. When, where, how, who. We'd meet tomorrow morning before seven and all grab a taxi together. He didn't know if both of us would get in, but did say that the process was relatively lax, especially for foreigners. 'We should be okay, provided they don't recognise you from the Thai news' but, as yet, it turned out we hadn't managed to get huge traction within Thailand itself. We should be fine.

I can't remember eating that night, or much on the flight at all. I was wasting away and Lara was getting really worried but there was simply no appetite, I would snack whenever the chance arose, otherwise it was coffee. And more coffee. Sleep that night was even worse than the past seven weeks, horrible. My head was pounding, every time I closed my eyes I thought my temples would burst. Running through my mind, over and over, was what I would say during the visit. I was worried that if I wasn't prepared enough, I might miss the only chance to make a difference and get this kid out. I spoke over FaceTime to Lara and the kids, assured them everything was great, there were no security issues. I told them not to worry and that it would all be straightforward. But I suspect, in truth, that it was me who needed the reassurance, just to see their faces, hear their voices.

At about 3 am, I woke. I'd been drifting in and out of sleep thinking about what to say and do and turned to thinking about the desired outcome of the meeting. What's the best way to make a serious statement, hit the front pages internationally? If I had the choice and if things go well, what would I ideally like him to say to help us get him out?

I grabbed the hotel notepad and pen and drafted questions for Hakeem to agree to, for me to deliver to the media. Where are you? Why are you not helping? Isn't my life worth enough? Another piece of paper. Come on, I know it's early but think. Concentrate, for god's sake. Several cups of coffee later with a wastepaper bin full of discarded attempts, I settled on three questions, wrote them in large letters so that I could show him and get his agreement. I drifted in and out of consciousness for the rest of the night, a very heavy weight bearing down on the pillow. Tomorrow would be one of the most important days of my life.

•

The next morning got off to a shocking start. Amnesty had warned me about what I was going to see in the jail and the effect it can have on people so while the mood was determined, it was also very tense. The film crews from SBS, Channel 10 and the ABC were all outside the hotel, waiting. We planned to all go to the jail together but *The Project* had booked their own van, wanting to film Evan and me en route to the prison, and there was some commotion about how we were going to accommodate all three networks. *The Project* had offered a fee for me to do a story for them which I had requested they donate to Nani so I had an obligation to both them and her and pulled the others aside, in no mood for turf wars. Guys, tell me what you need, I promise you that I'll give you enough to do your job well. Let's all work together. We need everyone onboard so deal with Evan, let me get on with working for Hakeem, and tell me when I'm needed. Evan and I travelled to the prison with Channel 10, filming on the way.

The plan was to try and be as covert as possible getting into the prison. This meant that we wanted the media crews to be careful not to attract any unwarranted attention. I wasn't sure how many guards would be patrolling the perimeter or whether, on seeing cameras, they'd throw us out immediately. The entire trip and now the campaign, with over 100,000 signatures of concerned people in Australia and around the world, rested on getting in. My mouth was dry and my empty stomach churned. I had my passport and wallet on me in case things went south, the Australian embassy's number in case of a diplomatic incident and Evan briefed to get us on the nearest train and out of the country at a moment's notice.

We turned off the freeway and drove in through the main prison gates shortly after 7.30 am. People go in these gates and some never come out, I thought. It's a massive complex and as you drive in there is a foreboding, monolithic building with a huge sign at the front with the prison's name on it. We turned right at a roundabout and drove for 300 metres or so until we reached a smaller building. This was it.

We parked the vans a hundred metres away, trying to stay incognito, and the media crews asked to get some shots of us walking down the path towards the main entrance. Sure, but please, guys, let's stay undercover here, not too close. We can't afford to get turned away now. Evan and I started walking towards the building, each with our own thoughts and, after a short while, turned around. Here they all were creeping along behind us, cameras on. Bloody journalists! You could see them all, trying to sneak from tree to tree behind us like a cartoon skit.

We couldn't help but laugh and it was a welcome break in tension. 'I don't think this is going to go down well if we're caught,' said Evan.

That's their job, mate. I work in the industry and we need them here. They'll take every inch they can. Let's get on with it, quickly, before someone realises what's going on.

Directly outside the building, there were gardens, motor-cycle taxi drivers, an area with small vendors cooking chicken on a stick, some fruit carts, another vendor selling ice blocks and a whole heap of people sitting around, waiting, and staring. We put our wallets, phones and passports in a set of old metal lockers, went through a metal detector, and we were in. No cameras or photos beyond this point, and there was a lot of signage to this effect plastered all over the walls. We then found ourselves in a foyer area with basic visitor seating, a waiting room of sorts.

There's a small shop, where they sell things that visitors can buy for the prisoners – socks, cough lollies, tea, coffee and other bits and pieces. 'We put our name down over there,' said Evan, at a window with guards behind, already aware of the two foreigners who'd just strolled in, all eyes on us as we approached. The moment of truth. Deep breath.

Evan greeted the guards in Thai, me behind looking innocent, glancing around to see whether anyone seemed agitated, aware. So far, so good. We were given a ticket with a time allocation, visitor room number, and a number of the telephone to use. It reminded me of a scene straight from the television documentary series *Banged Up Abroad*. Not a helpful thought.

In the small foyer area, there was also a counter where you could deposit money into the prisoners' bank accounts. And then, just off the waiting area, a whole row of rooms, maybe seven or eight of them, next to each other with numbered phones in each. Off to the side of these rooms, another smaller room where the lawyers can meet with their clients for much longer periods than our allocated 20-minute slot. Apparently, this was where Nat had snuck Nani in as her Arabic translator, during that first week Hakeem was in prison.

We weren't sure if they were going to allow both of us to go in, but we'd try. If not, Evan would wait. I was in his hands entirely which made me very uncomfortable. I'd known him less than 24 hours and was relying on him completely. The bell went for our slot. We both got in line, Evan flashed the ticket to the guard, who casually pointed across to the room. We were in. I sat down at a small bench with an ancient-looking black telephone and Evan stood beside me – no one seemed to care or pay extra attention to us. The walls were white and dirty, the screen in front of us reinforced glass, the telephone a type used decades ago. There was a matching telephone on the other side of the glass.

'You'll have to speak loudly,' Evan said. 'The telephones are hard to hear.' We waited. Checking my notes, my questions. Then a door swung open and prisoners started to file in and take a seat. Where is he?

When Hakeem entered, he looked over and saw Evan, who he knew. He'd been expecting to see Nat, his lawyer, who we'd coordinated the visit time with, so initially I think he was a bit confused to see us. It struck me how thin and gaunt he looked.

Evan had visited Hakeem the day before and explained who I was and that I was going to be coming to the prison within the following few days, but he looked cautious. He sat down on the other side of the glass, less than a metre away.

He recalls of our first meeting: 'The first time I meet Craig – Evan introduced [him], that was coming, the day before. I didn't know him. I didn't know who he was. I thought he was looking like someone else. He [came] with Evan but, so I know, I can trust him.'

He tried to smile, but it was strained, forced. The sound over the phone was very faint, so I was almost shouting, but we were sitting so close that we could almost lip read what the other was saying. I explained who I was, he nodded. I showed him some petitions and messages of support from home to try to communicate how much everyone was fighting for him, to try to give him reassurance and hope, and asked him how he was feeling. All he could talk about was that he didn't want to go back to Bahrain, he couldn't. He just kept saying, 'They will hurt me there, and I'm worried about my wife, if I go back to Bahrain, I will be dead.' He kept repeating these same messages over and over.

He also mentioned Salman's name. 'In Bahrain, they lie all the time . . . I am here because I criticised . . .' He was particularly frightened about the Bahrain Government's response to Evan's op-ed, which surprised me. 'They want to influence journalists, they won't stop, that's what they do,' he said.

I realised that sitting in jail, knowing that Bahrain was running a misinformation campaign and were willing to call journalists around the world was a terrifying prospect for a kid facing forced return and who knew intimately the lengths they would go to.

Evan had brought with him a letter from Nani, in Arabic. This moment is seared into my memory. I'll never forget it as long as I live. Evan stepped forward and pressed it up against the glass so that Hakeem could read it. His whole demeanour changed. Because of the vertical metal bars behind the glass, he couldn't read it in one go, so Evan had to keep moving the paper slightly from side to side so that he could see all of the writing. There was raw emotion on his face. In those few seconds, he had forgotten that anyone else existed in the world as he devoured the words from his wife, eagerly. A desperation I'd never seen from a human being.

That's what really touched me – his eyes, the softness of his voice and demeanour, the intense fear, his obvious love and concern for his wife. This was a young man who hadn't seen his wife for six weeks, hadn't spoken with her, was worried sick about what might happen to her, on top of dealing with life in a prison cell. As he read, I was fighting back tears as it hit me that he might well never see his wife again. Seeing him there, in an incredibly vulnerable moment, stripped to his bare essence, gave me a sense of who he really was. He could say anything he liked, but he couldn't hide his love for his wife, nor his fear. Later, everyone kept asking, 'What's he like?' – I could only answer with absolute honesty. He was a softly spoken, lovely kid. There was kindness there, and love in his heart.

Later, Nani would tell me that she had written in that letter who I was, that we'd met, that she trusted me and he should know that I was leading a campaign to get him out. As I said, smart woman, that one.

The clock was ticking away on the wall to my left. We had limited time and needed outcomes from the twenty minutes. Otherwise the whole trip would be useless.

I passed on messages from his teammates, his friends, explained that I'd met them, trying to gain his trust. We are all fighting for you, mate, we're going to get you out. Stay strong, don't give up, I know it's hard but all of football is standing up for you. We've got Robbie Fowler, Gary Lineker, the Matildas and Socceroos. Big stars, they're with you. Take strength from them. And I'm not stopping till you're out.

He told me about playing inside the prison. 'They asked me to play inside here, but why do I have to play in a prison? I want to play on the outside. I want to have a career.'

Yes, let's talk football, it's our connection. 'Your teammates tell me you're a right back – who's your favourite?' I wanted to get some targets to reach out to on social media.

'Sergio Ramos is my favourite,' he said. 'When I was young, I had a poster of Ramos on my wall, I wanted to be like him.'

Okay, I'll get onto him, and try to get his support, I promised.

Time was getting away, so I showed him the three questions for FIFA. I need to get them to act, I told him, and this has to come from you. If you're comfortable with it, I'd like to take these three questions outside and tell the world this is what you asked. It has to be from you, with your agreement, what do you think? A pause, this was the moment the campaign could hit the next level. I knew how powerful it would be if he was willing to play his part. He didn't know me, and I was asking him to place incredible trust in my hands.

Without knowing what the clever Nani had written in the letter, I held my breath and looked at Evan. I had told him he must witness the request and agreement. I didn't want anyone saying that I'd led Hakeem or put words in his mouth and Evan would be my witness. 'We can change the words, it has to come from you, Hakeem.' He read the text and nodded. 'Yes, please, say whatever you want, just get me out, I trust you.'

In the last few minutes, we asked if there was anything he needed to make life in the prison more comfortable. He told us that he didn't eat for up to 15 hours at a time inside but wasn't concerned for himself. He said, 'Please make sure Nani is okay, I'm so worried about her, give her any money that you have.' I told him that the PFA were helping her financially. Are you sure you don't need anything? No. We pressed again, surely you must need something, anything from the shop? 'Pair of socks maybe,' he said, 'to play football in the sand.' Fantastic, socks it was. You can have a bloody life's supply, mate. A warehouse full.

The bell rang, our 20 minutes was up. A guard came in behind Hakeem and all prisoners stood up. As he was turning to leave, I tried to leave him with hope. 'Stay strong, you're an international footballer. We'll get you out.' He smiled. It was a different person who left the meeting to the one who'd walked in. At least it felt that way.

Evan and I went over to the small prison shop to get some socks. They were out, bugger it! But we managed to get him some boiled chicken, some sweets.

I wanted to send in a whole heap of goods, but Evan rightly pointed out to me that if Hakeem had too much, he might become a target for the other prisoners or guards. Sensible young man. If it had been up to me, I'd have sent the whole shop in, if it contributed even just a little to this kid's wellbeing in that place.

By the time we collected our things from the lockers and got back outside I was gathering my thoughts. I stopped Evan and stood around the corner from the front gate, out of view of the media, thinking through what we had seen, reading the notes, the questions for FIFA, structuring the interview, trying to control the emotions. It was unlikely I would ever deliver lines on camera as important again.

Ready? Let's go, Evan.

The media crews were camped right in front of the prison, in full view of everyone. They were within about 15 metres of the prison entrance, far beyond the point where we had agreed. Typical, I smiled. We were in a good place now, though, locked and loaded. There were four or five cameras, including Reuters who would send it around the world.

I had decided that this moment was about condemning and challenging FIFA directly, not attacking Thailand. There were a number of reasons for this. Firstly, I didn't want to be counterproductive to Hakeem's ongoing treatment in prison or get arrested of course. I'd consulted Tim and Alex, as well as a former Australian diplomat who'd reached out through a mutual contact before I'd left Australia, about how to approach the Thais. The view at that time was that we still wanted their help, not to be too aggressive and to offer them a way out, a conciliation.

They had been caught in this difficult situation between Bahrain and Australia, through no fault of their own, just let the kid go, he's innocent and let Bahrain and Australia work it out between them. It was also important not to criticise the prison conditions too heavily. Doing that was guaranteed to antagonise the Thai Government and, I was advised, could lead to adverse impacts on Hakeem's treatment. Step carefully, but forcefully.

In relation to FIFA and Bahrain though, all bets were off. So, I fronted the cameras, started by explaining that I represented the current and former players of Australia as a former chairman of the PFA and captain of the national team, and let rip.

This young man hasn't seen his wife who he deeply loves, is being chased by a torturous regime seeking retribution and has asked me to deliver the following statement to Gianni Infantino, President of FIFA. I had to pause as I tried to deliver the lines, close to tears. I was choking them down, my voice wavering badly. Bloody hell, I was thinking, keep it together. I never expected to be so emotional and could never have anticipated how much meeting Hakeem, seeing his deep love for his wife and his naked fear would affect me. Like a delayed reaction, I just couldn't hold it back. Tears welled as I spoke: Where is Gianni Infantino? Where is FIFA? Where are my human rights?

This was the first moment that anyone back in Australia knew I was even in Bangkok, and these words had power. Delivered by a former international, who was clearly overcome by meeting the young player, challenging the global governing body, the most powerful organisation in world sport. That doesn't happen too often. Young journalist Matt Connellan from SBS and the others raced to get the grabs out on social media and the news that night and the footage went viral. What was that morning a relatively niche Australian story had gone global. And FIFA were on notice.

We travelled back to the hotel with the ABC filming. They wanted a personal insight into Hakeem, which was ideal. We still needed to make Australia and the world sympathise with him. To see him for what he was – a fellow human being in trouble. We could already see that, despite the intractable nature of asylum seeker policy in Australia, sport had enabled a different discussion; there was a face to the name and Australia cared, passionately.

Evan was coordinating the rest of the day, flat out on his phone.

Firstly, we went to the Australian embassy, where we met with then Ambassador-designate Allan McKinnon (now ambassador), Deputy Head of Mission Paul Stephens and a host of staff. The room was packed, in fact, a cast of thousands. The Australian Government is starting to take this very seriously, I thought. It's likely they'll want to assure me how hard they're working, keep me on side. No problem, but will they share, open communication channels? Ambassador McKinnon, of whom Marise had spoken positively, is an imposing figure in his mid-to-late fifties, with glasses and a professional demeanour one expects from a diplomat: courteous, careful with words and meaning. He seemed sincere to me, I liked him. Not the pomp and ceremony I've often seen in diplomats over the years. And Paul Stephens has an air of thoughtful, careful consideration when he speaks.

I knew they'd be well briefed on everything that had occurred on social media and otherwise, including from Marise, and thought we had a chance to build trust, depending on the feedback she'd provided. Let's see.

The meeting didn't start well at all, though. I was so horrendously tired, particularly with the draining emotion of the morning and knowing that everything had exploded back home and around the world. Where's the coffee? I poured myself a cup as I talked. People were glancing at each other with confused looks. What's wrong? I'd poured a large cup of milk. We all laughed but God knows what they thought. Is this guy really who we thought he was?

They needed to get me on side or at least make sure that I was going to go home and say they were doing their best. It was obvious by now from their point of view that I was a potential public threat and was capable of publicly calling people to account. They proceeded around the room, telling me exactly what they were all doing on Hakeem's case. They were very well prepared, synchronised. I was looking for advice and candour, though, not only diplomacy, and waiting for the moment when everyone was comfortable enough to open up. If they would.

I asked about the campaign. Nothing different there, all acknowledged the value of pressure on the stakeholders involved. Good. However, I told them I knew they were well aware of the social media campaign and needed them to advise me immediately if it started to become counter-productive in any way. If you're hearing anything adverse through your back channels, let me know.

I felt assured by the end of the meeting that they were genuinely concerned. Allan convinced me they were doing everything that it was possible for them to do and importantly he made clear that the campaign had played a significant role in at least ensuring Hakeem was not sent back to Bahrain quickly. The early noise was vital, it had helped them, it put Thailand in a position of uncertainty. That was welcome confirmation.

I did, though, form the impression that they were constrained in some way but I understood that, at the end of the day, they were only an embassy. There were a lot of constraints on them and in the diplomatic world, there's only a certain number of possibilities available based on directives from above. So I left knowing my role was to create an environment that would assist in broadening their possibilities. I also had a sense there was something more to this case than met the eye. What else could possibly be going on here? What was I missing?

I needed a photo of this first meeting to provide comfort to other stakeholders, to use as leverage and was careful to document each step of the way to keep the hundreds of thousands of people now following the case involved. I needed to let them feel that we were all taking up the fight together. We agreed what a tweet might look like, 'a productive meeting' etc., stepped in front of the Australian embassy crest, and snapped away.

That first, chaotic day, which had already been so incredibly emotional, challenging and revealing, was not over yet. We met Hakeem's lawyer, Nat, at Evan's workplace. APRRN is a refugee network based in a tiny, two-room office with one air-conditioned room. It had been hot as hell shuttling around the hectic streets of Bangkok and I closed the door, turned the air-con up to breaking point and took a moment to rest, close the eyes. We'd been going all day, and the heat and humidity were starting to tip me over the edge.

There were live crosses back to Australia or elsewhere around the world coming in by the minute, requests relayed by Evan, who was proving a major asset and every 20 minutes or so I'd pop the iPhone up, open Skype, and we'd go live to some country or other. I must have looked like death warmed up by then, but I felt an all-encompassing sense of injustice and weight of responsibility that we were all Hakeem had at that point, fuelled by anger and determination.

Of course that wasn't true, Hakeem had had a massive coalition, a team of exceptional people around the world, all working away, but it felt like we were his only chance, here in Bangkok, learning and adapting on the run. There was a powerful, driving sense of mission, of purpose. With BBC, CNN and Reuters on the case, we'd succeeded in breaking through the international barrier.

Nat walked in, smiling, shyly, we shook hands and sat down. I was under strict instructions from Nani to make a judgement about her competency. Nani had expressed concerns and I'd promised to form a view on her behalf and to find out about the relevant deadlines of the case. I was in discussions to bring another extraordinary Australian into the case, human rights barrister Jennifer Robinson from Doughty Street Chambers in London, perhaps best known in Australia as a longstanding member of Julian Assange's legal team. After connecting on Twitter, we'd met a few weeks earlier in Sydney to discuss possible legal avenues against Thailand, FIFA and the Australian Government, if necessary, including a potential compensation and damages claim for Hakeem. Jen is one of the world's finest practitioners in the human rights field, an expert in refugee law and Interpol red notices, as it happens, and we couldn't get information out of Nat for her to form a brief at that stage. I needed Nat's cooperation if we were going to bring a global legal team together.

First, though, I sat Nat down and interviewed her for the accompanying media. The campaign engine must be fed, and

I was playing dual roles. Nat must have thought, what the hell is this guy doing? Is this a meeting or a reality show? It was both. Then, to questions, off camera. How was she coping? Did she need any help? Where was the case at?

'I had no idea who he was,' Nat recounts. 'Evan told me he was a sport activist coming from Australia [with] a lot of followers on Twitter, and said he will be very influential and can do a lot of things to help [Hakeem's] case . . . I was willing to work with anybody who can give positive support to the case. So I said okay, I will meet with him. In the end, Mr Craig made such a big difference.'

Nani and I needn't have been worried about Nat. As with many characters involved in this story, I was soon to learn that Nat Bergman was another stroke of luck for Hakeem. She was clever, thorough, diligent and well connected. She was also very well respected in Bangkok's diplomatic circles, with several embassies, including the EU delegation, who confirmed in our meeting that they held her in high regard. Above all, it was clear that Nat was incredibly invested in Hakeem's case and, more broadly, in human rights. She really cared about him. She was, however, having a terrible time. Firstly, she hadn't yet been paid. Anything. There had been some kind of miscommunication with an advocacy group in the UK, who had offered to pay for her services. However now, almost two months later, it became clear that there might not be any money on the way. So Nat had essentially been donating her time on the case up until this point. Wow, I was impressed, it showed a deep commitment.

She was, though, completely overwhelmed. She admitted that the media requests had been constant and were escalating, an unwelcome distraction from the time she could spend on the case. When she'd taken the case on in December, she hadn't expected it to become the beast that it had. She was now a media spokesperson, as well as a lawyer, with all her other work beyond Hakeem's case piling up too.

'I was also working on two other cases at the same time and was incredibly busy,' Nat explains. 'On Hakeem's case, I was working four to six hours reading everything, and then answering emails, talk with reporters, the legal team and NGOs. I kept two days not working on his case and have to work on other cases.'

Evan agreed to help coordinate the media for Nat and I got in touch with John that night to let him know about the finance situation. He would find out what was promised, by who and, if necessary, find the money.

To that end, where was the fundraising campaign at, exactly? Disjointed, was the answer. One fund, by Hakeem's Melbourne lawyers, had $15,000 to $20,000 in it and I wanted to promote it aggressively to build a war chest. I wasn't comfortable raising money for an organisation that I didn't know, however, and with no oversight into its disbursement, so I asked John to get in touch with them, take over the fund, centralise any other efforts and send me the link to share on social media when the PFA had taken responsibility for it all. Then, I could be confident that probity was guaranteed. John paid Nat over the next few days, which was a relief for her, and for Hakeem.

Nat carefully explained that there are several discretionary levels for an extradition order under Thai law. The attorney-general may first consider that the request is political rather than genuinely legal, and thereafter the foreign minister may decide that it is damaging to Thailand's international standing and relationships. Excellent. We would focus on these two individuals and ensure that Thailand was aware that we knew of these opportunities to expel the case. 'So if they put the submission in,' Nat said, 'there's still a small chance.' What do you mean, *if*? Isn't the paperwork in, yet? 'Not yet,' she said casually.

Wow, what happens if they don't submit? Then there would be no case – he'd be free to go. I had to ask her several times. So, you're saying that if we get Bahrain not to submit that paperwork, he goes home? What's the date by which they had to submit? Eighth of February, exactly two weeks hence.

This meant that Bahrain was now the key actor. We had two weeks to get Bahrain not to submit their request, and it was over. What is the most likely case trajectory if it's submitted? I asked. 'Similar cases have taken from one to four years to work through the appeal process.' Four years! So Hakeem could be in that prison, sleeping on concrete for four years? 'Yes, I'm afraid so. Sorry.'

I started getting people following me and the campaign on social media to direct all efforts towards Bahrain and FIFA. Do not submit the extradition order, Bahrain. Infantino, you have considerable leverage in the Gulf region, make sure that paperwork does not go in. The date is 8 February, he's free if Bahrain pull out by that time. This quickly became the mantra, and the consistent message to that night's news back home and to the international media.

We would visit a number of embassies, intergovernmental organisations and NGOs over the first few days. These meetings were extremely important, both in terms of confirming support for Hakeem, but also in gathering intel. I wanted to know what Allan had not told me. Where were the missing pieces and what was the feedback on our own government's action, or inaction?

Each embassy had a different approach, some candid, others more formal, and critical information emerged. 'We would be delighted to assist when asked,' said one, 'because the safety of refugee passage through Thailand concerns us all.' Evan and I looked at each other. Are you saying that Australia has not formally requested your support in this matter? 'That is correct. We would expect the host country to lead a delegation or démarche to lobby Thailand, and we would be delighted to add the support of our government.' Thank you. We'll be sure to convey your message.

I had heard through Amnesty that the Australian Government had requested other countries to take the lead, which was highly concerning so this was consistent with that information. A piece of the puzzle fell into place.

I spoke to Evan. Listen, mate, you're doing a fantastic job managing media requests and these meetings, thank you, but I'm here to meet ambassadors or senior officials. Don't book another meeting with an attaché, I'm not interested. If I can't speak to decision-makers, I'll spend my time elsewhere. 'Got it, but it's not that easy, they don't know you and some will be concerned by your social media activity.' Just do your best and they will have seen the meeting with the Australian embassy on social media by now, that's what the photos are for, use them to your advantage.

Several officials went further, though, into new and completely unexpected territory that changed the destiny of the case. 'You must understand there are higher level concerns here that cannot be talked about in Thai society' and 'There are certain indicative factors here, for example, in the reactions of our Thai Government counterparts when we discuss this case, who become particularly agitated, which is generally a very strong sign that there are other, higher forces involved.'

Higher forces? Evan understood immediately and looked decidedly ill. I, on the other hand, wasn't clear. 'So are you saying that putting pressure on the Thai Government alone isn't going to be determinative? What are these higher forces? Inside, or outside of Thailand?' After the meeting, Evan filled me in. On the next occasion, I asked, 'Is it your understanding that the Thai king is directly involved in this case?' There was no time to play diplomatic games, I only had hours to get to the bottom of this. Hakeem had been in jail for almost 60 days. 'Of course, we can't be certain, but that is our understanding, yes.' Shit, what has this kid gotten himself into?

My mind raced. This is a scandal! Can I bring this out, speak about it, expose this to the world? No, advice was unanimous that it would be counterproductive to Hakeem's hopes of freedom and that I could be jailed under the 'lese majeste' laws under Article 112 of Thailand's Criminal Code, which states that an individual who 'insults, threatens or defames the King, the Queen, the heir-apparent or the Regent' may be jailed for a term of between three and 15 years. The Constitution of Thailand also states that 'The King shall be enthroned in a position of revered worship and shall not be violated. No person shall expose the King to any sort of accusation or action.' Fury was fast welling up inside. This is not right! Would two kings really trade the life of a young man? What sort of world are we living in here?

If all the rumours were true and King Maha Vajiralongkorn was involved, then how could the Thai PM withstand that influence? This would mean that all of the pressure on the Thai Government in the world could not possibly be enough. Football had now become a critical lever that had to be pulled.

Evan, who can tell me more about the Thai royal family?

'Phil Robertson is a local expert, we'll meet him in the morning.'

Excellent.

Then it dawned on me, are we at risk here? This was extremely sensitive information, people were being locked up for mentioning far less explosive royal matters. Our phone calls were now in hushed tones, everyone encouraged to use a more secure, encrypted application to communicate. There could be no risk of any leak from this point onwards, this has become serious not just for Hakeem, but potentially for us.

But whereas we'd been flying blind before, as it turned out, now the contest was equal. Given what we'd just heard, we had to win, and Aussies don't like to lose. By now I saw the issue in those black and white terms; it was a titanic contest, a struggle for one young soul between good and evil, law and lawlessness, rights and privilege.

All the government embassies we visited were willing to attend the next court hearing. It was clear this case was about much more than an individual caught between Australia and Bahrain. It was about the future of refugee and immigration policies in Thailand.

A message reminded me that there were worried family at home. 'When are you coming home? I saw you on the news, you didn't tell me you were going to the prison, remember that you've got a wife and children. Don't get yourself arrested, will you?' Trying not to, Mum.

I needed advice from an experienced, local source about the campaign tone and messaging. Were we being too strong? Might it push Thailand too far? Evan arranged dinner with the former Thai Foreign Minister, Kasit Piromya, and I listened to his advice and views. He wasn't sure about the royals but reinforced that this military government would only respond to pressure, so go as hard as possible.

One embassy provided the definitive view I was looking for. They recounted how, whenever a refugee or person was in trouble with the Thais, and the embassies or human rights organisations spoke to the media, Thai officials would complain that if only you would all be quiet, we could resolve the issue privately, everything would be fine. 'Why do you have to make such a noise all the time?' the Thais would say. The officials told me how a Cambodian refugee was detained. 'So this time we decided to extend trust and didn't say anything, trusting that Thailand would do the right thing. Within a couple of days, they were sent back to Cambodia. I wouldn't make that mistake if I were you.' Good to know. With some clamouring for quiet diplomacy, telling me I knew nothing about Thai culture, this was very important validation.

While obviously a cordial approach between governments is important for long-term relationship building, in this instance, in such a time-pressured case when there are incredibly powerful interests involved, the only option was volume. But I was being very careful to keep communication channels open.

If we'd initially hoped for some better intel on the case in Bangkok, we'd now been overwhelmed with new information. We'd met Hakeem in the prison and carried his voice outside the prison walls to the outside world, found out the Australian Government was not doing enough, that powerful interests were involved and discovered the paperwork from Bahrain wasn't in.

The other important aspect that I had learnt in these meetings with government embassies and NGOs was that Australia's willingness to help others was in question, and people were saying, why should we step up and help Australia, given your record on asylum seekers?

Some alluded to this, others simply pointed out that there had been a number of cases where Australia had been asked to get involved and had not done so. The Rahaf case, where Australia had hesitated and Canada had stepped up, was mentioned many times. We were now asking other nations to support a refugee we had said we'd protect. How did this make any sense? Given that we'd been told that some countries were waiting for Australia to ask them to get actively involved, it was not a pretty picture regarding Australia's international humanitarian standing.

After almost two months, the UN High Commissioner for Human Rights, Michelle Bachelet, had yet to issue any kind of statement, though this had become a highly visible, global issue. Neither had Filippo Grandi, the UN High Commissioner for Refugees, made a peep. I'm no longer surprised, I thought, given the UN reports into Australia's offshore detention system, in particular, and considered how to deal with the situation.

Back at the hotel the next morning, I sat down with Phil Robertson, Deputy Director of Human Rights Watch in Asia. Phil has lived in the region for more than two decades, but you'd be forgiven for thinking he'd only stepped off a plane from Boston the day before. He's a 40-something, short, stocky white male, and if you didn't take the hint from his thick, east coast American accent, you'd certainly get the message from his favourite topics of conversation. Baseball and US politics. Critically, though, Phil is fluent in Thai and an encyclopaedia when it comes to Thai and South-East

Asian politics. He knows who is connected to whom, who owes whom what, and where we needed to be directing the massive social media weapon we were now in control of.

Phil explained that we hadn't cut through enough in Thailand. The rest of the world was getting onboard, but we needed the Thais to agitate to their own government, which would also pressure the king. In Phil's view, we needed to get local clubs and players onboard. It was the only way to get through to a mass public audience in Thailand, who didn't necessarily empathise much with the plight of an individual refugee. Evidently, Thailand had their own shortcomings in the treatment of asylum seekers.

I had already reached out several times through close contacts to the President of the Thailand Football Association, who was another general, to no effect. When I mentioned this to Phil he suggested that we just rock up and doorstop them the following day. 'They couldn't possibly refuse, in Thai culture it would be embarrassing not to receive you.' We'd only just met, but that was my kind of thinking. I liked him already.

Phil showed me a tweet from a North Thailand football club, Chiang Rai, who were the first to come out in support of the campaign, displaying a #SaveHakeem banner.[1] With a military junta in power, that was quite some effort. 'We need more of this,' he said, 'you need to get big players onboard, EPL stars. Get in the local media and talk to Thai football fans. I'll help with some local contacts.' Evan, with the assistance of local Amnesty International Thailand colleagues, jumped on the phone and the local media started to respond with interest. Amnesty Thailand, via their social media and other networks, started having an impact engaging Thai university clubs and football fans.[2]

We needed different messages for different audiences: Australian, international, Thai, Bahraini, FIFA. We are all part of one football family, I'd tell Voice TV, web newspaper Prachatai and broadcaster Thai PBS. We are thrilled for your success at the Asian Cup recently, but succeeding on the field is not enough, we must all treat each other well off the field and if you mistreat our player, we take that very seriously. You cannot expect to be a member of the international football community and send one of our players back to torture or worse in Bahrain. That was completely contrary to the values of sport that we all share.

The aim, based on the advice of embassies and Phil, was to try and touch an emotional nerve. We love Thai people and our two peoples respect each other, but our patronage as tourists and our relationship diplomatically is at risk, and you're putting it there. Release Hakeem, and let's go back to being friends. The junta also needed to be challenged, though we'd need to tread a fine line for security reasons in that regard. Phil agreed to speak alongside me at the Foreign Correspondents' Club a few days later.

Throughout those hours and days, I would have many discussions about the Thai king. Can we get to him through contacts at Duntroon, Australia's military training centre in Canberra, where he studied? Could we get to him via contacts in Germany, where he grew up, owns property and spends much of his time according to the German embassy? All factors pointed to a deep financial relationship between the Bahrain and Thai kings, as well as vast commercial ties between ministers and the governments. There were literally billions of dollars involved. Media reporting since the campaign has revealed a lot more about the relationship between the two kings, although, as with everything to do with the royal family in Thailand, most of the information has been filtered through the quiet whisperings of government officials and senior diplomats.

I had been told that the Thai king, as a young man, did not have a strong relationship with his father, who the people loved. Reportedly 'privileged, unpredictable and a bit of a Don Juan', according to his own mother,[3] the king has been the subject of scandals and many a raised eyebrow. Apparently from time to time he would run out of funds, due to his lavish lifestyle and the Bahraini royal family were said to have provided financial support through access to investments at beneficial rates.

Rumours also abounded that Bahrain's friendship with Thailand had recently extended to assist the country mend an almost three-decade diplomatic rift with Saudi Arabia, Bahrain's close ally. The rift was due to a fascinating tale known as The Blue Diamond Affair, which I don't have time to go into now but certainly recommend further reading for anyone interested in million-dollar jewellery heists.[4] There was also reportedly a $1.6 billion commercial deal between the royal houses of Bahrain and Thailand that saw

Thailand's Crown Property Bureau sell a 60 per cent stake in the Kempinski Hotels Group for €1 billion to the Bahraini royal family. A *Sydney Morning Herald* article states that, 'Since 2004, Thailand's crown had owned 80 per cent of the 122-year-old group, and Bahrain held the other 20 per cent. According to the agreement struck in mid-2016, the shareholdings would swap: Bahrain paying out the Thai royal house and taking on the larger, 80 per cent share of the company.'[5] Could this be what was behind all of this?

Phil powered through the domestic media, which had impact. He was a white, middle-aged *farang*, but he was able to communicate about Hakeem's case in fluent Thai, reaching a much broader audience in Thailand than I could've ever achieved. We drank coffee and worked flat out, churning through film crew after film crew, print and radio. Waiter, another iced coffee, please?

Later that day of Wednesday, 23 January, devastating news came to hand amid all that was already going on. As I'd been running around, negotiations between FIFA and the players' body had been underway. Despite all the work it had taken to move the HRAB and the hope that we had following the seven recommendations to FIFA over the weekend, they'd agreed to just one, a letter to the Thai prime minister requesting a meeting. A meeting with Thailand? Where were the other six actions? I was furious and rang Brendan in a rage. How the hell did we go from seven to one, what's going on?

Brendan explains: 'I got a phone call from FIFPro saying, we've done a deal with FIFA and will be sending a delegation to Thailand. We're going to go to Thailand. Of the three targets identified in the recommendations, Australia, Thailand, and Bahrain, FIFA and FIFPro had gone from the softest (Australia) in their first statement to the second softest target in Thailand. They're all going to jump on a plane in hope of meeting the prime minister of Thailand, but in circumstances where the prime minister had not even responded or committed to a meeting, they couldn't go without him first accepting the invitation. I made clear that all seven recommendations were critical and must be made public to provide accountability and, when Craig called from Bangkok, he was not pleased.'

For Christ's sake. What is it going to take? Not pleased? I was incandescent. They're kidding, surely. We were finally making headway and someone negotiates this outcome? We've got the Thai king involved, a letter to the Thai PM is not going to do anything, it's unlikely he'll even respond. That's unbelievable. Can't happen, no way.

I sat up through the night writing an open letter to Infantino, sent and published online the next morning, calling on him, as president, to fulfil FIFA's obligation and demanding that a similar letter as that sent to Thailand be immediately sent to the Government of Bahrain to demand they withdraw. The letter highlighted Infantino's close relationship with Bahrain and their allies, Saudi Arabia, as well as the deadline for Bahrain to submit the required application forms to Thailand's attorney-general, as per Thailand's Extradition Act. FIFA had exactly 14 days to prevent Bahrain from submitting the paperwork.

I woke up to the final day in Bangkok, Friday, 25 January, with a splitting headache. I had been repeating the mantra to Bahrain and Thailand through the press that Aussies do not do defeat, and we're not going away. This fight is only going to get harder, I'd say. Later that evening, it would prove too true.

•

The morning started in a small bagel shop on the ground floor of the Foreign Correspondents' Club Thailand building. The heat was already stifling as I scoffed down ice coffees one after another and tried frantically to finish off an opinion piece for an Australian publication before Phil arrived. He was a bit late, which suited me fine. I pressed send to the publisher as Phil and Evan walked in, and we discussed what they had organised for the press conference in 20 minutes' time. Phil and I would speak and we spent a short time chatting about roles and process. I drained the remaining dregs of my coffee as we finished, can't let that go to waste, let Phil go ahead, took a deep breath to compose my thoughts and lines of argument, straightened the tie that complemented a fairly dishevelled suit by now, and walked upstairs.

I had continued to stay in touch with the Australian embassy throughout these four days in Thailand, which were starting to feel like four months. By Friday, I was comfortable talking about how strongly Australia considered Hakeem's legal case to be and that, if Hakeem was not released, it would damage the bilateral relationship between Australia and Thailand. It was not at the forefront of our strategy, but we did have a sense that escalating language about the countries' relationship, which is quite extensive from a trade and tourism perspective, was an effective means of ensuring the Thai authorities understood how serious we were and that we weren't going to let this go.

It was 10.30 am and the room upstairs at the Correspondents' Club was already full. By the time we walked in, there were three or four large television cameras and maybe 20 or more journalists. I wasn't sure how Phil would go as I'd only met him once. I needn't have worried. He was a force to be reckoned with, incredibly direct and assertive in his messaging about the collusion between the Thai and Bahraini governments, likening their relationship to two teenagers 'playing footsies under the table'.

It was all I could do not to laugh out loud as I looked at him sideways, thinking, this guy is fantastic. It surprised even me. Phil smashed the Thai Government, paving the way for me to target FIFA. There was no holding back. We were streaming live to social media around the world. The slogan of FIFA is 'For the Game, For the World', but in that press conference I asked FIFA – Whose game? Whose world? What about the world of Hakeem al-Araibi, is that not important? Does his life not have the same value as Gianni Infantino's?

I staggered off the stage, did a few quick interviews and looked forward to getting some rest that evening. I was heading back home tomorrow, we had done all we possibly could, Bangkok had well and truly delivered and I planned to collapse into bed early.

A RED HERRING

Given the debate around Australia's role in issuing the Interpol red notice was about to blow up in Canberra around this period, this is perhaps an opportune moment in the story to clarify the timeline of events and Australia's exact role and level of culpability here. Some of this detail was known publicly at this time, but much of it was pieced together long after the campaign was over.

The question that had gnawed away at the advocates working on this campaign, including myself, was how exactly had Bahrain known that Hakeem would be travelling to Thailand? They hadn't issued an Interpol red notice any time within the four years since Hakeem had left Bahrain, or in the two years since he had made public comments to the media while living in Australia. And yet, they issued one on 8 November 2018, just one day after Hakeem's Thai tourist visa was granted and 19 days before he was due to travel to Bangkok. An extension of this question was then, naturally, how did both Thailand and Bahrain know that Hakeem would be on the *exact* flight he was on, so that they could arrest him in Bangkok as soon as he and Nani landed? To answer these questions, we must make some educated guesses with the information that we have. Before we get to that though, let's look at what we definitely know Australian officials did (and didn't) do in relation to the red notice.

In the third week of February 2019, senior officials from the Australian Federal Police (AFP) and the Department of Home Affairs, including the Australian Border Force (ABF), fronted up to Australian parliamentarians in Senate Estimates to answer questions about their agencies' roles in Hakeem's detention. Their statements illuminated several key things, apart from their confusingly similar acronyms.

Firstly, it became clear that Australia had, indeed, blundered. Communications and database cross-checking between the separate agencies, both with differing responsibilities in terms of Interpol and immigration, had broken down. When Interpol issued Bahrain's red notice for Hakeem on 8 November, it went to all local contact points of Interpol globally, including Australia's, which is called the National Central Bureau (NCB). The AFP, following protocol, then passed that red notice on to ABF officers on 9 November. At this time, neither the AFP nor the Australian Interpol NCB were aware of Hakeem's protected visa status. Thirteen days later, on 22 November, Border Force assessed the red notice, ran Hakeem's details across the Home Affairs system and added his name to the Central Movement Alert List (CMAL) database. It was at this point that the system, critically for Hakeem, broke down. At this juncture, Border Force failed to send a 'true match' notification email, which apparently needs to be done manually, to the NCB, as per the usual process. This email would have included Hakeem's visa type, and, had this been sent, Australia would have been able to get the red notice rescinded by Interpol well before Hakeem travelled. This was at the heart of Australia's mistake. If the email had been sent, it is 'highly unlikely' that the AFP would have gone on to alert Thailand to the red notice's existence, as was pointed out in the Estimates hearings.[6] This is what the AFP did, just five days later, at 2.15 pm on 27 November, soon after Hakeem had attempted to scan his document through the SmartGates in Melbourne airport and was okayed to travel. They gave Thailand just under 11 hours to prepare for Hakeem's arrival. The thing was, Australia didn't just notify Thailand that Hakeem was travelling. Australia's NCB *also notified Bahrain.*[7]

Sport was always important for Hakeem. In 2009, when he was fifteen years old, he secured a spot in Bahrain's Under-18 national football team. He would go on to play in the Under-21s, Under 23s and then the senior team. The Bahraini royal family came to training sessions often and the team met them many times.

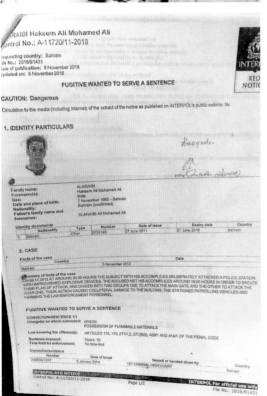

Left: The Interpol red notice, issued by Bahrain on 8 November 2018. It started a chain of events that would see Hakeem wrongfully arrested and jailed in Bangkok when he and his wife travelled there on their honeymoon. *Above:* Having been granted a permanent protection visa by the Australian Government in 2017, Hakeem was issued with a UN Australian Travel Document, which should have allowed him to safely travel overseas.

After visiting Hakeem in Bangkok's Klong Prem prison, I spoke to the waiting media, including the ABC, SBS and Channel 10 from Australia. Hakeem's story was now global and FIFA and others were on notice.

With Brendan Schwab outside FIFA headquarters in Zurich. If I needed anyone to advocate for my life, it'd be Brendan, hands down. He's possibly the most brilliant sports lawyer on the planet.

Brendan and I met with Fatma Samoura, FIFA's Secretary-General and number one on *Forbes'* list of the most powerful women in international sport in 2018. It was a frank and at times tense meeting – but we got our points across.

Speaking to the board at FIFPro's global conference in Amsterdam, just one day after our meeting with FIFA and eight days after seeing Hakeem in prison. As the global body representing professional football players, FIFPro needed to step up.

After a series of international flights and transport glitches, I made it to the second Opera House protest in Sydney, where I reported on campaign progress. By this time human rights organisations had mobilised in force and their supporters were all there, along with politicians, ACTU reps and sports stars. The message was getting through and public support was huge.

Deep in discussion with Evan Jones, program coordinator in Thailand of the Asia Pacific Refugee Rights Network. While Hakeem was in prison, Evan was his main contact, facilitating communications and visits from myself and others, and providing Hakeem with vital support, materially and mentally.

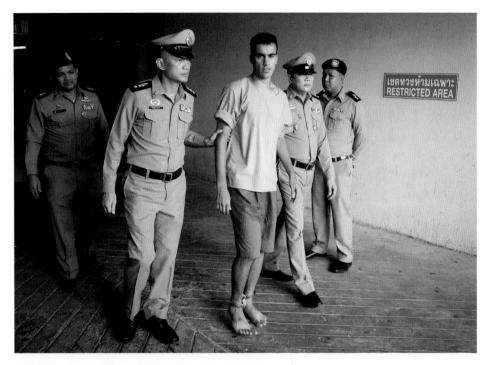

4 February 2019: Hakeem, flanked by Thai police, was brought into court wearing prison-issue clothing, barefoot and in shackles. His deep distress was obvious. Mainstream and social media picked up on the shocking scene. The world was aghast; it was the moment that Hakeem's case became real for people everywhere.
(PHOTO COURTESY AAP)

On the steps of the court following the hearing. Australian ambassador to Thailand, Allan McKinnon, supported by embassy staff and Hakeem's lawyer, Nat Bergman, addresses the waiting media. The Australian Government had made it clear that Thailand could and should act on Hakeem's behalf and release him.

So many people were key players in the campaign to free Hakeem. *Left to right:* Sahar Okhovat and Paul Power from the Refugee Council of Australia; Ghassan Khamis, Yahya Alhadid and Fatima Yazbek of GIDHR (the Gulf Institute for Democracy and Human Rights).

When Hakeem arrived home in Melbourne on 12 February, he was greeted by a very excited, energetic and emotional group of friends and supporters of the #SaveHakeem campaign.

Tim O'Connor and Alex Engel-Mallon of Amnesty International Australia with Hakeem in Melbourne, the evening of his arrival home to Australia.

Two days after safely touching down on Australian soil, Hakeem travelled to Canberra to meet Prime Minister Scott Morrison, Foreign Minister Marise Payne, and others who had assisted the campaign. It was a powerful statement for Hakeem, a young male Muslim refugee, to come to Parliament House and remind everyone what a strong and courageous country we can be for people who seek our protection. *Above:* Senator Marise Payne and Graham Perrett MP, Deputy Chair of the Parliamentary Joint Committee on Human Rights, with Hakeem at the celebratory football match played in his honour on the Senate Oval.

Scott Morrison takes a celebratory selfie with Hakeem and me.

On 12 March 2019, Hakeem became an Australian citizen. His certificate was presented to him by Marise Payne. Hakeem said, 'I owe this country everything and I will be so strong for Australia'.

Now, we can assume that Bahrain already knew that Hakeem was travelling to Thailand due to the extraordinarily coincidental timing of the issuance of the red notice the day after his tourist visa to Thailand was granted. This is circumstantial though, and there will likely never be hard evidence to prove the two events were correlated. There's also the comments made from Surachate Hakparn in early December that revealed 'The Bahraini government knew that he [Hakeem Al-Araibi] would be arriving in Thailand [on 27 November], so they coordinated with Thailand's permanent secretary of foreign affairs to detain him, pending documents sent from Bahrain.'[8] But even this is not hard evidence. Technically, the Bahrainis could've been acting on the information provided to them by Australia's NCB. Even without hard proof, there remains significant cause for concern that Bahrain and Thailand potentially colluded to make this happen. A warning to protected refugees ever thinking about travelling to Thailand, in any case.

What we do know for certain is that Hakeem went through a slightly unusual process to get his Thai tourist visa. He was asked to return to the embassy two times before it was granted on 7 November. One of these times he was asked to provide a copy of his flight ticket, which he did. As Evan Jones points out, 'Anyone with an Australian travel document travelling to Thailand for less than four weeks that needs to request a three-month visa would stand out to the Thai authorities ... Australian citizens can stay in Thailand for up to 30 days without a visa, so it would've been very unusual for an Australian travel document holder only going for a week's holiday in Thailand to need a visa ... only refugees really fit into this category.' Although Hakeem's travel document does not indicate that he is Bahraini, it does list his place of birth as 'Jidhafs', so it would not have been difficult to find out where he was from. It is highly probable, whether innocently or otherwise, that Thailand contacted Bahrain at the time Hakeem submitted his visa application, and that this was when the process to extradite him really began.

The day after Hakeem was detained and his story had hit the news, the Home Affairs department notified the AFP of Hakeem's protection visa status and the validity of his Australian travel document. Unfortunately, the relevant AFP employee had gone home by the time the email with the advice arrived in their inbox, so did not act on it until the following morning. It is noteworthy that this was the very first time the AFP was notified of Hakeem's visa status. Once acted on, it was also possibly the first time Bahrain discovered that Hakeem had a refugee protection visa. While the AFP insisted this gap in time between the AFP employee receiving and acting on the email had no impact on Hakeem's detention (as it occurred the day after his arrest), it clearly would have sped up Australia's notification of the invalid red notice to Interpol, which did not occur until an email was sent at 8.17 am on 30 November to Interpol's General Secretariat.[9] Even then, that email noted that Australia was 'conducting urgent inquiries with the relevant Australian authorities to confirm the refugee status of Mr Alaraibi'. It wasn't until 3.03 pm that a second email was sent with formal advice that Hakeem had a permanent protection visa.[10] Documents obtained via Freedom of Information laws reveal that a final, third email was sent by Australia at 10.54 pm, seemingly in desperation. It was titled as a 'follow up request' and politely asked for clarification regarding the 'effect that an existing refugee protection visa would have on an Interpol red notice'.

The red notice was finally rescinded late on 30 November from Interpol's headquarters in Lyon, France, in line with its own policies, which make it clear red notices can't be issued against a refugee from the country they fled. By then, it was already the morning of

1 December in Bangkok, the day that Hakeem and Nani thought they would be flying home to Australia. At this point, once the red notice was rescinded, Thailand had discretionary power to let Hakeem return to Australia. However, as of 27 November, Bahrain had formally requested Hakeem's extradition, meaning that Thailand now had an extradition request from a sovereign country, of which Hakeem was a citizen. It was Australia's will against Bahrain's, and Thailand was now caught smack bang in the middle.

Australians were, and should remain, aghast that our country's border protection and immigration systems broke down in such a way and played some role in placing this young man's life at risk. While Senate Estimates revealed that officials have gone some way towards addressing the system failures that allowed this to happen, nothing has led me to believe, categorically, that this exact situation could not occur again. I'm happy for it to be proven otherwise. Australia's continued participation in Interpol and the credibility of their systems, in particular, must be closely scrutinised moving forward. It was a clear failure of Interpol headquarters, as mentioned earlier, that the red notice from Bahrain was not analysed with due diligence before being issued in the first place. Further to Radha Stirling's longstanding research and advocacy in this area, Australia remains a contributor to an international policing system that is openly being used by authoritarian governments to return refugees and asylum seekers to them for punishment and persecution, despite Interpol's supposed policies to prevent this. That's all I'll say about red notices for now but, rest assured, this element of the story is far from over.

Back at the hotel in central Bangkok, Evan reminded me that we'd been invited to the Australian embassy that night for an Australia Day function. Not tonight, no way. I was so tired that I was falling asleep on the couch in the hotel lobby and, psychologically, I was already on the plane home. But in retrospect, I thought better of it. The embassy had been very welcoming and helpful, I owed them as much. It would be good to meet in a less official setting, and we might learn something in less formal conversation.

We rocked up to the function and I was immediately struck by the scale of it. It was huge. There were several large connected rooms in the massive function centre and perhaps more than 800 people. It was clearly a very significant night for the Australian embassy in Thailand.

A large portrait of the Queen of England, still Australia's head of state, was prominently on display and I found the emphasis on the English royal family throughout the speeches to be incongruous with accepted procedure back home. Then a song started and the congregation snapped to attention, military style, faces forward, dutiful. I'm not familiar with it, Evan, didn't we already have the Thai national anthem? 'The Thai *royal* anthem, Sansoen Phra Barami or "glorify his prestige" in English.' It was a chilling reminder.

I touched base with a few of the embassy staff that I'd met earlier in the week and it was clear they cared about the case and opened up on how much it meant to them. One of the women was in tears describing how she felt meeting Hakeem in prison. I empathised with her and may have had something in my eye, as well.

By late evening, we were happily heading for the exit; our official duties on this trip were at an end. As we made our final goodbyes, I was tapped on the arm by a senior official and, as we stepped away from the main group, he spoke in hushed tones.

'I've got some bad news,' he said quietly. 'Bahrain has put the paperwork in.' When? 'Late this afternoon.'

I was momentarily paralysed. This was the first time it hit me – Bahrain was speeding up. I'd started calling for the extradition papers not to be submitted, and they were in two days later. My mind was racing with the ramifications of this, my heart quickened and, for a millisecond, my face must have showed it. There was more.

'It gets worse.' Jesus. How much worse could it get? 'Our information is that Thailand is rushing it through. To skip the levels of executive discretion that exist under the attorney-general and foreign minister.' The world caved in. The kid was gone. I thought of Nani, of the promises I'd made to her.

Up until this point, the Thai Government had been using their judicial systems and 'due process' as the rationale for keeping Hakeem detained, despite the red notice being lifted. Now, 'due process' was out the window, a charade. Minister Payne had been informed and had already been in contact with her Thai counterparts to let them know the Australian Government considered this 'extremely distressing'. Bahrain was hitting back. I was devastated, but thinking it through quickly: options, options, options. I need to go to Zurich. We need FIFA to step up, it's the only way.

The next morning, I'd let Lara and the kids know first. Is everyone okay? She'd been keeping in constant contact about the security issues prior to my leaving and thankfully there had been no further scares. Sorry, my sweet, won't be back just yet, I have to go to Zurich. 'You know you have all my support, love you, everyone is fine here, go get 'em.' And Mum? Might leave that one to Lara.

There were, by now, what seemed like hundreds of interviews to do and Evan was flat out, so I'd need to coordinate them among everything else that was going on. It wasn't always a roaring success, frankly. Once, I had CNN on Skype on the phone about to go live. They'd had me waiting for a full 10 minutes, which is long but the opportunity to talk about the 'torturous regime' of Bahrain, the political nature of the case and how FIFA weren't doing enough to a global audience was too important. They'd tested, and tested again as the phone was propped up on a bookshelf in the hotel, staff and customers walking past. Then, with 15 seconds to go, the bloody phone fell on the ground! Luckily it didn't smash, as I hurriedly propped it up and hoped like hell they weren't looking at just half of my face. On another Skype interview I did, with Al Jazeera's *Inside Story* alongside a panel of experts, the hotel started turning the lights off in the middle of a sentence. I was literally sitting in darkness, on a very serious and well-respected global affairs show with an important reach into the Middle East and trying not to laugh at the absurdity of it all. It was that sort of campaign.

This is where Bob Icevski came into his own. An old friend of mine for 15 years with a deep love and knowledge of football, he owns a travel company and can be trusted to go the extra mile. He was about to go much further than that. He had already changed my flight home. I need another change, I told him over early breakfast the next morning, between interviews. 'Again? It costs money every time. How many more days will you be there?' No, I need to get to Zurich on the first possible flight. 'Tonight or tomorrow?' No, now. 'I'm onto it,' he said, 'call you back shortly.'

A message came through. There was a flight available at 1 pm. I had to leave the hotel within the next 10 minutes. For crying out loud, there goes the packing, I'll have to throw everything together! I called Brendan in Nyon in Switzerland, filled him in on the awful case updates and that I'd be arriving in Zurich tomorrow. Let me know if you want to come to FIFA House, I'm going on Monday. 'Do you have a meeting, Fozz?' he asked. No, I'm going to demand one now. 'Really? On email?' No, Twitter. 'Good job, I'll get packed.'

Bob spoke with the PFA for an upgrade to a business class ticket, he well knew the pace we were keeping up and thought I should arrive at FIFA looking a great deal better than I did presently. 'I saw you on the news, son, you looked awful. Get something to eat for god's sake. Did you only take one suit? I've seen that grey suit for a whole week on every interview you've done.' Yes, the week was a tad more eventful than I anticipated. 'Well, buy another one, for god's sake, it must be walking on its own by now. Do you have any warm clothes, you do realise you're headed into winter, right?' Stuff it, hadn't thought about that. I'll have to buy some when I get there. But I wasn't going business class. Not happening, mate, players' money, we're going economy. Change it back.

As soon as I got into a cab and headed for the airport, I drafted an email and tweet to FIFA and hit send. I'd either meet with Fatma Samoura or Infantino, or I'd hold a press conference on the steps of FIFA to explain to the world what was happening. International media had been alerted, and FIFA were on notice. In true Aussie style, we were going to gatecrash FIFA's party.

Orsat called after seeing the tweet and said, 'What the hell are you doing? Do you have a meeting arranged?' His job was to work with his counterpart, head of media at FIFA, and this was way, way out of the ordinary, bordering on crazed, really. Unless you knew the reality of the case. I filled him in. 'Got it, good call. While you're in the air, I'll work on it and we'll talk when you land.'

Then a call to Tim and Alex at Amnesty. I need the petitions in a PDF form, at least a portion of them, to hand over to FIFA either in a meeting, or to leave on their doorstep in front of the world's media. Send it on Dropbox so I can print tomorrow. Thanks.

I knew that FIFA had been given seven recommendations and chosen to do as little as possible, opting merely to pressure Thailand, a political minnow compared to the Gulf nations friendly to Bahrain and which did not require them to put any political relationships at risk. The paperwork was in. Hakeem al-Araibi was being cut loose, and the game would move on. He was to be collateral damage. But not this time.

If I had a breath left, football was going to fulfil its duty to this young player. I sent two more tweets to let FIFA and Bahrain know that I was aware of the game being played and prepared to let the world know. The Australians were coming, and not for a barbecue.

@Craig_Foster Jan 25 Will be in air next 12 hours. Please share with all major news outlets. The game is trying to leave this young man behind and we can't let it happen. Football must step up now! I'll explain case, polity s fully to media Monday 2pm #SaveHakeem

Any international media please contact @WorldPlayersUtd or @thepfa for information, background. I'll brief fully on why Hakeem is a political prisoner, why football is not doing enough, why FIFA will be held accountable for this life if they do not act now. See u in 12 hrs.

Chapter 8

FIFA HOUSE

26–28 JANUARY 2019

It was minus 4 degrees in Zurich. This had not been part of
the plan when I'd hurriedly packed my suitcase a week ago.
I'd come from 30 degrees in Bangkok, had nothing warm
and it was snowing outside. All I had was one suit, a very
messy suitcase and a head full of logistical questions. Bob
had booked accommodation for me while I was in the air
so when I turned my phone on, mercifully there was a text
waiting with information about how to get to the hotel. There
were even instructions on how to get to the nearest H&M
store. I grabbed the first jacket I could find, a horrible-looking
thing, and then called Orsat.

His FIFA counterpart, then media chief Fabrice Jouhaud,
had contacted him to try to get a handle on what was going
on. This was most unusual, not how FIFA did things at all,
Andrew. Orsat let him know that he could get in touch with

me but that I was independent and he could not influence the chain of events that I had set in train. I would follow through on the threat to hold a media conference on their front doorstep and it might well be in their best interests to arrange a meeting for Monday, despite the extreme short notice.

'Fatma Samoura is very busy, you understand.' They weren't convinced that anyone would attend a press conference for this guy from Australia who was showing up with three days' notice, demanding a meeting with the world's most powerful sporting body. They were confident, or hopeful at least, that there would not be many journalists there on Monday.

However, the tweet had reached not just the international media, but around 800,000 people. Orsat let them know that more than a dozen major media outlets from all over Europe had already confirmed they were attending. Er, they'd get back to him shortly. By the time I landed, he'd created a WhatsApp group chat with FIFPro and FIFA's media teams, as well as FIFA's human rights lead, Federico Addiechi, and me to arrange logistics. We'd broken through.

Their tone changed. 'Would Craig be open to a joint press conference, if we are able to find time to meet?'

Orsat called me. 'What do you want to do?' Say no. They, rightly, want to bring me in, shut me down, make a joint statement and move on. Tell them I'll make my own statement, meeting or not. I held the leverage and wasn't giving away an inch. 'How amusing' was Fabrice Jouhaud's response. FIFA were off balance, scrambling to respond.

Operating remotely from Amsterdam, Orsat managed to secure a meeting with the Secretary-General of FIFA, Fatma Samoura. I let her know by email that the most brilliant sports lawyer on the planet was coming too. If I needed anyone to barge into FIFA House and advocate for my life, it'd be Brendan Schwab, hands down. I thought back to the myriad meetings we'd had together over past decades with football officials. Somehow, we'd arrived back here again but this time the stakes were much, much higher.

•

I called Schwabby: it's on, get over to Zurich asap. He'd be there in the morning and asked me what I thought about the AFC statement. Which statement? The AFC had issued a release while I was in the air stating that AFC Senior Vice President Praful Patel 'was asked 18 months ago by the AFC Executive Committee to handle matters involving AFC's West Zone to ensure there were no accusations of a conflict of interest involving AFC President Sheikh Salman bin Ibrahim Al Khalifa'.

What the? Brendan Schwab explained that members of the Advisory Council of the Centre for Sport and Human Rights had suggested this. They thought that if Salman publicly announced his recusal, then that would somehow 'get him out of the way'. But it was 'in the way' that I wanted him. There is no conflict of interest when it comes to saving a player's life, rather it was an admission of complete failure to uphold the responsibilities of office. It was staggering that a FIFA official – bearing in mind he is the most senior official of the AFC, which includes Hakeem's home country of Bahrain as a member – could even purport to be recused from their human rights obligations. Has anyone even heard of such a thing?

It was an admission by the Centre for Sport and Human Rights, if nothing else, that Salman was an impediment to a successful resolution. In which case, how could he remain in the position? They should have been calling for his head, not offering him a way out.

The FFA Chairman, Chris Nikou, had met with Salman at the Asian Cup several weeks ago. Had this supposed recusal been raised at the meeting? Where was the outrage from the Australians who'd evidently been duped? The whole thing was a mockery. Still, I knew Salman would get away with it but the scandalous nature of it only served to highlight the plight that Hakeem was in. This was the level of people charged with protecting him, for Christ's sake.

Salman had sat tight in his position not saying or doing anything publicly for a full 60 days, and then, the very day *after* Bahrain had submitted Hakeem's extradition papers, the AFC has decided to announce his recusal? Has he waited for Bahrain to translate all their paperwork, then stepped away? The case for the affirmative was damning.

@Craig_Foster Jan 26. This statement betrays every principle of international sport governance. Admission of conflict, morally bankrupt, investigation required in due course.

I wasn't the only one to notice the AFC's actions. On 28 January the *South China Morning Post* published an article with the headline 'Is AFC that inept and naïve to think "conflict of interest" absolves Al-Khalifa of his duty to detained Bahraini player?' The article noted that 'Not once has AFC called for Hakeem al-Araibi's release, not once has it condemned those responsible for throwing him in jail.'[1]

There was, though, some welcome news. Just the day before, Brendan had written on behalf of World Players United to the IOC. We'd been trying to get the Olympics involved for weeks by now, and he'd particularly made reference to the demonstrated commitment by the IOC to support refugee athletes and that safe passage of refugee athletes around the world was under threat in Hakeem's case. The IOC issued a statement within 24 hours. Great job, mate, but we need them to pressure Bahrain and Prince Nasser, head of their Olympic committee. I told you about the royals, we need pressure on both the Bahraini and Thai royals. ASAP. 'Got it. Leave it with me.'

The next day, Sunday, 27 January, we planned. And planned. I did say he is meticulous. We had points, and diagrams, and highlights, and fallbacks. Well, he did. I had my own thoughts on how to handle the meeting and was organising them in my head throughout the day, thinking through the entire case. It was a rare respite, a day sitting around in a hotel, time to think, put the pieces together, look at weak points, where Bahrain might hurt us, how the connections were forming, recent events, what I could reveal or could not.

I also thought about how to manage the meeting, where to bring Schwabby in. We'd worked together over a long period and could bounce off each other on the run, but here we had extremely limited time and needed a resolution by the end of the meeting. Hakeem depended on it. No mistakes, no wasted time, no obfuscation from Fatma, no second chances. Get in and out with the outcomes. And what were they, exactly? We needed FIFA to understand that I knew the full dynamics of the case and the disregarded recommendations and that simply taking the path of least political resistance by attacking the Thai prime minister, who was under royal pressure from above, was never going to be enough. They must accept the extreme urgency of the matter given what we knew about Thailand expediting the case through the discretionary legal steps and they needed to get over to the Gulf and sort it out. Now.

Orsat was in touch, FIFA had agreed to an hour-long meeting at 12 pm, but I'd told the media two days before that I'd front them at 2 pm. I smiled. They wanted to meet for an hour then Fatma would have an opportunity to speak ahead of me, and leave. She'd set the agenda and we'd lose the advantage. Orsat had already informed the international media; what should we do? Get back to them, mate, change it to 1 pm. Things will keep changing as they try to wrestle back control. Keep me informed.

•

I was up early on Monday morning, pumping in caffeine with interviews aplenty, amid final moments to prepare. There was nothing but extreme focus, concentration. We were going to get an outcome from this meeting for Hakeem and

Nani, and I didn't care what I had to do, or say, to get it. Brendan and I went over our meeting strategy one last time during breakfast, point by point. Have we missed anything? Where are the traps that might be set? Then it dawned on me that though I'd pledged to deliver the petitions of the people, I'd forgotten to actually print them amongst all the other priorities. The 50,000 signatures cost over $500 to print. I put it on Brendan's room. As any Aussie worth their salt would.

Importantly, Orsat had been chasing high-profile players, constantly. At 1.24 am Zurich time that morning, Gary Lineker sent out a simple but powerful tweet saying 'Come on @FIFAcom sort this wrong out.' The timing was perfect. We were going to walk into the meeting with that ringing in Fatma's ears and they could not know whether more may be waiting. Pressure rose again.

Then, about an hour before the meeting, Bahrain reacted, again. 'Have a look at this, Fozz, they're talking about us. It's terrifying,' Brendan said. Interior Minister and another royal family member, General Sheikh Rashid bin Abdullah Al Khalifa was quoted in a release saying that, 'external interference in the internal affairs of Bahrain is unaccept-able. Those raising unfounded doubts about the integrity and independence of the Kingdom's judicial system are not only interfering, but also attempting to influence the course of justice.'

Given their immense political connections they must have thought it preposterous that these Australians had marched into FIFA and they clearly knew that I was very well briefed. They'd certainly seen all the photos from the embassies, and my public comments told them that I knew exactly what they were up to. I thought it fantastic and was really energised by it. They were in a panic, scrambling to pre-empt the media that they knew we would soon generate. It also broke on the international news wires that Bahrain had submitted the extradition paperwork in Thailand the preceding Friday, which they'd clearly leaked before I might speak about it publicly. They were reacting to our timeline, again. They had scarcely veiled public threats from one of the far too many generals now infesting this case, but we had the upper hand.

It also highlighted the escalating desperation of Bahrain to win this battle. It seemed as though the very credibility and control of the royal family was being put to the test and while I had ensured that Middle East politics and religion were completely avoided in the campaign – to us Hakeem was simply a young man in need of help and nothing else was relevant – this concerned me deeply because it meant Bahrain would do everything in its power to win. By now, a large number of Bahrainis were constantly in touch through social media, giving support and cheering us on, and it was becoming evident that for many of them, Hakeem represented a figure of hope, even of resistance. But if Bahrain was now fighting to extradite not just a kid who had spoken out against them but a growing symbol of anti-repression, we knew this fight would go to the death. Being so vocal, aggressive and opening themselves to further international condemnation, said as much. The stakes were suffocatingly high.

The air was heavy in the cab en route to FIFA-Strasse, very quiet, both of us running through key points, rehearsing and planning. As two long-time player rights activists, we knew exactly what we were walking into. FIFA, and all political organisations like it, rely on the seductive nature of power. Trading benefits for causes. I have said many times since that if we were so inclined, we could have compromised that day, even a fraction, gained political capital with FIFA and personally benefited in many ways. That is how the system works. They would soon realise, though, that we were not there to trade anything for Hakeem's life. Furthermore, I was prepared to do it at any cost, regardless of how many relationships I had to break, if necessary. It would be best to work with FIFA to free Hakeem but if doing so meant any compromise on them doing their job, I'd happily work against them. The choice was theirs.

I had the currency of information, and the world's eyes trained intently on them. They had an escalating situation which could become extremely damaging and an Aussie they could trade nothing with. As we drove quietly through Zurich, I reflected on what FIFA House was supposed to stand for, the most impressive and opulent sports headquarters on the planet which was built from money generated by the greatest players in history. It's time these administrators stood up for another one, Brendan. He looked at me and nodded. I was preaching to the converted. He wrote the manual.

FIFA's head of human rights is the suave Argentinian Federico Addiechi and we walked in the door of FIFA House to textbook treatment. Bring them in, make them feel comfortable, show them the splendour of FIFA, try to shape the conversation, put out some fires and placate if possible then bring in Fatma for a photo op, some diplomatic language about how we're doing our best of course, you must understand the issues, though you couldn't possibly because we're FIFA, don't you know. To Federico Addiechi: no offence, Federico, that's your job, but we have ours. I pushed back cordially but firmly. When Fatma gets here, I'll take you both through what's really happening.

Fatma had held the post of secretary-general, the most powerful position in FIFA's management team, since 2016, the first female to hold the job that earned her the number one spot in *Forbes*' list of the most powerful women in international sport in 2018. A former Senegalese diplomat, she is also no stranger to the plight of people seeking refuge. Her former positions within the United Nations have included senior roles covering complex humanitarian emergencies in Kosovo, Timor-Leste and eastern Chad. She reportedly earns around 1.3 million Swiss francs per annum (more than 1.8 million Australian dollars), just shy of Gianni Infantino's presidential salary of over 1.5 million Swiss Francs (over 2.1 million Aussie dollars). Players' money.

Before Fatma arrived, the press was ready and waiting. She entered the room like a head of state. The shutters blazed as she smiled and introduced herself. We shook hands and a photographer snapped the moment which, to me, succinctly captured the meeting and the campaign. Fatma, accustomed to deference, smiling. Brendan dutifully smiling for the camera. And me? Well, Australians don't do genuflection well. At all.

I shook her hand, oblivious to the cameras and looked at her as if to say, we're not here for small talk, Fatma. It was the lobbying duo from hell.

Photos over, I told all the media to leave the room so that we could get down to business, thanked Fatma for her time and told her I was there to tell her exactly what was happening in Hakeem's case, including information she did not know.

You've seen social media, I told her, and know the phenomenal support from back home. I am not the Prime Minister of Australia, so I don't speak for the country but I do represent millions of Australians who feel extremely strongly about this case and I am accountable to them. I am going to inform you fully about what is going on here so that, afterwards, you're accountable to me. And either you are going to act appropriately and we'll get this kid out together, or I will speak to the world's media downstairs about what is going on.

I've brought information from Bangkok that is extremely worrying so your letter to the Thai PM is not enough. The key here is the Bahrain Government and royal family so Gianni needs to get across to Bahrain and sort this out or call the Saudi royal family, with whom he has close commercial and political ties, and get them to solve it. His silence is not good enough, the president is obligated to use his leverage, now. Our advice from a range of credible sources is that Hakeem's life is in severe danger if he is returned. Further, I was advised by very high-level government sources on Friday evening that Bahrain had submitted their paperwork for extradition and that Thailand are moving to expedite the case through several discretionary levels. You need to step up now.

Fatma left the room and shortly returned.

From there, the meeting ebbed and flowed through a range of points. Brendan was, as usual, superb. At times, Fatma and I were getting heated, not shouting but very assertive, and Brendan would interject, ask a question, change the tone. Federico played his role well. When Fatma was struggling to manoeuvre out of the questioning, he'd start slowing things down. 'We must understand, Craig, that FIFA has been . . .' etc. etc. Thanks, Federico, but a kid's life is at stake and we're here to speak with Fatma.

We were controlling the agenda when the head of media, Fabrice, got involved from the corner of the room. 'Well, Craig, can I ask why the players don't do something more, hold their own protest? Why must it always be FIFA?' Brendan, lightning on the uptake: 'Good idea, Fabrice, are you saying that we have FIFA's mandate to hold a global protest next weekend across the world's major leagues to mirror the wearing of orange armbands in Australia, for example? That would be very worthwhile, thank you.' 'Oh no, Brendan, this is not what I meant of course.' We knew what you meant, buddy, now sit down. That bit was just in my head.

Fatma asked why I was fighting so hard for Hakeem, not other players, like the Nigerians in trouble in China, for example. 'Fatma, are you saying that I should not be trying to save this kid's life? I don't understand the question and, yes, I'll be delighted to help save others as well. Let me know how you'd like to proceed in that regard but our immediate focus in this meeting is to get this kid out.'

Fatma pointed to the work done by her and the organisation for the Afghanistan women's team, who were found to be victims of sexual abuse, as evidence of her strong commitment to human rights. Congratulations, I'm thrilled at the positive outcome and I can see how strongly you feel about the issue, Fatma, but this case has governments like Bahrain and royal families involved which have far greater political influence. I'm here to ensure that FIFA act irrespective of these factors.

I went for Salman. You should stand him down immediately. 'How is that going to help get Hakeem out?' Fatma asked. That's not the point, Fatma, the man is a power-broker in one of FIFA's global regions and is therefore accountable to FIFA's Human Rights Policy. And I do believe that holding his organisation to account would both demonstate your commitment to the human rights policy and enforce a new standard of official conduct. We argued the point, strongly. I told her that we wanted him gone and would not stop until it had happened.

Brendan raised the recusal and its timing, coming the very day after Bahrain submitted its paperwork. 'You can't prove causation,' said Federico. They were well aware of the inference.

Infantino needs to speak up, I said. Fabrice, again. 'Now, Craig, we can agree that noise and shouting is not what FIFA is known for and, of course, you must understand the cultural nuance of Asia and Thailand.'

I did not shift my gaze from Fatma. 'Fatma, I'll guarantee you that I'll not take offence at your head of media inferring that I lack cultural understanding, despite having lived in South-East Asia for a number of years as a player and taken advice on campaign tone and messaging from a vast range of actors including a former foreign minister of Thailand, my own government and ambassador to Thailand, all of who are in concerted and indeed vociferous agreement with the approach taken.'

'No, no, Craig, that is not what I meant.' I knew what you meant, mate, that'll be enough from you. I didn't say that last one, either.

We discussed the issue of sanctions at length. FIFA needed to force Bahrain and Thailand to act and one of the most powerful tools is sporting sanctions, an Asian Champions League or national team ban. Fatma would not contemplate it. Her background as a UN diplomat informed her belief that sanctions do not work. Tell that to black South Africans, I thought.

Federico thought that, under FIFA's regulations, sanctions weren't permissible. Brendan, as always, had done his home-work and argued that there was a legal case that could be made. Irrespective, sanctions should be considered on the basis of policy, we believed. 'I'm happy to work with your legal department to enable it in accordance with existing regulations,' said Brendan. 'It will be necessary in similar cases in future.'

According to advice in Thailand the week before, even the threat of sanctions could be enough to get Thai fans activated, which was critical. Fatma stood firm but we made it clear that in our view the option was still on the table. We'd anticipated this and knew that it would be a key message in the press conference to come.

I told Fatma we should get out to Bangkok straight away, visit Hakeem in prison to make a strong statement of FIFA's intent, meet with the Thai PM and get Bahraini officials to Zurich by the end of the week, by which time I'd come back to meet as well. Obviously, I was going nowhere near Bahrain. But how could the FIFA Secretary-General turn up when her letter hadn't even garnered a response? Fair enough.

We'd been going back and forth much longer than anticipated by now, almost an hour and a half, Fatma needed to leave shortly and the media were waiting. Fabrice asked, 'Are you going to speak with them, or shall I tell them to wait a little longer?'

Fatma, we can agree on the following points and I will communicate these to the waiting media. She would raise the urgency to 'emergency' status to indicate the importance that FIFA are placing on the case, FIFA was to make a public call for meetings with members of the royal family of Bahrain and their goverment as well as Thailand, and we all agreed that we wanted to see progress this week. Privately, she'd have Infantino speak to Salman at the Asian Cup Final four days later. 'Yes, I must go, Fabrice will assist with the statement.'

We marched downstairs, composed our thoughts, burst into the sunshine and a blast of freezing cold air and strode across to the media centre, quickly structuring what we'd say. Almost two hours had gone, we had achieved what we wanted, and now it was time to deliver a message to Bahrain down both camera barrels.

We are delighted that FIFA have recognised the emergency nature of this case and that more needs to be done, immediately, I'd say. This young man is in grave danger and football has not done enough to date. Fatma Samoura and FIFA have resolved to call for immediate and urgent meetings with the highest levels of both countries including governments and royal families and we expect progress within the week. And I specifically mentioned the disagreement on sanctions but that we believed that penalties for both Bahrain and Thailand were necessary and must remain on the table. 'Are you satisfied that FIFA will make every effort in this case after your meeting?' came the reply. FIFA have committed to agreed actions and a timeline and I am happy to work with them to see a successful resolution of the case; nevertheless, the only acceptable outcome is that this boy has his rights upheld and is granted his freedom and you can be sure that we will hold FIFA to their undertakings.

I then handed the stage to the global athlete union boss to add his carefully structured, informed and articulated comments. All the while, Fabrice stood in the corner watching. He'd lost control of the messages, but a shared statement was the next best outcome.

Press conference over, I'm staying until we get this statement, Brendan. Agreement on broad principles is one thing but negotiating language is going to be laborious, the detail is where it'll get watered down to nothing. There's still a long way to go before we're in print, mate. We need Orsat. I got him on the phone from Amsterdam and took him through what we had agreed upstairs. I want you to call them and let them know you'll handle the statement for us, we'll be in the lobby doing work and interviews. 'How long will you be there?' he asked. As long as it takes. It was about 3 pm. By 7 pm, we still had no agreement, the cleaners were moving in and lights were going off. Stubborn bastards, these Australians.

As expected, Fabrice stayed out of it and put a proxy in charge, a lower level media executive who would come down with a printed statement. I'd take it, tell him to email it to Orsat, get on the phone and edit on the run with him, negotiating language, order, quotes, have Orsat email it back, and wait. Then, instead of emailing it back to both of us, the process would repeat.

FIFA were drawing it out, wasting time, but why? They wouldn't mention the Bahrain royals, it would be the 'very highest levels of Bahrain and Thailand'. Fair enough. We wanted to hold them to progress within a week, as agreed. Deadlines can reflect poorly if not met. That's fine. Finally, as lights went off, we agreed, shook hands and left, tired and elated. By 10 pm, now back at the hotel, it was clear the statement wasn't going out that night. We needed it though and I'd not back off until we got it the next morning, to put Bahrain on the defensive again.

It was clear from the Bangkok meetings that, by now, it was incredibly difficult for Thailand to send Hakeem back to Bahrain under the glare of the world and our leverage in getting FIFA to the table publicly would provide further protection against the worst. But we believed that Bahrain wanted, at a minimum, to tie him up in prison for anywhere up to four years, something which was apparently common practice and which would still be a warning to others who might speak out. Bahrain could win in two ways. We had only one, and time was our enemy. I needed that statement.

I was drained completely as I finished the last call for the night with Orsat, sat at the dinner table with Brendan and just started to relax and rest the mind. A glass of vino tinto might be nice, I thought. But Brendan wanted to do a thorough review of the meeting. Mate, it's 10 o'bloody clock. 'Six points we had, Fozz,' and he checked off one, two, three, four, five and 'we didn't get to six but you covered this anyway in your earlier engagement with Fatma. Outstanding meeting, well done.' Bloody lawyers.

I was planning to stay the following night to see Schwabby's family in Nyon when Orsat mentioned that the FIFPro global conference was on the following day in Amsterdam. Really? Will all the board members be there? Can I speak to them? 'Yes, I'll make it happen.' Another flight. Bob, sorry to wake you up, what time is it there, mate? I knew full well.

The following morning, Marise Payne's office issued another statement saying that 'Australia remains deeply concerned by the ongoing detention' of Hakeem, and that the Foreign Minister 'has also conveyed her deep concern about the matter to Bahrain's Foreign Minister, Sheikh Khalid bin Ahmed Al Khalifa, and asked Bahrain not to proceed with the extradition request.'[2]

And finally, our joint statement with FIFA came through on email. But not before the AFC issued their first publicly supportive statement, mirroring FIFA's language.[3] I had to smile. After I'd attacked Salman, and Brendan had mentioned the blatant inference from the recusal timing, they'd had the AFC draw up a statement before releasing ours. Not bad, Fabrice. Squeezing everything out of a difficult situation. The Aussies had achieved what we were after, though, and in the space of just three days after Bahrain had submitted their paperwork and tried to clandestinely rush the case through, we'd hit back with an almighty counterpunch.

Chapter 9

AMSTERDAM – GENEVA – SYDNEY

29 JANUARY 2019, AMSTERDAM

'Hey buddy, how are you? Give me a hug,' these were my first words to Orsat as I pushed his iPhone out of the way, embarrassed.

I'd just walked out of the arrival doors at Amsterdam's Schiphol airport, trundling my small black suitcase along beside me. True to Orsat's communications background, he was there at 6.30 in the morning, filming. I was delirious with lack of sleep and food, a starved zombie, and there he was, capturing it live on camera and sharing the footage around the world. Apparently, he'd been recording the sliding doors opening and closing for half an hour before I actually came out. Serves him right. An hour would have been better.

There weren't enough high-profile players supporting the case publicly and Hakeem desperately needed them. A lot more pressure could be applied, especially with Thai fans, if we could get high-profile players from Europe and the UK onboard. FIFPro's board members are either responsible to some of the world's most high-profile players as heads of the main global unions or, in some cases, are ex-players themselves. If we were going to get their overdue support, this was the place, and time.

We visited FIFPro offices then headed to the beach club conference venue outside Amsterdam. Orsat is a highly skilled professional and briefed me thoroughly. I watched some of the meeting dynamics, observing the characters from the corner of the room. 'Go slowly, Fozz, many will have interpreters and it takes time to get from you through two people to the recipient. Many speakers make that mistake. If you want to reach them, don't speak at your normal pace.' Afterwards, the interpreters would make a point of thanking me for my sensitivity which allowed them to work properly. That was the difference between making an impact, or wasting a trip. I would never have thought of it.

'You are going to need to reach them emotionally,' Orsat told me. 'It's too distant for them, they're not across everything. Tell them what happened in Bangkok and make them care.' They won't be left wondering, I assure you, I said. As fast as everything was moving, it was actually just eight days since I'd been in the prison with Hakeem. The emotion of it was still very close to the surface.

Hakeem al-Araibi needs you. All of you. He is a player and that means we, this room, this organisation has to do everything in its power to save him. You have no choice, only responsibility. I'm going to tell you the real story, and you're going to join with me to get this kid out. Because he's one of us.

Eyes were opening, heads turning my way, I could see I was having an impact. We're a chance here, I thought.

You represent the players and you don't realise the power that you have. They're running *our* game . . . I stopped and pointed to the ex-players whom Orsat had briefed me about, including Geremi Njitap, a former Cameroonian footballer; Real Madrid legend, Damiano Tommasi, a highly respected defensive midfielder with 25 caps for Italy; Caroline Jönsson, a former goalkeeper who made 80 appearances for Sweden in the early 2000s; and of course Francis Awaritefe, who'd been lobbying hard before my visit. I was tired and emotional by this point, as I told them that they were allowing FIFA to get away with a grossly inadequate response for a player in grave peril. Our young brother. He needs you and the players you represent. Now.

The world players' governing body had not been doing anywhere near enough. And, aside from seeking the board's support, I was there to let them know in no uncertain terms that the issue hadn't been prioritised, and now was the test of how they would respond to the confronting reality.

Jonas Baer-Hoffmann, a young German in a senior position, wanted to talk afterwards. I was in no mood for double speak. Jonas mentioned what we all knew, that Hakeem's case was the 'Bosman' of sport and human rights, referring to a game-changing case by a Belgian player, Jean-Marc Bosman in 1995, that changed the shape of the entire European transfer system in football when he challenged the freedom of movement by a player at the end of their contract. Really, Jonas? That's interesting that you say so because, if that's the case, what resources has FIFPro committed to the effort? What have you actually done to press this young man's rights and to ensure that FIFA steps up?

You do realise that the seven recommendations from the HRAB that went to FIFA somehow turned into one. After what I told you today, you now understand the gravity of the situation. That means that Brendan and I went to FIFA and got agreement to the rest of the recommendations, to deal with Bahrain, in particular. If we hadn't, the kid could lose his life. Do you understand the position that agreeing to only one recommendation placed this young boy in? Who agreed to that? How is it that the players' organisation is not throwing everything at this case?

In my view as a former chairman of a member union, I explained, the organisation had become too dependent on relationships with FIFA executives rather than remaining completely independent and policy and principle driven. The relationship between the two entities should be grounded purely in respect for the strength of the player movement and the quality of its research, policy, and people.

The #SaveHakeem campaign should help drive much-needed internal reform, I told board members, and I'm happy to help you in that pursuit by contributing to a full review of the campaign after we get him out. I also made sure they were fully apprised of the conduct of Salman throughout, which obligated the organisation to hold him to account for the future wellbeing of players and the game.

Afterwards, I headed to the lobby with Orsat. The ex-players, in particular, came straight over to pledge their support. Within just a few days, Njitap and Tommasi had tweeted their personal support and Chelsea legend Didier Drogba and Juventus superstar and Italian national team captain, Giorgio Chiellini had backed the campaign thanks to the two FIFPro legends. Brilliant work, guys, precisely as former players should conduct themselves. The impact was immediate, and huge. Of course, behind the scenes, Orsat was working hard to amplify these voices. He would send me screenshots showing who'd made a comment any time of the day or night. Quick, respond to this one, or that. I'd jump online, say thank you and reiterate the key campaign messages or actions that day. Others would then re-share and amplify these comments. Thanks to Orsat, we had multiple time zones and continents covered.

Back home, more players jumped onboard, as our entire profession became more active than ever. Former Australian captain, teammate and Lazio star, Paul Okon, who felt very strongly about the case, reached out to his former teammates such as Frenchman Olivier Dacourt. Rebekah Vardy, wife of Leicester City striker Jamie, also pledged her support. As Jamie plays for Leicester City, which was bought by a Thai billionaire in 2010, this was important for Thai fans.

Back in Thailand, Chiang Rai United FC President, Mitti Tiyapairat, posted on the club's Facebook page that there should be no reason for any footballer to be imprisoned without proper legal reasons. 'To take a footballer and lock him up is to ruin his life, particularly when there is no reason in law to hold him,' wrote Mitti. 'I think we need to come out and demand his release.' A well-known university team in Thailand spoke out, and another. It was snowballing.

Meanwhile, a week earlier, Sayed had been in touch with a draft statement for Nani to release. It came through one morning on email. I was stunned, and worried. I thought Nani wasn't going to do any media. Had she been pressured? Was this what she really wanted, or did she feel compelled? Would her family suffer? I emailed her to ensure she was comfortable. 'Yes, Craig, it is okay.'

In between meetings, in cabs, hotels and cafes, I spent some time editing the statement to make sure it hit the emotional mark. It was written by a lawyer, dry, but I'd met both Nani and Hakeem and they were gorgeous, soft and loving people. Tell the emotional story, I told her, about how you felt, what Australia means to you both, the support of your new country, who your husband really is. It was one of the last major bullets that we had in the holster; it could not be misfired. The letter was published that day and received global coverage, including on CNN. Just a week later, Hakeem's mother would also release a statement so Sayed was working very actively and effectively in the international media.

Stay and see the family, it's been years, Orsat was pleading. Sorry, mate, it's been wonderful to see you again, but I need to get back to Switzerland to see the International Labour Organization (ILO) with Brendan, please give my love to famiglia. Clearly, I wasn't doing too crash hot on the social side, but at least we were making headway.

A 4.30 am start the next morning, to Geneva to get the UN moving more quickly. En route to the airport, I caught up by phone with former Australian Rugby Union international (Wallaby) and prominent Australian author and columnist Peter FitzSimons, who I liked and respected. Peter was now firmly onto the case, inspired by what he was seeing, and was writing a piece for that weekend. That was when I knew #SaveHakeem had moved beyond our own sport, and the campaign. It was now a cause.

30 JANUARY 2019, GENEVA

I landed in Geneva and went straight to the ILO offices. Brendan had secured a meeting with Director-General Guy Ryder, who he'd met previously due to their involvement in international labour relations as well as the Centre for Sport and Human Rights. I was also aiming to connect with Michelle Bachelet, the former Chilean President turned United Nations High Commissioner for Human Rights, as, to date, neither she nor Filippo Grandi, the High Commissioner for Refugees, had said anything strong publicly about Hakeem's case and we had been trying to get through to them by various channels to issue a media statement calling for his release.

After all, Hakeem was a recognised refugee and the only thing that Grandi had said was what had been referenced by IOC President Thomas Bach in the IOC's statement released just a few days prior. I thought I knew why and needed Guy's help.

Brendan controlled the meeting. At the opportune moment, I went to the issue about Australia's human rights record. Guy, I understand from a number of our discussions that there's some concerns with Michelle Bachelet and Filippo Grandi around Australia's refugee policy and treatment. But you can see what we're doing here – the whole country has now stepped up for this single refugee. I think that demonstrates that the policies over a long period of time by the government don't reflect the feelings of a large number of Australians and certainly I'm one of these. I need your help, and the help of Michelle Bachelet, to get this kid out.

I then gave him an undertaking that, once we achieved a positive outcome for Hakeem, I would do everything within my power to help change Australia's disgraceful offshore detention policies and help restore our damaged reputation as a compassionate and humane country.

Ryder was by chance meeting a Thai Government official later that afternoon on labour issues and would raise the case and find out whatever other information he could. He also assured us that he'd raise the issue with Michelle Bachelet that same day and discuss what steps they could take. The involvement of the Thai king did not surprise anyone.

It was lovely to see Brendan's wife, Megan, and Henry, one of their four children, who's a mad football fan and a mean player to boot. I'd been going flat out, it was a very early morning start and I could barely hold a conversation by this time. We ate in a local Nyon restaurant, and I rushed outside for a live cross on the phone to a Middle Eastern network.

We were done here, and a meeting with Bachelet was going to take time. By now I had heard from GIDHR and Amnesty back in Australia that plans were underway for another Sydney Opera House protest, along with a demonstration in Melbourne on the same day. It would be great to make it back for the Opera House protest and report publicly to the Australian people, who had been so amazingly supportive, what I had learnt and promote the messages we needed them onboard with. When is it? Friday. Ah that's right, we'd talked about using the Asian Cup Final as a major campaign milestone for Hakeem's case. Is it that time already? What is today anyway, Schwabby? Wednesday. I know that I was going to stay, mate, but I've got to get back to Sydney, sorry. I've got to be there. What's the time? Early afternoon. I need a flight tonight. Bob!

'There's a flight at 6 pm via Frankfurt and Bangkok, into Sydney Friday morning just after 7 am, just enough time.' Quick, I've got to get going. Traffic would be hitting peak shortly, better to take the train, said Schwabby. Now, I'm the first to admit that I'm hopeless at travel. I was also running on low and didn't trust my navigation skills at that point so I quizzed Brendan again, and again. Which train? Which platform do I change at Geneva?

Arriving at Geneva station from Nyon, I jumped across to platform four as advised and onto the final train for the short journey to the airport. Sydney, I'm coming home. Then I fell asleep. I was woken up by a ticket inspector. He looked at my ticket, back down at me, and said, 'Where are you going, sir?' To the airport, of course. Luckily he spoke

English well. 'You're going the wrong way,' he said. What the? Bloody hell, what do you mean, I thought I was only 10 minutes away from the airport.

'This train goes for 40 minutes, you are heading to Lausanne.' Christ almighty, how much longer till we arrive? 'Another 20 minutes, sir.' Oh, no, how long until the next train back to Geneva and when would it arrive? 'Thirty minutes and that will arrive, excuse me a moment while I check, at 5.30 pm, sir.' My flight leaves at 6 pm. How long would a taxi take back to the airport? 'At this time of the day, approximately 40 minutes, sir.' Thank you for your help. I'd get to the airport at best, after five. I was in deep trouble and would miss the Opera House at this rate. Bob! I might need a later flight. 'For god's sake, I'll get onto the computer, get into a cab and tell him to floor it.'

The driver was sympathetic and put his foot down all the way. Bob was on the phone throughout, searching for later flights but my taxi arrived just after five and I raced inside to the ATM with the driver in tow. How much? '250 Swiss francs.' Geez, nearly 400 bucks. No time to change notes so here's three 100s, do you have change? 'Yes, sir, back in the car.' Oh, hell, take the 300, thank you and have a great life. Upstairs, racing frantically to find the check-in counter, flight closing on the screen. Just made it, thanks, guys, lifesavers. 'You must hurry, sir.' Do I have five minutes to change out of this suit? 'No, sir, you must check in now.' Okay, here you go. This suit has been going non-stop for a full two weeks, and this shirt has had more than a few quick once-overs with the deodorant, pity whoever has to sit next to me.

Relieved, emotionally spent but elated to be on the plane and heading home to see family and friends. And campaigners. We needed politicians there in Sydney and Melbourne so before I collapsed, I sent a few tweets asking them to come to the protests and another to Peter Khalil MP, to get them organised. Your responsibility, I told him. I felt as though I had done all that I possibly could.

When I landed in Bangkok, I had a text from Bob. 'Call me urgently.' Thoughtfully and not one for giving up, he'd arranged business class for the final leg, Bangkok to Sydney. 'You're going to have to speak at the Opera House, the place has gone crazy back here. If you don't get any sleep, you've no chance of making sense.' For once, I couldn't argue.

1 FEBRUARY 2019, SYDNEY

A huddle of trade unionists from the ACTU, including its general-secretary, Sally McManus, who had been extremely active on the campaign, awaited me at the arrivals gate at Sydney International airport. I had slept, not much but enough to feel alive again. I did a brief video interview for them on a phone, as well as I could anyway after the week that was, and called on everyone to get down to the protest later that morning.

It was fabulous to see Lara after everything that had happened, a sense of warmth, love and security as we hugged, a relief that everyone was okay after the worries just before I left. We rushed back home, and Lara grabbed me a suit. It didn't fit, and my belt wouldn't go that tight. Another one, bugger. I grabbed a pair of pants, grabbed my son's belt which was considerably shorter, pulled them in as much as possible and the jacket would have to hide the big kinks in the back.

Unlike the last time we were there, a good-sized crowd had already gathered at the Opera House. From the coloured shirts and signs, it was clear that the human rights organisations had mobilised in force – GIDHR, Amnesty International, Human Rights Watch, the Refugee Council of Australia – their supporters were all there. Many introduced themselves and put faces to names; we'd been connecting on social media for months but this was the first chance to meet and it was wonderful to feel the positive energy, to join the group having traversed the world alone.

Olympians Nikki Dryden and Natalie Galea had also come to speak, and my old colleague Simon Hill from Fox Sports in Australia was there. He'd been involved with Hakeem's story back in 2016 and was very active putting UK journalists in touch throughout the campaign.

There were red ACTU flags everywhere. A number of MPs, including Peter Khalil, who'd come up from Melbourne. Good thing too. I pulled him aside and told him the confidential details that I hadn't released, what I'd learned in the past week alone. You need to let Bill Shorten and Penny Wong, who had made a number of welcome, strong comments in recent months in the Australian media, know that this thing is serious and we need all hands to the wheel.

I was hopeful, though, that the message might have already reached them. The day prior, 31 January, Victorian Premier

Dan Andrews had posted a long thread about Hakeem's story, including a photo of a note he'd handwritten to let Hakeem know that all Victorians were standing with him.[1] Dan Andrews is one of the most Twitter-savvy politicians in the country, with more than 103K followers on his account. His post, and subsequent call for people to attend the Melbourne gathering, was seen and shared by thousands of people within hours.

The message had certainly got around Sydney as well – the media and public throng at the Opera House was huge. It was very special to see everyone and there was an overwhelming feeling of camaraderie, that we were fighting for something real and right and striking a blow for Australia's lost humanity in many ways. That's how I felt, anyway. Many people who had been hurting about asylum seeker treatment, and didn't know how to make a difference, jumped on the campaign to help Hakeem. I think it was a huge driver of the campaign; people could do something tangible instead of shouting about government policy. I was feeling so proud of everyone, enjoying the togetherness after a week of solitude and stress. Then it was time to speak.

This speech was easy because I'd met Hakeem only 10 days ago. I'd seen his eyes, felt his fear, knew his wife, knew about the royals and the paperwork, had been to FIFA and fronted the players' body. I could have hit autopilot. By now, all guns were on Bahrain to withdraw their paperwork and the Thai PM to exercise his executive discretion and let Hakeem go. We knew the PM had the ability to expel the case. I let the Thais have it in regard to their membership of the football fraternity, without mention of the king, which was to be avoided at all costs, and got stuck into the torturous regime of Bahrain. All was going well. We were fighting the good fight, taking it up to them. A great turnout with a strong outcome.

Then, predictably, we got sucker punched. Again.

Just hours later, my phone lit up with calls and social media erupted as news emerged from Thailand that the case had been committed to a court hearing on Monday morning, 8.30 am. My mind raced back to Bangkok, when the paperwork went in, and to the Bahraini statement on the morning that we saw FIFA. Now, when we'd been really gaining traction, Thailand had escalated the case. What happened to the discretionary levels? Jesus, the embassy was right. It was on in three days!

This also meant, of course, that FIFA had been unsuccessful. Infantino was to speak to Salman and the Bahraini royal family a week ago at the Asian Cup Final; the governing body thought they could get a solution within a week but Fatma was now being elusive. Infantino had utterly failed. FFA and the AFC had made some statements and, for all the talk of 'behind the scenes diplomacy', it had been a complete waste of time. The case was speeding up and getting more serious by the day. We knew where the pressure was coming from for the Thai PM. And the Bahrainis were digging in and fighting like hell.

Were they reacting to the campaign? Trying to put me under pressure? Making it look as though I was pushing them too hard? I wasn't sure, but it was extremely worrying. We must stop that court case at all costs!

We called Evan in Bangkok. What the hell is happening? Monday morning? 'Yes, they've done that so there's no time to get a permit, which is required to get inside the court. We're all scrambling to try to get permission, Nat is frantic, and we're all over the place.' Okay, I'm coming over. Meet me on Sunday night at the hotel. I'll text details – and please keep me updated.

I worked on SBS that night and the following, taking Sunday night off again to fly back into the tempest as I watched the weekend's #SaveHakeem A-League round, a welcome show of solidarity and collaboration between the PFA and FFA. Brendan called to suggest that Francis might accompany me to Bangkok. He'd been chasing his FIFPro board for emergency funding and thought it would be worthwhile to represent the global players' body. Great idea. I have known Francis for 30 years, he's a very close friend, is deeply committed to the players' cause and can provide another voice in the media as well as institutional representation. I emailed Fatma to let FIFA know that Fran would attend the hearing on FIFPro's behalf and it would be appreciated if they'd do the same.

Bob called, this time not only about flights but also security. 'Do you think it's safe? A lot has happened in recent weeks and we don't know what Bahrain is capable of. Best to be safe, you've got a family to worry about.' Good question. After the recent press releases by Bahrain and their obvious connection with Thailand, I really wasn't sure. I called the embassy in Bangkok for advice. Do I need security? Is it safe? Yes, we believe the profile of the case and yours in Australia and here now, means you're safe. Nevertheless, we'll pick you up at the airport and that'll give us an opportunity to discuss the hearing on the way to the hotel.

We had come so far, discovered so much, fought with everything we had and yet, as we boarded the plane, could we really be about to fail? Was it all for nothing, after all?

Chapter 10
PEOPLE POWER

We had amazing, compassionate and brilliant people involved right throughout this entire affair. But for all their work, without social media, particularly Twitter, we would have struggled. In many ways, Hakeem was saved by all of our phones. Social media allowed us to make such an incredible noise, to be proactive or reactive, and it was severely damaging to vested interests. What the campaign achieved against overwhelming odds, royals, government and a military junta was simply phenomenal.

Apparently, I had around 70,000 followers back in November 2018. Measly for a public figure really, and not something I'd ever been motivated to try to build. To me, it was an organic community of people that grew predominantly out of shared love of football or other social causes that I believed in, not a marketing tool per se. In less than three months though, #SaveHakeem and associated campaign hashtags[1] were tweeted 2,107,423 times and my tweets received more than 30.4 million impressions during the campaign. So how did this happen? Surreptitiously. Through a team of amazing everyday people who stepped up to help out. And quite possibly got Hakeem out.

Prior to November 2018, Twitter was a promotional tool for my broadcasting work at SBS. I'd seen both its positive power in social change movements like #ridewithme and #BlackLivesMatter, but also the corrosive reality of trolling when my co-host at the World Cup in Russia 2018, the outstanding Lucy Zelic, was shamefully abused on social media because of her pronunciations of players' names.

It didn't take long to realise, though, that social media would be central to freeing Hakeem. It allowed us to engage with members of the public, the media and the main decision-makers directly in a discourse rather than just pushing information one way. This is important because a campaign is about emotional involvement where people are seeking a conversation, to feel a part of something and engage more deeply with a subject, especially its key advocates. And engage they did.

By early January, I was spending huge chunks of my days and evenings online, and while the campaign was growing, the amount of time and energy needed to keep up with it was extremely difficult to manage across multiple time zones. I needed help, so I spoke to John at the PFA and others about formalising some kind of media or online team to assist. I was thinking of a group of professionals that I would be able to feed messages to directly, so they could help drive the campaign online. A combination of factors, not least limited time and resources and the chaotic nature of the case, meant that this wasn't possible. But in the meantime, something else, something quite extraordinary, came to my aid. And it changed the entire campaign.

I started to get contacted by people who were following the campaign and constantly asking, 'What do we do next?', 'We've done this, what can we do now?', 'Where can we get more information?', 'How can we make a difference?' In early January, I decided that I needed to provide these people with some direction. That's when I started to publish daily campaign updates. They were typically drafted in the early mornings and the late evenings, and concentrated on giving people concrete actions, specific targets and key messages. I also let people know who else had got onboard with the campaign, using high-profile supporters to build credibility and excitement.

In response to these updates, it quickly became obvious that there was a group of people who were spending the same long hours as me, if not more, pushing the campaign online. I started to see the same Twitter handles coming up, hour after hour. These people were very supportive, knowledgeable, offered help and creative ideas. Everything I posted, they responded to directly and shared. They were on message and, perhaps most importantly, they agreed with the tone of the campaign that we were developing and shaping. These anonymous people became incredibly valuable and fulfilled the role of an organised, paid digital and social media team perfectly. Except they were also hugely passionate and emotionally involved in Hakeem's story, which made them far more valuable. We started to collaborate closely, and I guided them on where we were going. I was getting intelligence daily from government stakeholders, human rights organisations, PFA and football contacts around the world – which shaped the narrative of the #SaveHakeem hashtag – and this team brought it to life. I have often wondered what their support would have cost at commercial rates. Easily several hundred thousand dollars, I'd imagine, but throw in their passion, which can't be bought, and they were simply priceless.

It started individually but once they had grown in number, we created a direct messaging chat group and added others as we went. Apparently, they also created a parallel chat group that excluded me, so that they could interact among themselves and send private jokes. I could have done with a joke or two throughout the campaign, but they made the right decision, thankfully. They kept it all business with me. Well done, guys, and thanks.

One of the strengths of this group was that their tones were all different, spanning from polite or emotive, fact-based and direct, which created a powerful mix when we were targeting particular individuals or organisations. We maintained a constant balance in the campaign between asking and demanding, agitating and conciliating, and this group, with their range of personalities, helped strike that difficult balance. In effect they, crucially, enabled me to play a diplomatic role while ensuring the stakeholders that I was working with were put under the necessary pressure to act.

They became our secret weapon and, in my view, we wouldn't have succeeded without them. Incredibly, I never knew who these people were or met them during the campaign. I did meet a few over lunch on the day of Hakeem's return to Pascoe Vale and, as the club thanked everyone involved in the welcome home ceremony, I introduced them to Hakeem. I told him that these anonymous, wonderful people had saved his life. It was a very nice moment for everyone, as you can imagine. I arranged for Alex from Amnesty to meet up with the larger group in late March 2019 and discover who they all were. Our secret social media team that allowed us to create the biggest online storm Bahrain will likely ever see. Unless they try it again, that is, I say with a wink.

MEETING #SAVEHAKEEM'S PEOPLE-POWERED SOCIAL MEDIA TEAM – IN THE WORDS OF ALEX ENGEL-MALLON

We met in a narrow noisy café near the train station in Parramatta, in Sydney's west. It was a pretty strange circumstance. I was basically going on someone else's blind date with people they'd been communicating with closely for weeks, exclusively about someone else, that none of them actually knew. From the outset, it was clear that Craig's online impression of them as completely different characters was 100 per cent accurate. They're a spectacular hodgepodge of ages, cultural backgrounds, genders and interests. We ordered coffees and exchanged a few awkward pleasantries to break the blind-date-once-removed ice. It wasn't long before we were talking like old friends. In fact, the conversation soon became so animated, with everyone jumping in over each other to throw in perspectives or make a point, that at times it was hard to keep up.

Jo and Duncan live in Hobart, Tasmania, where they've lived for the past three years. Duncan is originally from Toowoomba, up in the sunshine state, and works in communications. He's mid-forties, tech-savvy and has a gentle but excitable manner that perfectly befits his Twitter handle '@StarkRavingDuncan'. He was the only actual football fan among the group. Jo is from Melbourne, sharp as a tack. Her pixie-like features are framed by bright red glasses, jangly earrings and short, neatly cropped hair. She's quite tall but her height's emphasised by loud multi-coloured Christian Louboutin stilettos that clip the ground smartly as we search for a table. Jo works as a consultant and, at one time, was paid to write about the politics, business intricacies and regulations of Formula One. This interested Craig, given the importance of the Formula One Grand Prix to Bahrain since it was first hosted in 2004, and the amount of controversy it has since attracted in relation to the human rights abuses and protests with which it has been associated. The couple heard about Hakeem on the radio while driving to Launceston, about three days after he was arrested in Thailand. Jo remembers thinking the case would be resolved by the government quickly, like many of us did, but when a few days later they learnt Hakeem was still there, they started to engage.

'I've been involved in a lot of human rights things, so this was really an extension of that,' Jo reflects. 'But there are particular human rights issues I'm interested in, especially arbitrary detention, and that's what this case was. I also have particularly not liked the way that the Gulf states have used sport to gain respectability and credibility with Western countries by spending money . . . they do it in motor sport, in football, golf . . . all the big, wealthy sports, and then they sit around a table with these really rich stakeholders, whether they are actual government officials or just people with a lot of money and influence. I really despise the fact that they are using sports to get this access and legitimacy. Hakeem should never have had to fight for his freedom, because he had the right to be free.'

With Duncan's interest in the game and the politics involved, combined with Jo's legal training and interest in human rights, they made a dynamic duo. They spent evenings together on the couch, side by side, tweeting away, bouncing ideas and information about the campaign off each other. They went through emotional highs and lows, and tag-teamed each other to strategically target people in different Twitter conversation threads. 'We became so involved . . . it ended up being like a full-time job, it was like 20 hours a day of tweeting,' says Jo. 'I actually ended up having to visit the osteopath for Repetitive Strain Injury on my wrist from using my phone too much. I'm not even kidding!' she laughs. One night in January, Duncan arrived home to find Jo in the kitchen with a large whiteboard, storyboarding the timeline of the Interpol red notice. She had printed off research she'd done about Thailand's legal system and extradition laws, and used her university legal training to identify the key legal points and arguments. This research would eventually form the basis of a 64-tweet thread that picked apart a Thai foreign ministry press release in early February, which features later in this story.[2] They even went to the trouble of getting the tweet translated into Thai language.

Another member of the group with legal training was Rawan, a Sydney-based human rights and refugee lawyer with Palestinian heritage. She's in her early-mid thirties, has intelligent eyes and a personable, generous manner. She has followed the Bahraini independence movement for many years. 'I follow Bahraini activists just generally because I support their cause. I saw them tweeting items about Hakeem and I just started picking up things. They had tweeted about Hakeem's case and the protest and hunger strike they were organising outside the Thai consulate in Victoria, which was very early in December.'3 Rawan connected soon after with GIDHR and offered them legal advice and support on the case. At the time, she was also busily setting up a not-for-profit organisation looking at conducting investigations and prosecutions into international crimes, known as universal jurisdiction litigation. This type of legal action results in cases being brought against the likes of the Saudi Crown Prince Mohammed bin Salman.[4]

Trish is from Katoomba, the largest town in Australia's famous Blue Mountains. She's the eldest of the group, with locks of curly hair and a hardened, almost conspiratorial tone. Razor sharp, she's careful and calculated with her words, clearly sceptical of how they might be used. She's followed FIFA and the politics of the game for a long time, but has no direct interest in the sport itself. Fascinatingly, Trish had never used Twitter before the campaign. She had signed up in early November, primarily to start accessing news she couldn't get in the mainstream media. Evidently, she took to it like a duck to water. I had seen this woman in action, and she was born to tweet. She spoke in depth about analysis she'd done of FIFA and Bahrain's messaging throughout the campaign to determine what strategies they'd adopted at different times, and she explained some of the tactics she had used to influence different stakeholders. 'When counter hashtags and chatter about boycotting Thailand started, I was really worried it was going to derail the campaign. I was careful not to feed into anything that seemed against the Thai people, but I did do research to find all the businesses owned by both royal families and tweeted at those – I will not go on holidays, drink your beer, I will not stay in this hotel, I will not eat this product – things like this. The aim of the boycott hashtag was not misplaced, but when it was being used by people as an off-the-cuff reactionary thing, it gave a reason for the Thai people to become defensive and could have potentially had a negative impact.'

Trish and Sara, also a member of the group, were obviously close. They finished off many of each other's stories and spoke about how each other's messages boosted their morale and strength when they were feeling particularly low or exhausted. Sara works in inventory management and comes from Toongabbie, a small suburb just outside of Parramatta. She's dressed all in black, with a dark rinse of purple through her hair and a thick accent that gives away her Bosnian cultural roots. She'd never been interested or involved in any human rights or social justice campaigns before this one. She explains: 'I don't remember how I heard about Hakeem, I just remember being really angry about the police involvement in it. Surely they did not do this to a kid, a refugee? I looked into it but couldn't find a whole lot online, so I went on Twitter to see, is anybody talking about it? It was more, why is this kid in this situation, and what are they doing to help him? So I searched and I found Craig, a lone wolf, posting his little letters to global leaders, and I thought, okay . . . I'll start following his lead. It felt like Craig was alone and he needed our help. At first I thought, what am I doing here? I know nothing about FIFA, about the politics of football. I'm from Europe, I'm Bosnian, I watch World Cup every four years and have a drink, yes, but . . . I'm not really interested in it. I think part of me not wanting to know about, you know, problems of the world, comes from the fact that I've come from war. I've seen my fair share, I don't really care for the politics of left and right . . . I'm not interested at all. All I saw was a kid that's detained somewhere where he shouldn't be, and nobody was doing anything to bring him home. That was the extent of it. The politicians made no effort to talk to the public about it. If this was their child, he would be home by now. So yes, I didn't know what we were doing . . . I was just following Craig's lead. So if today he was talking about FIFA, today we're talking about FIFA . . . I'm in waters I've never been in before, all I can do is follow the lead, so if he started with that, then we would start with that. Simple.'

Beyond a strong sense of this being the right thing to do, Sara also happened to have an unusual penchant for Obama GIFs. She loved using them in the group's private chat, which they used to support each other, exchange strategically useful information and generally 'talk shop'. 'We started another group without Craig so that his phone wouldn't melt,' laughs Duncan. 'Yeah, we were all a bit hyper, running on adrenaline and about 40 coffees a day,' adds Jo. So where did the Obama GIFs come in? 'There's a GIF for everything. It's a tension releaser,' Trish explains. 'It's Sara's thing, and we all just jumped onboard. Sometimes people would be abusive to us online, so we'd jump into the group, share it, have a laugh with each other, and then jump back into the public forum again.'

At some point everyone started to refer to Craig as 'Dear Leader' in jest and adopted a whole range of nicknames they used privately for other personalities that popped up in the campaign. 'We named someone "Quadbike", for example . . . because they started tweeting authoritative statements about Hakeem's case when, in fact, they had no real knowledge about it at all.' We all chuckle. The group then revealed a detailed knowledge of the spikes of content that had boosted the campaign on Twitter, some of which I wasn't even aware of, and I'd been monitoring things very closely.

For example, they had seen the degree to which the 'Paul Pogba selfie story' had significantly boosted campaign activity in the third week of January, the day after Craig visited Hakeem for the first time in prison. A young Aussie guy called Patrick tweeted about a train trip in England where his parents had shared a carriage with some players from Manchester United. Apparently they had been a bit noisy during a game of Uno, which led Pogba to apologise to Patrick's parents by offering to take a selfie with them. Patrick's father had agreed, but only out of politeness, because he had no idea who Paul Pogba was. Patrick, an e-sports commentator, used the story's instant popularity online as an opportunity to link people to content about Hakeem's campaign.[5] There was also viral content that had been organically produced and shared by people online to support the campaign, including a meme of someone mowing their backyard with a colossal tornado whirling towards them. 'Thailand' was captioned under the person mowing, and the tornado was aptly named '#SaveHakeem'. We laughed together at both the randomness and the combined power of it all.

There are a few other members of this core group, including Shell from Shepparton in Victoria, and Madeleine from Melbourne, who couldn't be at the café that day. There are also some others who wished to remain anonymous for different reasons, who contributed social media graphics and other multimedia, and who were extremely important in amplifying the campaign. What is important for everyone to know is that all of these people were incredibly brave because they were happy to hold everyone publicly to account. From politicians in Australia and members of the Bahrain Government and royal family, right through to the King of Thailand, the Government of Thailand and the President of FIFA – they had no boundaries. It's also important for people to understand that they didn't do this without personal cost.

'The trolling was pretty horrific,' explains Duncan. 'Everyone in the group was very focused on the campaign messages so, because of my experience with digital campaigns, I took on the job of diverting and diluting the trolls. There were many Saudi and Bahraini trolls, I'm assuming probably from a troll farm[6] outside Saudi somewhere. You can tell immediately, because their English was different and they were pushing exactly the same lines as the Bahrain Government ... so this is organised, government-led stuff, right? The car outside Craig's house, that's government stuff, this isn't just individual people. They were trolling to control the narrative ... my strategy, particularly with the trolls from Thailand, was to hit them with the counter-arguments until they were exhausted ... or at least put the counter-arguments there, so if someone else then picked it up and read the trolls' message, there was an argument there countering it. I was taking away the people trying to negate the campaign. From my experience with anti-racism digital campaigns, you can't just leave things there, un-countered. I knew I was never gonna change the mind of the racist guy or the government-paid troll from the UAE, but I am going to leave a record of a counter-argument to say "this is why you're wrong". This cuts out and negates their influence if you do it right, and this campaign was so diverse and coming from so many angles, it was worth doing.'

But the harassment wasn't restricted to the online world. 'Members of our group were harassed by people from the Middle East ... it actually ended up happening in phone calls to their home landline,' explained Trish earnestly. They claimed to be from the UAE and were talking about the person's family, threatening them for the messages they were posting online. We still don't know how exactly they got the number. I also had a few people trolling me throughout, even after the campaign ended, saying that Hakeem was lying, that I was wrong about the case ... I tracked where they were from and it was clear some of them were working together.'

It was also a hugely challenging experience for all members at a personal level. 'This campaign was an emotional rollercoaster,' said Sara. 'There were days of desperation and tears . . . but no matter how busy Craig was, he always picked up on when we were feeling down and would post something that would inspire and give hope. I now have Craig's and Hakeem's picture at my desk at work. Craig restores faith in humanity, Hakeem represents hope. I smile every time I see it.'

They also, ironically, faced challenges from within. The group laugh as they remember certain points where people outside this core had almost steered the campaign completely off-course due to infighting on ideological or seemingly unrelated issues. There was an online spat at one point, for example, with people who argued that the hashtag should be '#FreeHakeem' instead of '#SaveHakeem', because of the 'white saviour complex' inferences of the latter term. This was despite the fact, as has been noted earlier, that it was Hakeem's own friends from the Bahraini community in Melbourne who had first used the '#SaveHakeem' tag, and that there was a real danger of diluting the campaign's whole online momentum if people were using different tags and messages.

Within the core it became clear that they too had divergent views about many things, including the relative effectiveness and hazards of calling for sanctions. You'll recall this was a hotly debated topic between campaign strategists offline and with FIFA. I was surprised at the level of detail and information they all had to back up their various positions and admired the amount of time and energy they'd put into their thinking. They were all agreed, however, on one thing. It was the huge diversity of grassroots voices and community groups who had got engaged in the campaign that won the day. Twitter just provided them with the perfect platform to channel their energy. People power at its best.

The hashtag was 11 years old when #SaveHakeem kicked off. Since its creation, it has successfully been used to set media trends and news agendas right around the world. Likewise, it has both supported and enabled pro-democracy and social change movements. As mentioned in Chapter 1, social media certainly played a strong role in the Arab Spring protests back in 2010. The protest movements in Libya, Tunisia and Egypt were dubbed by many as 'Twitter Revolutions', because of the role the platform played in enabling protesters to share information and organise activities.[7]

Twitter has a reasonably high penetration in the Australian market, with around 4.7 million active users, although this is dwarfed in comparison to 15 million Facebook users. Thailand is a comparable story. Twitter hasn't historically enjoyed the same level of attention as other social media platforms like Facebook (49 million users) and Instagram (13.6 million users),[8] although it has certainly seen growth, increasing from 2.7 to 4.1 million users between 2014 and 2019.[9] Today, however, Thailand is one of the fastest-growing markets for Twitter in the world. This is not surprising, given the country ranks in the world's top 10 countries for social media usage, and also now has one of the most powerful 4G networks and among the fastest internet speeds in the region. Twitter had also recently enabled a language function, allowing Thai users to write and share content in their native language. The timing of the #SaveHakeem campaign couldn't have been better.

Nuttaa 'Bow' Mahattana is a high-profile human rights advocate in Thailand who 'contributes 40 per cent of her time to political activities, 30 per cent to raising her 10-year-old son, and the rest to freelance jobs as a special lecturer'.[10] The softly spoken 40-year-old has worked part-time as a university lecturer since she became an activist after the military coup in 2014, led by General Prayut Chan-o-cha. She is now the leader of 'We Vote', a pro-democracy movement that campaigns on civil and political rights issues, including fair elections and the right to public assembly. This work has earned her a grand total of five major lawsuits to date.

'Social media is the only strong channel available to Thai people to communicate,' explains Nuttaa, emphasising that social media platforms, including Twitter and Facebook, enable people in Thailand to share news due to the more limited ability for government to control it. 'There were many who feel like me about Hakeem's case but they . . . are afraid of activism, that it will get them in trouble.'

Nuttaa became interested and active on Hakeem's case in mid-January, pushing materials about his case out in Thai on her YouTube and Facebook channels, where she has more than 90,000 followers. Originally she had hoped the football clubs and community would lead the campaign, but when she saw this wasn't happening, she decided to get involved. She started a separate petition in Thai language on Change.org. 'The platform was so onboard,' says Nuttaa, 'that they put their own money in for advertising the petition to a wider audience.' This petition, which Nuttaa would eventually present publicly to the Human Rights Commissioner of Thailand, Angkhana Neelapaijit, in early

February, played an important role in ramping up the pressure in Thailand. Many Thais, including the commissioner, had been outspoken on Hakeem's case since early December, but the petition showed the extent of public support from within the Thai community and added much more power to their message.

This petition, combined with Amnesty International and GIDHR's petitions, had grown to more than 160,000 signatures in total by the time of Hakeem's court hearing, an increase in more than 100,000 since I had met with FIFA in Zurich less than a fortnight prior. It was clear from the names and postcodes alone that people from all over the world were now engaged in calling on the Thai Government to do the right thing.

Petitions can sometimes be problematic in social change campaigns and if you don't get enough people signing them, it can reflect incorrectly on the importance of the issue or case concerned. There are also so many campaigns out there in the world, I do understand why people can end up thinking, 'What difference is my signature really going to make?' In the case of this campaign though, I can assure you that petitions were critical to the campaign's success.

The immense size and scale of these petition figures, combined with the online and media attention the campaign was receiving, meant that we could use them as significant leverage with government and sports governance stakeholders. We referred to the petitions over and over again, in meetings, in media interviews, and in social media posts. This was just one way that people engaged with the campaign, but it was an important one. As Nuttaa put it, 'this showed that this [was] the work of global citizens and that we can influence . . . [it] highlights the need to take action [as] only then can we make things happen and improve human rights for everyone.'

Chapter 11

SHACKLES

A car from the Australian embassy met us on our exit from customs in Bangkok. I was pleased to see the commitment of the embassy staff, including the ambassador, Allan McKinnon. All into a van, brief pleasantries and straight into the case. Time was weighing heavily, and we needed to share information, coordinate messages and be as prepared as possible for tomorrow. I briefed Allan and Mark Warnock, a young, talented staff member who had been right at the centre of the case from day one for the consulate. He'd visited Hakeem in prison, providing briefs on everyone involved for our government, and theirs, including me. Allan needed to hear how things had progressed with FIFA, and I needed to know what our best approach would be the next morning at court.

The ambassador would attend the court hearing himself in the morning and confirmed that a wide range of other embassies, including all those that we'd visited the week prior, also planned to come. I knew that Mary Harvey, the CEO of the Centre for Sport and Human Rights, and the centre's chair, Mary Robinson, had also been active with the government members of their Advisory Council and we'd have a good showing.

I was interested in messaging. Where are we at? What's the latest strategy? There'd be a circus at court, it was massive news by now all around the world and Mark, who spoke Thai, had prepared a statement for Allan to deliver. Bravo. We knew the Thai PM could expel the case and, importantly, while the Thais had been consistently on message that the case was in the courts and would have to run its course, their attorney-general had publicly confirmed otherwise a few days earlier, either deliberately or by accidentally breaking ranks. Was he indicating a fracture among different interests inside the Thai Government on the handling of the case? Perhaps. Irrespective, we would use those comments tomorrow.

Pressure on Bahrain was critical, to isolate them and let Thailand know that no approach had been made to Australia in the past four years for Hakeem's extradition. Now, all of a sudden, they want him back? From my end, it was time to raise the volume on sporting sanctions.

The embassy had provided legal support to Nat and also, critically, the Australian cave divers, Richard Harris and Craig Challen, had reached out to DFAT and asked if they could be of any assistance. This was sensational news. The key was how to make best use of it? Calls for their help had been deafening over the past month but I felt uneasy in making them feel they had to do something. They'd already saved twelve kids and their coach, and were known to be very humble, disliking the limelight. My view was that they'd do something in their own time although I admit that our social media team spent some time targeting them and applying some pressure to get involved. It was decided that correspondence from Richard and Craig should be sent in such a way as to avoid any chances of it having a negative effect. These two were so revered in Thailand that no one wanted them to be seen to be disrespectful in any way, which could be counterproductive.

I was pleased to receive an email from Federico advising that he would represent FIFA at the court hearing and that he'd provided the official match sheet to Nat from the game played at the same time as the offence that Bahrain alleged. I wasn't sure why it took until 2019 for FIFA to highlight the official match sheet in support of Hakeem's case, when he had been involved in a legal case five years earlier in full view of them, but that's another story. FIFA being in town was important and I let Allan know that we'd all need to work on Federico regarding sanctions. Let's get a meeting in the next two days, and work on him while he's in town.

That night, as we all met in the hotel lobby, I spoke to Prince Ali of Jordan, one of the most respected football officials globally with a strong record of speaking up for human and players' rights. He'd been active in the past few weeks, and we'd touched base to coordinate. As part of the broader royal cohort across the Gulf region his knowledge and advice was valuable. Evan, Fran, journalist James Massola (South-East Asia correspondent for the *Sydney Morning Herald* who'd been all over the case from its early stages and was experienced in this region, having covered the fairly recent cave divers episode in Thailand) and I synchronised timings for the morning. But in terms of detail we were flying blind.

Nani had sent an email with a message to give to Hakeem the following morning if I saw him at the court. 'Everyone prays for you and my heart is with you,' she said. 'Be strong, you're innocent. I'm waiting for you to come home to Australia.' I posted some of it on Twitter to let people know what we were experiencing together and was in tears as I hit send. After two and a half months, with close personal relationships forged through an intense and traumatic time, emotions were now completely raw.

Evan, who was by now visiting the prison almost daily, was concerned about Hakeem's mental state and how much he understood what the hearing was about. He had visited him on Friday and Hakeem had been physically quite unwell. He had asked Evan for medication and told him that he was having difficulty eating and sleeping. At the time of his visit, Hakeem hadn't known yet about the papers being submitted, as this news was only released publicly much later that afternoon. So he understood that Hakeem had now received that information during a follow-up visit from his lawyer Nat on Saturday.

Nat remembers the conversation well. 'I wasn't sure if they would let me in, because lawyers aren't allowed to visit the prison on Saturdays. I pretended that I was a family member, and somehow the guards let me in. When I first told Hakeem about the scheduled hearing on Monday he seemed pleased and thought it was good news. He thought he would get to put forward his case to the courts. But when I told him that we weren't sure what the outcome would be and that the judge could potentially rule that the extradition orders from Bahrain were valid, he became visibly distressed. It was my job to calm him down and brief him on what to expect. He was my client and I needed to prepare him as best I could for the hearing.'

For my part, I was extremely worried about the fact that Thailand had expedited the process. It was an awful sign and I thought there might be a chance the court would send him back to Bahrain tomorrow. Especially because things were escalating around the world so quickly. They want to get rid of the case, but how? Sending him back to us, or Bahrain? It was horrifying.

Evan mentioned that Hakeem might be brought to the courthouse wearing shackles. Really, what do you mean? In handcuffs, like before? 'No, the ankles.' Like slaves from 200 years ago? 'Exactly.' All of us were horrified, swearing and carrying on. How the hell can that be possible, how does the international community stand by and allow people to be treated this way? I looked at Fran with a raised brow. We can make something of this. We need to be there early, to get a position right in front. If this kid is in shackles, we are going to broadcast it to the world. That might be our chance. What time does the court open? Seven am. Hearing is 8.30, he'll arrive shortly before. We're there at 7, 7.30 max, put the alarms on. And bring your phones.

MONDAY, 4 FEBRUARY 2019

At Klong Prem prison, Hakeem heard his voice called over the loudspeaker and was directed outside to where a white prison bus with wire mesh on the windows waited. A guard stopped him near the door, knelt down, and wrapped metal leg irons around each of his ankles. The two rings were connected between his legs by a short, shining chain. Once the guard had locked them into place, he motioned for Hakeem to get on the bus with the other detainees. Hakeem climbed awkwardly up the steps and another guard handed him a piece of paper with English writing scrawled on it. The note informed him that he would be the last person to get off the bus when it arrived at the courthouse, and he was to sit and wait until called by one of the guards to move. Hakeem felt a rush of hope. He thought it might mean that there was a lot of media waiting there, and hoped that was why he was being treated differently to the other detainees.

The bus trip lasted a lifetime. He remembers: 'It finally stopped and I could see all the media waiting outside for me. There were so many and I was so desperate to say anything I could to them about my case. I was like an animal with these shackles around my feet, but I didn't commit any crime, not in Thailand and not anywhere. When they told me it was my turn to get off, I felt sick and wanted to vomit. I walked out and there were so many people, I felt like I was on show in a zoo. My mind was racing. I could see faces that I knew from FIFA, but I couldn't remember their names. It was all a big loud blur. And then I heard one voice above the others. It was Craig. He was yelling out to me that Australia supported me and that I must be strong. I was very excited to see him. I saw him taking a photo and told him to send a message to my wife that I will be strong.'

•

When we arrived at the court, journalists and camera crews were already milling about. They had started to set up cameras around an entrance underneath the building, where we were told that vehicles typically drop prisoners off. Evan, find out where he arrives, quickly, so we can set up. It was furnace hot. I felt like we were in the bowels of hell, with bars everywhere, guards all over the place and crews starting to jostle for position underneath the building. We need to know whether we can get into court as well, mate. See what you can do.

The authorities had set up rows of yellow metal barriers, marking out a short path from where the vehicle transporting Hakeem would stop and where he would be brought to the entrance gate. Francis and I got in place, then changed, and changed again. An opening right near the entrance into the holding cells opened up, and we pounced. Quick, Fran, let's go, hurry! The crowd started to grow quickly around us as the minutes ticked by. A crew was starting to set up behind us and I could see it coming, working in television. 'Would you mind if I get this camera in here, next to you?' Yes, I would, not happening, sorry. Fran, you're here. If you move an inch I'm going to rip your head off. He chuckled, nervously. This was our spot and I'd be carried out in cuffs before anyone was getting anywhere near it. We had a perfect view down the tunnel where the van would pull up, could see the entire walk, and into the cells to our right.

I was sweating buckets and on edge like never before. This was the most grave, worrying circumstance I had even been a party to. Was this kid really going to turn up in shackles and barefoot like a scene from centuries ago? Media crews wanted comments and interviews and we obliged to get the message out about this inhumane injustice, all the time guarding our position with our lives.

News came that the bus was close. Tension rose, guards snapped to attention, cameras were turned on, necks craned. People pushing forward from behind, we stood our ground. The detainees came off one by one and filed past us into the building. Where is he, can you see him, Fran? There he is! Fran started filming. I hit live on Twitter, praying that it worked as all hell broke loose.

Like the others, Hakeem was dressed in a prison-issue light pink shirt and maroon shorts that came down to his knees. His ankles and the shackles on them were completely exposed for all to see, his feet bare on the concrete floor. I remember thinking how dazed and vulnerable he looked, in contrast to the severity of the officials who surrounded him in their pressed military uniforms and polished shoes. All the other prisoners had walked alone, but they surrounded

Hakeem with five guards. What is he, a mass murderer? It was barbaric!

When he walked towards where we were standing, I could feel my heart pumping, emotion erupting everywhere. I was trying to capture the whole thing live, but had no idea whether it was on, or if I was holding it steady enough. People were yelling over each other, trying to get him to turn for their cameras and Hakeem yelled to them as he walked. When he was just a few metres away I started shouting to him as loudly as I could, 'Your wife sends her love, Hakeem! Australia is with you. Stay strong, Hakeem, we're with you!' He walked past towards the metal gate and I just kept shouting, overcome with the horror of it all. 'All of Australia is with you! Be strong, buddy!' I'd never been so emotional in my life. Here was a kid, who was innocent, had been in jail for over 70 days and five guards led him in shackles, no shoes. What f#@*ing century was this?

Once they were inside, the guards locked the gate and absolute chaos ensued. They'd walked out of sight and we didn't know where they had taken him. Evan was nowhere to be seen and we didn't know if we could get into the courtroom or what the process might be to even try. Guards, media everywhere. My mind was going through the possibilities. What was to be gained from the overkill of guards around him? Were they trying to demonstrate Thailand's authority and let us know that they were the ones in charge? What decisions have they already made? Did this mean that they were about to put him on a plane to Bahrain? Or Australia? I found Evan, who was clearly in shock. He'd been the one who'd visited Hakeem the most by now, apart from his lawyer, Nat, and the raw emotion from seeing Hakeem like that was plain on his face.

Let's split up, keep your phone handy and try to get inside the court. We needed to find Nat or someone who could explain what was going on. We went upstairs to ground level, and people were everywhere. Federico came over; we were all stunned by what we'd seen. I kept my eye on the Australian diplomats. If anyone would get in, it was them. Then a message came through that the original courtroom had changed, and the case would now be heard in a much larger room that we were allowed into. Evan received a text message from Nat confirming: Room 704. What the hell is happening, this is getting crazier by the minute. Didn't you say, Evan, that they'd never let us in? Why the change? Everything was a worry.

We raced to the head of the throng and sat down near the front of court, which was soon packed to the rafters. I was pleased to see Allan and his staff there. Representatives from more than 13 countries were in attendance, there to let Thailand know that Australia wasn't the only diplomatic relationship at stake here. I wasn't sure if this kind of country-to-country support was typical in the diplomatic community, but was assured that it was extremely rare. Federico was seated nearby. Many Thai and international non-government organisations were also present, including Thailand's Human Rights Commissioner Angkhana Neelapaijit. Bahrain Government officials from their embassy were sitting at the back, stony-faced.

The tension was palpable and we shifted nervously in our seats. I looked to see if anyone had phones out. Some did, so I took a photo and shared it, wanting people around the world to be there with us, to witness this atrocious violation of human rights. I couldn't shake the feeling that this was some kind of show, but to what end? Meanwhile, the video we had shot live on social media went viral. Within just a few hours, it was viewed over 100,000 times. The world was aghast. Within 24 hours, the #SaveHakeem hashtag skyrocketed to over 500,000 tweets. It was the moment that Hakeem's case became real for people everywhere, all around the world. Many said they cried, seeing a young man dragged into court in this way. No one could ignore what had happened. It had to have an influence, I thought, this is going to change things. Just how much, we could never have anticipated.

Hakeem was led into court, still shackled and flanked by two policemen. He sat down at the front right of the room next to Nat, an Arabic translator next to him. We later discovered that the court alleged they had run out of Arabic translators that day, so this translator had been brought in from the Bahraini embassy. Unbelievable! Talk about a fair trial! If it wasn't so shocking, it would have been comical. Hakeem remembers: 'I was watching this interpreter when they introduced him to me. He couldn't look me in the face ... and was too embarrassed to meet my eye. He was definitely shocked by the amount of people in the room. It was clear that this was the first time so many countries had attended a case like this and that he hadn't been expecting it.'

The court proceedings lasted for just under an hour. Evan and Phil sat on either side of me and tried to interpret what was happening. There were huge piles of paperwork being shuffled around and Hakeem was asked to sign a lot of documents. About halfway through, Hakeem stood up and addressed the audience with a short speech in Arabic. We obviously couldn't understand exactly what he said, but we could make out 'Sheikh Salman' and 'Bahrain' repeated several times. Shortly afterwards, the prosecutor stood up and formally opposed bail on the basis that Hakeem was a convicted fugitive and a high flight risk. Nat was now talking. Later she'd report that the prosecutor asked for the case to be brought forward. They were trying to rush it through. She pushed back. 'I only received the submissions that day and needed the whole period. The submission was huge.'

I was constantly on to Phil and Evan for information. What's happening? What are they saying? They relayed that the judge had determined Hakeem would be remanded in Klong Prem for a further 60 days, until 22 April. I was more relieved than anything. The prospect of him being sent to Bahrain was much, much worse. This at least gave us a further window in which to try to stop the case proceeding altogether.

Hakeem was led out. He stopped and turned back to us. 'Please tell my wife I love her, please tell her to keep fighting for me,' he said. My chest tightened. 'We will, mate, we will, don't worry, be strong,' I said. With a brief nod, he turned and was led out by the guards. Evan recalled this moment, weeks later: 'He was only a few metres away from us and it was the first time that I'd come face to face with him, without glass or prison bars in between, and I remember the irrational thought popping into my head as I eyed the guards with him – police officer number one is Mr Pudgy, he wouldn't be able to put up much of a fight. Number two is Mr Old and he wouldn't be able to do a lot either. Maybe I could just grab Hakeem and we could run off? It was stupid, I know, but it was the first thought that came to me. Yes, we were seven storeys up in Thailand's biggest and most secure court, but here he was, almost close enough that we could touch him. It was my instinctive reaction. Just to get him out of there and protect him. The thought lasted all of two seconds, and almost instantly I went back to feeling completely helpless.'

We all started to file out when, unexpectedly, the female prosecutor was asked a question on her way out of the court and stopped and answered. Everyone rushed over, including every government official in the room. She was incredibly open about the case and fielding questions like it was a press conference. A range of diplomats asked about specifics of the case and the day's decision. When a moment presented itself, I recalled Allan's words yesterday in the van and asked her whether it was accurate that the Thai PM had executive discretion to expel the case from court? 'Yes, that's correct.' So, are you saying that this can happen at any time, including after the 60-day period, and throughout the court case itself? 'Yes, as I said, under the Thailand Immigration Act, executive discretion is available to the prime minister at any time until the final determination of the case.' I looked at Allan, who looked as surprised as I was. This was extraordinary. Here was the prosecutor contradicting the Prime Minister of Thailand, who'd been adamant in contradiction on this point in public, along with most of his officials, for weeks.

Outside, the media were in a frenzy. I've taken part in some spectacular sporting occasions and seen plenty of media scrums, but this was literally life and death, and everyone felt the gravity of what had just happened. We all spoke to the media, and I was ripping into Thailand's membership of global football and calling on FIFA for sporting sanctions, as was Fran, strong and on message, representing his constituents, the players, well. As I looked to my right, our embassy people, Allan, Mark and other staff had assembled on the court steps with Nat in between, with a massive media throng looking up at them. This was a critical moment, and I was thrilled and felt a sharp sense of pride at seeing our ambassador standing with Nat, protectively. I'll never forget that image.

We had been fighting for months, and the Australian Government had stepped up, and were saying to their Thai counterparts: we're behind this young man all the way. Mark spoke fluent Thai and delivered his prepared statement to powerful effect. It was only nine sentences long, but in diplomatic terms it was a sledgehammer. The actions of Bahrain had put Thailand in a very difficult position, in particular during what is 'an important year' for the people and country of Thailand. This was a subtle reference to the auspiciousness of the year for Thailand, due to the new king's forthcoming coronation ceremony, and translated to the strongest possible language that could have been used by a diplomat in Thailand who wished to remain in Thailand.

Allan followed up with a brief statement in English. The main thrust of his message was that Bahrain had made nary a peep for the four years that Hakeem was in Australia and now took the opportunity to request his extradition in an opportunistic manner that put Thailand in a difficult position. He also stressed that confirmation had just been received from the public prosecutor that Prime Minister Prayut could set Hakeem free at any time, and that Australia was respectfully asking that he allow Hakeem to return to his friends and his family in Australia. It was now on the public record. The Prime Minister of Thailand had the authority to stop this whole thing and Australia, one of their most important trading partners and regional allies, had requested that he do so.

Journalists James Massola from Fairfax Media and Anne Barker from the ABC expertly steered the conference. Should Thailand be suspended from playing at an international level by FIFA? Will Australia consider sanctions against Thailand if it fails to act? Allan McKinnon dutifully circumvented their questions, letting them serve their purpose. FIFA and sanctions were now a part of the public conversation. Federico was there too and was repeatedly asked by journalists about FIFA's position. While his presence was significant, it was clear that he had not come with any authority to explain FIFA's views or that they had hardened in any way. Showing up was not enough, we needed more. I spoke to the embassy, we need to meet tomorrow with Federico. 'We'll make it happen.'

Aside from sanctions, there was one other football angle that we pushed hard and which had been suggested by Minky Worden at Human Rights Watch. I hadn't been aware that Thailand was reportedly preparing for a joint World Cup bid with Indonesia and Vietnam for 2034, and it seemed preposterous that they could be considered a credible candidate if they disregarded the human rights of a player in this way. We went in hard, no way they could host the big dance with this form!

And there was always, always the spectre of lasting consequences hanging menacingly in the air as the case kept moving forward, inexorably. I stayed at the court for several hours, waiting to broadcast live on CNN and also joined *The Project* live where well-known host Lisa Wilkinson threw the question that I had been anticipating. 'Are you comfortable that the tone of the campaign isn't pushing Thailand into a corner, Craig?' That was the question that I'd seen building through social media on many minds back home. I can assure everyone, I replied, that I am constantly taking advice from a broad range of State and non-State actors on messaging. There are a range of factors which I can't reveal that are extremely worrying, very powerful forces restraining this boy, and I'm confident that we need to be as strong as possible in relation to the Thai Government and Prime Minister, though always respectful to the Thai people.

That was the best I could give at that time. And I well understood that, on the outside, it looked as though it was all spontaneous, emotional. Yes, emotion bubbled over at times, but the underlying strategy was thoroughly planned. The further we went, though, the louder these calls became. I felt like I was being pulled deeper and deeper into the fire. One thing was now perfectly clear, however; we would either ultimately succeed, or I'd personally go down in a ball of flames.

After the circus had moved on, I spoke with Federico, who agreed to come to the embassy the following day, and let Mark know that we'd need a coordinated message to push for FIFA sanctions. Turns out Federico was waiting for a meeting with the Thai FA President, who hadn't responded. Don't hold your breath, he was also a general, handpicked. FIFA had been going on ad nauseam about how they, and the AFC, were 'working behind the scenes with all football stakeholders'. They couldn't even get a meeting. You're FIFA, for Christ's sake! What sort of show were these people running?

TUESDAY, 5 FEBRUARY 2019

The following morning, I had a car booked so I could visit Hakeem again. And promptly slept in. A British television crew were going to be there at 8.30 am. I woke at nine. I didn't even know if I could get in to the prison later, what are the rules anyway? I put on a black and yellow #SaveHakeem t-shirt from Amnesty. There's no secrecy anymore, if they throw me out, fair enough. There was an interview to do on site and, anyway, I was too stuffed to care. Head down, keep moving forward.

En route, I phoned Federico to let him know when the embassy meeting was scheduled. Evan was busy and I had to take the train. Given my recent experience on trains, I wasn't thrilled. It took twice the time it should have, but I made it. I jumped a taxi for the last bit. Thank god for Google Translate. And for the great man, Australian rock legend Jimmy Barnes. His wife Jane is Thai, as every Australian worth their salt would know, and I'd seen her support on Twitter. Jimmy called to let me know they felt strongly about the case, had some contacts who might be helpful, provided some views based on a much greater cultural awareness than I would ever have and we'd get together in a few days when I was back. I was pleased – it sounded positive in terms of background knowledge and, hell, it was Jimmy Barnes, people, come on! It was a welcome feel-good moment. I was half lost, going to the prison by myself, unable to speak Thai, with zero idea whether I'd get in.

As I stepped up for an interview in front of the prison, someone was calling. Hang on, give me a minute, please. It was Scott Morrison's office, could I speak with him? Of course, put him on. His staff had evidently seen on Twitter that I was going in to see Hakeem and wanted me to pass on his best wishes and assure Hakeem he was doing everything possible so that a resolution would be found.

At one point, Scott made reference to the fact that Hakeem should have been more careful about where he travelled. I'd read his comments to 2GB radio the weekend prior, where he had seemed to suggest that Hakeem bore some responsibility for his situation. Hang on a minute, Scott, how is he supposed to know there is an issue in relation to travelling to Thailand unless he gets the information? He'd been to the country before without a problem and had tried to check he was safe with the Home Affairs department before leaving. Surely you're not blaming him? He backtracked quickly, emphasising that this wasn't his intention. Scott had made his views very clear at the highest levels in Thailand and everyone was working overtime to crack this case. He did warn me that things were going to take a while though, likely a few months, and that while he was confident that things were moving in the right direction with Thailand, I shouldn't expect that it was going to happen quickly.

'Please let him know that I'm doing everything possible along with Marise, and our embassy,' he said. I will, Marise and Allan have been fantastic, my compliments to them both.

We discussed the case specifics a little more, and Scott advised me that he was planning to write to the Thai prime minister a second time because he was really disturbed to see Hakeem in shackles like that. I was pleased to see that he confirmed this later that evening on Sky News, saying: 'I'm respectfully reminding the Thai prime minister that Australians feel very strongly about this, very, very strongly.' Bravo, Scott. His willingness to step up so publicly at this critical moment meant that Thailand could be in no doubt about how important the outcome was to Australia. His statements that day were further emphasised by a media release from Marise Payne, formally stating that 'The Australian Government continues to advocate on behalf of Mr Alaraibi at the highest levels in both Thailand and Bahrain.' The level of public engagement by then, the public sentiment was so strong that the prime minister could be confident that he had the support of Australia behind him.

'And if you'd like to let people know we've spoken, that's okay.' No problem. Even PMs need social media promotion, it seems. It would not be often that a refugee has the PM call to personally wish them the best, I thought, certainly not in Australia in recent times.

At home in Australia by that time, calls for a parliamentary inquiry on the Interpol red notice had exploded. Many MPs reached out to me directly, and I knew human rights organisations had been in close contact with MPs from all sides of the House. They were starting to ask uncomfortable questions. Naturally, Scott would have been fully briefed about the AFP's role in warning Thailand about Hakeem's destination and its failure to get the red notice cancelled prior to his travel. His recent advocacy on Hakeem's case told me he now knew that, at some point, the truth was going to come out. Inside sources informed me that Minister of Home Affairs Peter Dutton had even written to his counterparts in Thailand in an effort to repair the matter.

I was aware that Amnesty had also followed up and received new advice regarding Australia's ability to grant Hakeem citizenship, which the Minister for Citizenship, David Coleman, and his staff had said was not possible to pursue back in December. After initial advice from Dr Kim Rubenstein, the author of Australia's Migration Act, it appeared that this was now, in fact, a potential opportunity that could be taken, but the minister's office had been slow to respond to Amnesty's follow-up inquiries.

It was also evident that the government remained under immense pressure in relation to the Medevac Bill, which was due to come to Parliament's first sitting in only a week's time. It seemed likely that this would be the first time in almost 100 years that a sitting government lost a vote on the floor of the House and, as they stared down the barrel of this historic defeat, all factors pointed to a need to get Hakeem out as quickly as possible, or risk political damage.

We were playing this for full value, wherever possible, as Scott Morrison or any other politician would only expect.

•

'After the court,' Hakeem says, 'everything changed. I was moved into VIP room and could see the television and newspapers like Mr Big. Every day after the day at the court, the prison guards took pictures and videos of me, everywhere I went. It was for publicity. They took me to the hospital, they took a picture. To show that they are taking care of me. I'm not sick. This was funny because, before the court, I was sick, but they didn't take me to a doctor or hospital then. They asked me if I was sleeping well. I said no, and they stopped filming at this time. They only filmed the bit when the doctor was speaking, telling me that I am very healthy. After that they took me to the kitchen and also took a video there, to show that all the prisoners are cooking and eating healthily. They didn't ask me questions anymore. That week, I did not hear anything more about my case, but the way they treated me changed a lot.'

•

The Klong Prem prison guards recognised my t-shirt; one of them stopped me on the way in and asked if he could have it. That was surreal, waiting to see a prisoner caged for months with one of his captors wanting to wear his shirt? Hakeem had reached a level of notoriety in Thailand now – I just couldn't quite work out if that was a good or bad thing.

After court the day before, Evan said they had upped the security on Hakeem's visiting privileges, and I was only one of five people allowed in to visit him. We assumed this was to try and control the media visits. All of the evidence was so contradictory as to what the Thais' intentions were.

Hakeem mostly wanted to talk about Nani. Was she okay? Was she safe? He had also seen the news of the Sydney Opera House protest from the previous Friday on television and in the newspaper, as well as yesterday's appearance in court.

My only aim before I left the next day was to give him hope. We spoke about the court case and what it all meant. He told me that he'd been expecting the 60-day outcome because Nat had briefed him well the previous Saturday. She had told him that it would be a key part of the court process; that the prosecutor would ask him whether or not he agreed to be extradited to Bahrain. At which point, she advised him, he was to answer 'No'. What he was nervous about, though, was if it really was just 60 days. He was also concerned that the information from Bahrain about the conviction appeared to have changed from previous court documents that he had seen; he said Bahrain was changing their story, again. Really? Wow, I'd have to get that looked at with Nat.

Above all, after passing on a message from Nani, I told him not to worry about the 60 days. Forget it, I said to him, I'm not interested in 60 days. We want you out today. If not today, then tomorrow, or the next day. One day at a time, we're fighting for you with everything we have, buddy, be strong and don't look too far ahead. In the ensuing days, an ABC journalist would relay to Hakeem reported comments from the Thai Government that his case could take up to six months and wrote that Hakeem was devastated at the news. No kidding, I was furious! We knew it could take up to four years, what was the point of taking the only thing he had, his hope? It was all I could do not to lash out when I read that piece.

Even the prime minister is fighting for you, I told him. He just called to pass on his best wishes and strength. His eyes lit up. 'Really, the prime minister?' Yes, and the foreign minister. The ambassador here is strong, very experienced, we've got an unbelievable team battling for you and we don't stop, mate, once we're in the fight, Bahrain won't beat us. If Aussies know one thing, it's how to compete, and win. I was trying to convince myself as much as him.

He was in far better spirits than the last time and, as on the last occasion, his greatest smiles were for news of his wife, and the engagement from the football community. When I told him about Drogba and Chiellini being in his corner, he was so excited. We parted with him smiling, less frightened. He looked emboldened. He knew the size of the campaign, and that the big artillery was out through sport and government. I felt hopeful for him, protective and fiercely determined. I only went into the prison twice, but each time I emerged with enough drive for years of campaigning. Shackles, Jimmy Barnes and the PM. Each day seemed more crazed than the one before:

> @Craig_Foster Says he's training inside prison to be ready for @pvfc_official 'Tell them I'll be strong, ready to play…'. Pushups, running without shoes. The smile when he heard about @chiellini @didierdrogba never seen anything like it, a footballer's passion never dies #SaveHakeem

> @pvfc_official Our hearts are broken @Craig_Foster. Tell him we are waiting, we registered him today for the 2019 season. He is No 5 on the team sheet and his shirt is waiting. #SaveHakeem

•

I headed straight to the Australian embassy in a cab to meet Fran, who'd been meeting with the Thai players' association in his role as a vice president of the global body, and Federico. By now, Orsat had been in touch with news that FIFA weren't pleased about media coverage after the hearing yesterday. Apparently, they felt they'd not been given credit for sending someone to Bangkok, and were upset that we talked so much about potential sanctions. We had made it clear that we believed sanctions were not only possible, but morally necessary, and Brendan was preparing a detailed submission to Fatma laying out the supporting factors.

FIFA wanted FIFPro to rein in the messaging about sanctions, but Orsat made it clear that FIFPro wasn't in control of me. I was independent, and FIFA should speak with me directly. They were the peak global body, there was a player in prison fighting for his life and all they could worry about was receiving credit for getting someone on a plane to Thailand? God help us. This was a real opportunity for them to stand up and show the world what they truly value. It could be a positive step for them, I thought, if they'd respond from a position of principle.

Journalists were sending messages about the rapid rise in sympathy from Thai football fans, and that talk of sanctions was mentioned by many of them, rightly worried their club or country would be banned from competition. In other words, the more FIFA tried to shut down talk of sanctions, the more we talked it up, and it was working.

In the lobby, Federico dutifully took up the issue, not knowing I was fully briefed, and waiting. 'We do not think that sanctions are possible and for this message to be so loud, and no credit given to FIFA, well . . .' Come on, Federico, get real. Your job is to be here, a kid's life is on the line for Christ's sake. In any event, if you want to control the message, or play a part in it, you need to get in touch with me. It's little use carrying on after the fact. I am happy to work with you if you are committed to acting appropriately. We believe sanctions are both possible and necessary. We argued back and forth, with Fran getting involved as well.

We were prepared and synchronised in the meeting room upstairs. Allan opened up with a review of where the case was at for Federico and we came to understand the Australian

Thai cave heroes had sent their letter privately to the Thai PM, and the embassy felt that it had been very well received. We all nodded to each other: this was what we wanted to hear and I was particularly impressed by how Allan had managed the situation. He quickly turned the conversation to sporting sanctions, and how helpful they would be. The conversation lobbed back and forth between us. We spent a lot of time working on Federico and it seemed as though he had come round somewhat. It wasn't often that ex-players would be working closely with their country's government on a player's case, and Allan made sure to validate this relationship. Federico had food for thought, we had political currency from the divers. Good meeting.

Better still, a glance at Twitter showed that after yesterday, the Thais were under incredible international media and diplomatic pressure. They had rarely seen a case like this, or this level of international condemnation. The whole world seemed to be falling in on them.

The campaign hashtag was well on its way to more than a million tweets and on the Twitter analytics heatmap[1] Thailand was now lit up like a fireball. The video of Hakeem in shackles had blasted like a meteor into the conscience of the Thai people as well. We finally had our cut-through and the impact ricocheted around the world.

Activist Bow Nuttaa Mahattana connected with me on Twitter. We had met the previous day at the court and I'd congratulated her on her work setting up the public petition. Her message conveyed the impact the shackles had in real-time on the ground in Thailand:

@Craig_Foster When I told you about our #SaveHakeem petition in the court yesterday, there were less than 2000 signatures. Today it's close to 15,000 and counting. More Thais stand for Hakeem now. We're too slow but hopefully not too late. Please join us.[2]

So many Thais were upset at the footage of Hakeem in shackles that a #BoycottThailand hashtag was now thriving from within Thailand. Thai media is not permitted to show prisoners in restraints and the *Bangkok Post* airbrushed the shackles out of pictures. This only enraged everyone more, thinking the Thai authorities were trying to misinform their citizens.

Unedited images, however, travelled far and wide on social media, and prompted a strong reaction from the Thai public. Also, many people wouldn't realise that amazing advocates like Bow were working hard behind the scenes, using Hakeem's case to highlight broader and longstanding human rights issues with their government.

A lot of the online traffic was generated in response to retaliatory comments made by Immigration chief Surachate Hakparn, who responded to criticism of Hakeem's shackles and bare feet, saying the practice was in line with international standards. He was, rightly, eviscerated.

For months we had been spending countless hours typing away, sharing, advocating, but after the shackles the campaign had a life of its own. Thailand's Corrections Department Director-General, Police Colonel Narat Sawatanan, also rejected media reports that Hakeem had been wearing 'shackles', stating that they were instead 'leg restraints' which could be 'locked and unlocked'. Every comment was attracting the most intense outrage, incandescence.

Such was the building pressure that even Thai PM, Prayut Chan-o-cha, got in on the act, calling for everyone to respect the court process and intimating that this was an issue that needed to be solved between Australia and Bahrain. When a PM is reacting publicly, we were in with a chance, and it was happening faster than we ever thought possible. Was he thinking about an exit? Had the pressure got too much for those above, or had the letter made a difference in royal halls of power?

Whatever the truth, both the prime minister's and Hakparn's Twitter feeds were smashed by human rights groups, including within Thailand. High-profile Thai political figures, including former deputy prime minister Chaturon Chaisang, also weighed in and called for Hakeem's release.

Then 'Big Joke' Hakparn changed tack. He responded to an Australian embassy tweet publishing McKinnon's statement delivered at the courthouse the previous day, tweeting, 'We hope that Hakeem will be able to go back to be with his family and his wife in the coming days.' For us, that was the shift in position that we were waiting for. It was all or nothing now, or so it felt.

Prime Minister Scott Morrison noted he was 'disturbed' to see Hakeem in shackles, and, of course there was a 'Hakeem' question in every press stop, which was ideal as more and more comments hit the public consciousness.

As always happens, though, a counter movement started. #SaveThailand began to attack the Australian Government because of their role in the Interpol red notice, to defend Thailand's legal system and the Thai people against calls for boycotts, and to attack Bahrain for putting Thailand in this position.

Some just used a combination of these to make exasperated statements, like this one:

> Thailand dilemma, we sent [Hakeem] to Bahrain = Australia boycott us. We send him to Australia = Bahrain boycott us. #SaveThailand #SaveHakeem

It didn't matter to me whether people felt for or against the campaign by now, only that they drove the social media storm higher and higher. Bahrain was now in the middle of one of the largest public spats that any of us had ever seen. They wanted silence and secrecy. They now had all of football, and much of the world, smashing them from pillar to post.

People were ready to throw outrage at anything and anyone, such was the emotion. Victorian Super Rugby club the Melbourne Rebels excitedly announced their newest commercial partnership deal ahead of the 2019 season. It was with Thailand's national carrier Thai Airways.[3] Big mistake. I had to laugh. Talk about timing! Football fans piled onto them, which only helped keep the issue raging. But the rugby players of UK and Australia had been fantastic, and this whole campaign had been about bringing everyone together, not dividing them along sporting or any other lines, so I reached out to thank them when they'd issued the obligatory apologetic press release. Mistakes happen, they handled it extremely well, I thought, and I wanted rugby to know that

I valued their support. Sporting tribalism runs deep, but not when our player is in jail and rugby had stepped up. No way. I'll return the favour anytime.

Some rugby fans rightly responded that Thai Airways was also a sponsor of the Western Sydney Wanderers, who quickly removed a Thai Airways sponsorship board from its grandstand ahead of that Saturday's match against the Central Coast Mariners. That's people power. It was now having very real commercial consequences, and Thai companies were being affected.

We had long been considering both a tourism and corporate campaign to encourage a boycott of relevant companies, including Thai Airways of course, which entailed a range of graphics and social media material ready to go from the first few weeks back in mid December but, so far, had decided not to action it. Going that far, I felt, could severely damage not just the diplomatic relationship, but the person-to-person ties between us and potentially put the livelihood of ordinary Australians, and Thais at risk. It had to be very much a last resort. In recent weeks, though, the PFA had been working with Sally McManus and the ACTU on a broad campaign to be activated through the national union member network and we'd been discussing when to action it. I still wasn't comfortable that the time was right, so the fact that it came organically from the community itself was very welcome.

According to live Twitter analytics site 'trends24', the three hashtags #BoycottThailand, #SaveHakeem and #SaveThailand dominated the feeds of Thailand's 4.1 million Twitter users.

Thai media reported that 'Big Joke' would be meeting with Australian ambassador Allan McKinnon the following day 'to explain the extradition proceedings and discuss possible solutions'. The Thai Government had also reportedly asked Australian authorities 'to send documents regarding Mr Araibi's refugee status in Australia, and the reasons why it is against his extradition'.[4] Interesting. Nat also received an inquiry from the attorney-general's office as to whether she'd like to apply for bail, which had been refused at the court hearing. Positive signs? It certainly looked that way.

Then, another about-turn. At 11.56 that night, Thailand's Ministry of Foreign Affairs released a statement reporting the Thai prime minister's view that this case was a problem for Bahrain and Australia to resolve. Who releases a statement at 11.56 pm?

It placed blame at Australia's feet for the Interpol red notice, saying erroneously that it had been issued by Australia, and reiterated that Thailand's 'Executive Branch cannot interfere with the judicial process'. This was despite the fact that Allan had only the day before reiterated that the Thai Government now held the discretionary power to release Hakeem.

It was important because there was a lot of uncertainty on social media about who was right. Should Australia be so vocal when it was really our fault after all? Some Thais or sympathisers started going in hard. I had avoided sharing the actual red notice earlier in the campaign, as it stated that Hakeem was a 'criminal' and I felt would only feed the trolls' narrative but we had long exceeded any need for sympathy and now shared it online. It proved that the red notice had been issued by Bahrain and left Thailand's statement in disarray.

Late at night, I received a copy of the FFA letter sent out to Australia's Olyroo players, our Olympic Under-23 team, to let them know they'd been selected for a scheduled camp coming up. I couldn't see what the issue was. I was so tired. I messaged back to the sender, what's the point? Look at the venue, came the response. Oh Jesus, you're kidding me. I shook my head, it was, where else? Thailand. After 70 days of incarceration of one of our own players and a campaign of unprecedented scale for a footballer, Australia had still scheduled a tour there? Stupefying. I was spent. I'll give this to someone else, I thought. I had enough fronts to fight.

WEDNESDAY, 6 FEBRUARY 2019

Following media and online reports of the Olyroos' letter, the next morning FFA's website announced the decision to cancel a tour to Thailand. The statement noted that their plans had been reassessed 'due to the ongoing detainment of Australian footballer Hakeem al-Araibi' in Thailand. The retraction was welcome and ironically fed into the threat of sporting sanctions perfectly. It looked to Thailand as if sanctions were already starting.

There were still levers to pull, though. I had requested a meeting with the Thai ambassador to Australia, Nantana Sivakua, in Canberra the following week where I'd take a delegation of high-profile athletes and hand over the public petitions outside the Thai embassy with Amnesty and GIDHR.

We'd also been discussing the possibility of bail, in which case Evan had offered his apartment for Hakeem to stay and himself as guarantor if necessary. Fantastic kid. Nat had thought it might cost around US$30–50,000. Now, she had been told it would be closer to US$200,000. John confirmed that he was lobbying FIFPro to get this money and that the PFA would give what they had. Unbelievable commitment by our players.

THURSDAY, 7 FEBRUARY 2019

By Thursday, it was clear once and for all that football's soft diplomacy had failed, miserably. Every official had talked about working behind the scenes with the relevant bodies of AFC, FFA, BFA and the Thai FA. Just over a week earlier, following our FIFA meeting, the AFC had issued their only statement in the 77-day saga. The AFC Vice President, Praful Patel, stated that 'through the AFC Administration, there has been a constructive dialogue with many of the relevant bodies in this case, including the Football Association of Thailand'.

Really? The Thai FA President, Pol. Gen. Somyot Poompanmoung, refused even to meet the FIFA representative following the hearing, three days earlier. Then, after Chiang Rai FC and others again raised the #SaveHakeem banners on social media, the Thai FA issued a warning that under Article 4 of regulations governing the Thai FA and members, pertaining to actions or symbols of a political and religious nature, anything in violation of this rule, including the display of photos or banners, may result in suspension from activities or membership.

It was finally laid bare. The game of football not only would not enforce their obligations under FIFA statutes, they'd crack down on others doing so. I sent it to Fatma with a renewed call for sanctions.

With the global outcry, diplomacy between Australia and Thailand was evidently well and truly behind us. Australia had decided that Hakeem was ours, and our government wasn't taking a backward step. In response to Thailand's statement of two days ago, the Australian embassy in Thailand released their own. Only 10 short sentences in English were required to make Australia's feelings known, but it was also translated and published on the embassy's site in Thai, to ensure the message was clearly received. It can't have failed to be.

'Due to misreporting on the matter, the Australian Government would like to clear up confusion regarding the INTERPOL Red Notice issued against Hakeem Alaraibi,' it read. 'Australia never issued a Red Notice against Mr Alaraibi . . .' And, 'The Australian Government has said unequivocally on many occasions that Hakeem Alaraibi should be returned to Australia, where he is a permanent resident with protected status, as soon as possible.'

'Misreporting.' 'Confusion.' 'Unequivocally.' A statement like this, by such a senior diplomat, is not made lightly. When we saw this statement released it was clear to us that the embassy, as directed by Marise Payne and Scott Morrison, had been told that this had the highest level of importance. But while punches were being thrown, back and forth, I just wasn't sure who might land the knockout blow.

The Prime Minister of Australia had already been in direct contact with Prime Minister Prayut at least twice, and the Thai PM had still chosen not to exercise his discretion to release Hakeem. Whatever other conversations that had occurred since Monday had also not worked. Thailand had tried to pass the ball into the court of both Australia and Bahrain, but Australia had now lobbed it straight back. We all held our breath and waited to see who would crack.

FRIDAY, 8 FEBRUARY 2019

'It's the biggest bombshell in Thai politics in more than a decade!' screamed the news headlines. Our worst fears came to pass. Intense media attention on the campaign since Hakeem's court hearing on Monday had placed enormous pressure on the Thai Government and boosted the momentum and impact of the campaign enormously. The only thing that could possibly have competed with the size and scale of this story now would be some kind of outlandish Thai royal scandal.

You guessed it. An outlandish Thai royal scandal.

Thai Princess Ubolratana Mahidol had announced, via her Instagram account, that she would be running for prime minister in the forthcoming national elections in Thailand. This pitted her against the incumbent, General Prayut, and the announcement electrified Thailand. It was unprecedented for a Thai royal to engage with Thai politics in this way, and she had aligned herself with a party affiliated with exiled prime minister and tycoon, Thaksin Shinawatra, considered by many to be anti-monarchist. She was hugely popular in Thailand and this, combined with her royal pedigree, made her an instant front-runner in the upcoming national elections. If we all thought that recent events were from *The Twilight Zone*, this was another level. How would this affect the campaign?

Less than 24 hours later, the princess was forced to back-track from her announcement and withdraw her candidacy. Her brother, the king, had put an end to her candidacy in a sharply worded statement on Friday night. 'Even though she relinquished her title according to royal laws,' he said, 'she still retains her status and position as a member of the Chakri dynasty.' The story was over but it highlighted that the elections were completely unpredictable and we'd have to stay across everything that happened. And to expect the unexpected.

I had flown back from Bangkok the day before and was due at the Pascoe Vale season opening function in Melbourne, in honour of Hakeem. I couldn't make it as I had to keep my work commitments up at SBS, so I connected by Skype with well-known football journalist, David Davutovic, the MC. The club function room was packed to the rafters. Hakeem was on everyone's mind. As I was holding down the rising emotion, coming just a few days after the shackles incident, I told them that we would never give up. Australians will go to the end for our player, your mate, I told them. I couldn't reveal what I knew but said we were really up against it but our resolve was far greater than that of those trying to take his life. Even over Skype I could feel the positive energy and support which no doubt I really needed at that time. It was marvellous to see our community so united, so together in pursuit of the lost soul of the sport.

I was more determined than ever and already planning the next few months of the campaign. I had reached out to football friends in Malaysia to bring their royals into the conversation and was considering contacting the Queen of England. If FIFA won't step up, maybe it will take another royal family to intervene? Nothing was off the table and no one was escaping without being roped in if they had anything to offer.

I went to work that night utterly spent. Interestingly, though, I received a response from Thailand's ambassador to Australia, who had been coordinating dates with me for a meeting in the coming days. Now she abruptly pulled out due to 'unforeseen circumstances'. In light of everything else, we weren't sure whether to interpret this as a good or bad sign. Either way, I was now incensed that FIFA had made no difference whatsoever and set about writing another letter to Infantino, who as president, under the FIFA Statutes, is supposed to be a 'vanguard' of human rights. Vanguard or rear guard?

SATURDAY AND SUNDAY, 9–10 FEBRUARY 2019

I was at home in Sydney when I received a text from the embassy in Bangkok. Would you be available to speak to Allan? 'I hope you've got some good news for me?' I told him.

As it turned out, he had. Embassy staff had been in discussions with the Thai Government throughout the week, amid all the public posturing and issuing of statements, keeping communication channels open, searching for common ground. Amid Morrison's public comments, the letter from the cave divers Richard and Craig, Marise's veiled threats and the gargantuan public outcry, discussions had been underway with the Thai Government about a solution.

The door was open to resolve the impasse and this needed space in which to breathe, without another major crisis, if possible. Scott had been asked to tone down the commentary, he would go quiet now, the point had been made and it would be helpful and appreciated if I could do likewise. The Thais would know that the embassy was in control of affairs and Allan could communicate to the Thai Government that the Australians, both the government and the loudest and most troublesome voice in the public campaign, would turn the volume down as a sign of goodwill. 'We think a solution can be achieved in the next 72 hours,' Allan said. That would be Tuesday.

I had been preparing to launch another full-scale offensive against FIFA. It had been two full working weeks after we had met with Fatma, and there had been nothing. It was clear that we hadn't shifted FIFA on sanctions, and Fatma wasn't being forthcoming about any discussion or resolutions reached between Infantino and Salman. She kept saying 'I haven't heard back', 'I've been busy', and 'I haven't had the chance to speak to Gianni yet about his discussion with Salman'. Infantino needed to speak out. In the meantime, he'd been confirmed as the only candidate in the FIFA elections, which meant he had a new, unchallenged mandate. Issues around Salman's support were no longer relevant.

Allan mentioned the threat of sanctions, and FIFA. I told him that I wouldn't send the letter. He could tell the Thai Government that I would back away from pressuring FIFA to rain sanctions down, for the moment. Though I couldn't let on to them, I asked the Twitter team to keep up the advocacy but to ensure they adopted a more positive tone. They went from calling for boycotts to 'please do the right thing', 'Australia and Thailand should respect our friendship and goodwill'.

The discussion led me to believe that the Thai attorney-general would consider making an announcement to the effect that some new information had come to light, the courts and attorney-general had again reviewed the case as a result and determined that, via some legal reasoning, the case should be dropped. It would still take several weeks, but this was light at the end of what seemed an infinite tunnel.

From this point, things moved extremely rapidly. I was sent an article the next day from a Bahraini activist, published by the state-run 'Bahrain News Agency' and the headline read 'HRH Crown Prince receives the Minister of Foreign Affairs of Thailand'. The article was only two paragraphs long, but it revealed that Bahrain's Crown Prince Salman bin Hamad Al Khalifa had been visited by Thailand's Foreign Minister Don Pramudwinai, at Gudaibiya Palace.[5] It reiterated the two countries' 'deep and longstanding ties' and also stated that during the meeting they discussed bilateral relations between the two countries and 'reviewed areas of mutual interest'.

A separate report from the Bahrain News Agency said that Bahrain's Prime Minister, Prince Khalifa bin Salman Al Khalifa, had also spoken separately with the Thai Prime Minister, Prayut Chan-o-cha, on the phone. Later reports in the Thai press covered the whole visit as 'secret diplomacy', as they only learnt about the visit when Bahrain's News Agency published a photo of their foreign minister holding hands with Bahrain's prime minister. It was also revealed that the phone call between the two prime ministers had in fact occurred during the meeting itself.

It was on. A deal was being negotiated. Social media rightly went for the jugular, as did people all around the world. This is evidence of the trading of lives, we all know this is about Hakeem al-Araibi, they said. It was, and I fully concurred. But it was not about sending him back, as they assumed, but sending him home. To Australia.

Several days later, the *Bahrain Mirror* confirmed that the meeting specifically discussed Hakeem's release and confirmed Foreign Minister Pramudwinai's recollection of the meeting where he was told that Bahrain did not want the issue to continue, especially since Thailand was preparing for an important event – the coronation of the new king.

The article quoted the minister, 'In light of our excellent relations, Bahrain wanted Thailand, which has gained nothing from this conflict, not to remain under more pressure. We would like to thank Bahrain, which has special relations with us on all levels including the royal family, for helping solve this problem smoothly,' he said. The last line of the article also added an important, final piece of information, and confirmation. 'The Thai PM revealed that his country's king called on the government to deal with this problem.'

Given what we'd lived through, though, no one could be sure where it was going to end. While Hakeem languished in prison, not knowing what would come of him, he was being traded between two monarchies. An agreement was being made which had nothing to do with international law, refugee conventions or human rights. Pure and simple, it was the trading of one young man. As elated as I was, the whole affair was abhorrent.

On Sunday, I was also contacted by two sources close to the ground in Bangkok who informed me that a press conference was being scheduled for Tuesday morning and Thailand's attorney-general would be making a statement. The whispers on the ground were that Hakeem might be freed. Could I really dream that Hakeem would get out, after all he'd been through? All the anger and tears? In the past two and a half months, Hakeem had never been closer to being a free man but we'd seen things take a turn for the worse in a heartbeat too many times before.

Chapter 12

FREEDOM

'Der ball ist rund und das Spiel dauert 90 Minuten.'
'The ball is round and the game lasts 90 minutes.'

Words of wisdom famously uttered by Sepp Herberger, coach of the German side that won the 1954 World Cup, meaning with football, as with life, anything is possible.

MONDAY, 11 FEBRUARY 2019

'You've got a message,' said Lara, frantically. 'It's from Marise Payne.' It was mid-afternoon in Sydney and I was at home recovering from a late shift at work. I grabbed the phone and saw that I'd missed a call from the foreign minister's office.

Unable to reach me, Marise sent a text asking me to call her office urgently. She was heading into a meeting but her staffer, with whom I had spoken several times, would be available. I raced upstairs, tripping over in my haste. This could be it, Lara! It's Monday, one day ahead of deadline but we saw the meeting in Bahrain yesterday. My heart was in my mouth as I picked up the phone.

'We think he's going to get out tonight.' Even having been prepared, I was stunned. 'Don't say anything publicly yet, but the embassy is preparing to get him back home; looks like it's going to happen but let's just ensure he gets on the plane and in the air. Until then, anything can happen.'

We then went on to discuss the importance of messaging, once a positive outcome had been confirmed. They requested that I not be too triumphal in tone and asked that the public campaign consider tailoring our messaging, ensuring that we were respectful to the Thai Government and people. I was left with the impression that Australia's bilateral relationship with Thailand had been significantly damaged by this case and agreed it was important to encourage conciliatory messaging from the campaigners around the world who had, ultimately, made this all possible.

I didn't let Evan know, or anyone else except Lara. We were close to tears together, hoping beyond hope. He's so close, Lar, so close. We can't even tell Nani, but it's better that she doesn't live through that heartbreak again if it doesn't happen. We sat, unmoving, watching social media, waiting for a call for several hours. BBC journalist Jonathan Head, who I'd met in Bangkok, was hearing about the press conference tomorrow, that the attorney-general was rumoured to be ending the case.

Then, suddenly, at 6.58 pm, I received a message from Jonathan that shot our adrenaline through the roof. 'He's coming out!'

'I think so. How do u know?' I replied, not wanting to give anything away.

It's happening, Lar, it's real! It took 12 minutes for him to reply. The longest 12 minutes of my life. The Thai International Affairs Department had confirmed that the criminal court ruled for the extradition order to be withdrawn. The prosecutor, who had been so forthcoming and fair to us that day in court, said she had been contacted by the Ministry of Foreign Affairs that morning and told that Bahrain was no longer interested in the extradition request.

As a consequence, the attorney-general's office determined that the request 'no longer served the public interest' and it was dropped. I called Evan. 'Mate, what's going on? Jonathan's messaged to say the court is ruling? Is Hakeem in court? Is he definitely out?' Evan was only just aware the press statement had been released and was trying to get hold of Nat on his way to the prison to try and locate Hakeem.

My phone beeped with a second message from Jonathan. I told Evan to keep me posted and hung up. 'He will be out today we think. Likely on the Thai Air flight to Melbourne midnight tonight.' Jonathan shared the incredible news on his Twitter feed and media outlets around the world were going crazy. I sat down, and tears streamed down my face. They just couldn't stay in anymore. The weight of the world had lifted. But we had to find out where Hakeem was and make sure he safely got on that flight. It wouldn't take off for another four, nailbiting, hours.

•

Evan Jones was at his office when he heard that the press statement had been released by the office of the attorney-general saying something along the lines of 'Bahrain was no longer pursuing the extradition of Hakeem'. His immediate reaction was to be sceptical about the vagueness of this statement. It didn't explicitly say, after all, what this news actually meant for Hakeem – that he would now be released or deported to Australia – it just said that Bahrain was no longer pursuing the extradition.

He remembers his initial reaction distinctly: 'So we thought, what does that mean? Is that effective immediately? Is there going to be a court process or was he just going be charged with something else under Thai law? Will he get moved from the remand prison to an immigration detention facility? We had no idea. I called some journalists who I knew had contacts inside the office of the attorney-general and could speak to some people relatively high up. Within about an hour, both of them had got back to me and confirmed that he was definitely getting out today. But no more details than that. They didn't say when, they didn't say how. Evan rang Nat straight away. 'What's happening with Hakeem?'

'I don't know,' she told him, 'I've got like 700 phone calls, I've no idea what's happening! I'm going to call now and figure it out.'

By coincidence, Nat had a court case near the criminal court that day that finished at 12. She was having some lunch when a journalist called. 'He said, do you know Hakeem is being released?' she recalls. 'No, but that news is good,' she told him.

She continues, 'They didn't need to talk to me even if they wanted to withdraw the request to extradite. A lot of people were texting me after that. So I walked over to the criminal court and saw the prosecutor walking about the building with the warrant to release Hakeem. I rushed over to speak with them and asked them for a copy of the documents, but I didn't get this until a month later. They said that I couldn't go with them to the prison to release him, so I just got in a taxi to follow them there. They took the van into the prison and I did not get to see him. They told me to go in a different car with the immigration police and we could follow the van to the immigration centre. But they are so tricky . . . they changed the location but didn't tell me any more details. Luckily, the policeman who I was in the car with needed to pick up Hakeem's passport from the attorney-general's office. Then we went straight to the airport and arrived at a VIP check-in area. I walked in with them as far as they let me and managed to overhear what flight he was on. I was afraid that they were going to release him, but that Hakeem would not be sure where he's going. The immigration police told the Australian embassy that they would make sure he understood this, but I still did not even believe [them]. I wanted to see him walking into the gate with my own eyes.'

Some journalists who had gone to the prison had by now sent word that they'd seen a car exiting Klong Prem. It had a lot of security around it and blackened windows, so they had all assumed that Hakeem was inside. When Evan heard this, he assumed that they were taking Hakeem back to the immigration detention centre where he'd spent his first weeks in Bangkok, which was standard procedure when deporting individuals. So he went directly there to hang around and see if he might be able to find out what was going on.

'Hakeem obviously had no visa because his visa was cancelled, so the normal process for anybody who's serving a prison sentence in Thailand once you've finished your sentence is you have to then be transferred to the IDC because you no longer have a valid visa in the country. Then you spend time in there until you buy your own ticket and you go home to your country. So obviously if you don't have money some people can spend another five years in the detention centre until you deport yourself out of the country. So that's what I thought, he'd have to go back to the IDC to go through processing, that could take a few hours and then he'd go to the airport.

'But when I had been at the IDC, after probably an hour and a half, rumours started to float around that he'd been taken to the Australian embassy. Another circulated was that he'd already gone straight to the airport. I didn't really know at that stage but I thought, just practically, well, the car from the prison to the IDC should have been here by now, as it's less than 45 minutes' drive away. I would have definitely made it before the car would have gotten here and no car's come in, so I thought the rumours could be true. Practically it just didn't make any sense to me that the Thais would take him to the embassy, so I took a guess, and jumped in the ABC's car and headed to the airport.'

Shortly after, Evan tried to phone Nat again, who hadn't been answering calls since they'd spoken a few hours previously. It was just after 5 pm and, this time, she answered. He discovered that she was already at the airport and that Hakeem was already airside. She didn't know exactly where he was, but she knew he was in there and past immigration. She asked Evan not to tell anyone this information, and she'd been told not to say anything.

'I think the Thais had obviously told the Australians that they didn't want it to be a media circus, so then I just kept that close to my chest. I knew what flight he was on then . . . When we got there, all the major outlets were there, Sky, BBC, Reuters, everyone. I went to meet Nat immediately, and she said that she'd been asked not to do any media. The Aussie embassy had told her to please be quiet, don't say anything because it's all very sensitive it's all very hush, hush and they didn't want anything to happen that could potentially screw it up. They said, "Look everything's organised, everything's set, please don't say anything that might jeopardise this at all."'

Evan and Nat then discussed if one of them should try and get on the flight with Hakeem. It appeared that, because the Australian embassy had been told to back off, he was going to be put on the flight home all by himself. Evan tried to book himself a ticket on his phone, but because the flight was departing in less than five hours' time, he had to buy it in person. 'So then I just walked up to the Thai Airways ticketing office and said, "Can I just jump on this flight please at this time?" And they said, "Yeah no problem." Funnily enough, I didn't have my credit card, so Nat used her credit card to buy my ticket.'

Nat laughs, remembering, 'I was going to go in with him but maxed my credit card buying the roundtrip airplane ticket to Australia for Evan. So I bought a different ticket to go to another Asian country, because I couldn't afford a ticket to Australia. I got a last-minute price, not roundtrip.' Nat had purchased a one-way ticket to Japan, just so that she could get through immigration and potentially see Hakeem. Understandably, she wanted to say goodbye to him but, more critically, she wanted to ensure he definitely got on that plane.

Evan recalls how last minute it all was. 'And then they asked me, "When do you want to come back?" And I said, "Oh jeez I don't know, two days I guess?" So I didn't really have a lot of thought behind it.' Evan sent me a message asking whether the PFA might cover the cost and, of course, John agreed immediately.

After buying the tickets they headed to the departure gate. Nat was being harassed by the media pack and dutifully refused to say anything. Hakeem had already obviously gone through to the other side of the airport and most of the media had figured that out by then, so Evan was the only one left standing who could comment with any degree of authority on the case.

'So I held a media conference in the middle of the airport . . . "Did I know where Hakeem was?" I just kept quite vague, saying, "My assumption is he's on the other side." "Do I know what flight he's on?" "No idea." "Do I know why it's happened?" "Not sure, but it's great that the Thai

Government's taken this step, blah, blah, blah." I had the plane ticket in my back pocket by then and felt a bit guilty for lying to them, but at the same time I knew that if I said I'm going on the plane with him, that would have just opened up a large can of worms. I just tried to keep it all positive ... because, yeah, I was a bit worried about how things were going to turn out.'

Evan then headed through security and met up with a contact from the Australian embassy. They sat down to have a coffee and debrief about the day. 'They did seem a little bit clueless as well as to how everything was progressing ... they were told explicitly that they weren't allowed to be seen to be anywhere near the gate and they were told to not interfere ... that Thailand wanted to do it Thailand's way, in Thailand's time, so the staffer seemed visibly anxious about that. He even said at one point in time, "Oh ..." because Nat was going to come to the coffee shop as well, and he said, "Oh if that's the case I'm going to go then, I'm going to disappear, okay bye." And got up and left. He was worried that even being seen sitting near Nat, if someone picked it up, could have been seen as the lawyer and Australia colluding to put pressure on the Thai authorities or something. He was that jumpy.'

At around 10.30 pm Evan reconnected with Nat near the departure gate. All the journalists were there and Nat recalls, 'Evan told me that the Australian embassy were very sensitive about me being seen with Hakeem. I said, "What are you talking about, he's my client?" It was very frustrating. If anyone should have access to Hakeem, it was me, his lawyer, but the Thai and Australians, nobody was letting me see him!'

Evan understood her frustration but told her that it might be best if she kept out of sight. 'We never know,' he said, 'I don't think the Thai Government would do anything but it may also cause a scene and it may also, if you just annoy the wrong person, these things can switch and they'll make up some other reason for detaining him or whatever.' After they chatted, Nat left the departure gate area and went upstairs to an executive lounge area, where she had sight of the gate through a large glass window.

'I'm lucky because I have a Star Alliance card, so I went and stayed in the executive lounge. It was the most expensive two glasses of wine I ever had,' she laughs, 'but it was worth it!'

•

At Klong Prem prison, Hakeem had been oblivious to all of this. His experience of the day had begun with a visit from a high-ranking policeman, whose name and exact position he can't now recall. The officer told him that he was going back to Australia at midnight, but Hakeem didn't believe him. 'Because they had lied to me before,' he says.

'I went back to the prison . . . and some hours later, they called me over the microphone speaker to get clothes. The law in the prison is that the prisoner has to shave his hair and beard before going out, so I went to shave. I was looking for Mr Big too. He had privilege to go everywhere within the prison with his special access card, and I did not know where he was. I finally saw him and told him I was going to be released and going back to Australia. He was very happy for me and said he liked Melbourne. He had studied there in 2004. We exchanged contact details and said farewell.

'After that I got ready and they took me outside. I was put in a van and they took me directly to the airport. When I arrived, I was put in a VIP room. I went in by a private entrance into the airport, so that no one could see me. Then I was just waiting. I sat in that VIP room for around six hours. I was scared because I didn't know, will they send me back to Bahrain? Then they took me through an electronic door for scanning. I went through immigration very fast. There was no line. My passport document was stamped and they took me to another room inside the airport. I was by myself there with some police.

'After a long time, I asked for a lady's phone . . . one of the police that sat close to me. I asked her, can I borrow your phone? She gave it to me . . . this was maybe at around 10 pm. I called Nani. She was waiting for my call. When she answered she had seen the Thai calling code and knew it was me. It was the first time I heard her voice in 70 days. She was very, very happy and I was so happy too. I wanted to make sure they were taking me back to Australia and she told me I was coming home to her. Now, when I heard my wife say it, I knew it was true.'

After he hung up, Hakeem asked if he could take a shower. 'They said yes, and I was so happy. It was the happiest shower I ever took,' he says.

Then at around 11 pm, he received a surprise visit from Immigration chief Hakparn. 'He came to the room and he brought nuts in, bowls of nuts and snacks. He told me more than five times that I could eat the nuts. He had media with him, and he knew they would take a photo when I ate. So, with all cameras in front of us, I just did as he said, and ate the nuts so they could take the photos.'

It appeared that the Thai Government wanted one last media opportunity, before they put Hakeem on the plane home. It didn't stop with nuts though.

'In the room he also brought me a football and asked if I would sign it for his son. They took a photo of me signing it with him. I was thinking, this feels so crazy. You have me locked in prison for all this time and now you are taking my signature and photograph? It was very strange. And then, they took me out of the room and put me in a golf cart with Hakparn. The golf cart went really fast . . . I felt very cold from the wind blowing and the air-conditioning, as I was only in my t-shirt. We stopped, and Hakparn took off his jacket and told me "Wear this." I remember thinking, nice jacket, but it's too small for me, I'm too tall.'

Meanwhile, Evan was in the departure lounge and Nat was upstairs at the bar, waiting for Hakeem to arrive. Evan remembers, 'It was just like a regular flight, everyone was lining up to go on the plane. Some people were a bit confused, as there was so much media standing around. I did a short interview with the ABC and then everyone else had boarded . . . I was one of the only people left so I thought, well, I'd better board too. So I walked towards the gate and loitered for a bit and then there was still no one, still nothing and I thought, oh jeez, maybe they're going to put him on a different flight or send him via Hong Kong or something . . . because they knew that the media had picked up on what flight he was probably on. But then I saw police coming out shooing all the media away so I thought, oh okay, if they want the media to go away then obviously I think he's coming now.'

Nat was watching from above through the glass windows. 'In other deportation cases, they only have two police officers, but they had almost ten to escort Hakeem. They waited until everyone was already boarded the airplane, cleared the gate and then Evan was also there. And then, I saw him! He didn't see me, but I got to see him walking into that gate!' she remembers excitedly. 'I took a picture and felt such a big relief, it was really relief . . . then I walked out of the lounge and the security people asked me if I missed my flight. I thought quickly and said that I'd got too drunk in the lounge, had a fight with my husband and missed my flight. They looked at me strangely and then they made me go through an offloading security process to get out of the airport. It took me about an hour to get out!

'The next day I did not move . . . I did not move for two weeks. I just stayed home being lazy and did the most minimal work possible. My life was so quiet, finally . . . no journalists calling. It was wonderful . . . Every now and again, Evan texted me . . . "How is not-so-famous Natalie today?" he would say, and it made me laugh.'

Hakeem was shocked to see Evan waiting for him in the departure tunnel.

'He wandered over,' Evan recalls. 'When he saw me, he had a bit of a smile and said, "What are you doing here?"

I just said, "Oh I'm on your flight, let's go, we're heading to Melbourne." And he looked a bit, still a little bit in disbelief, that it was really happening, but I think seeing me there he realised that it was all okay. He just had the policeman's jacket and a plastic bag with him, he didn't have any luggage or anything, no phone and didn't have his wallet . . . Nani had taken all that when she had left Bangkok.'

'We were the last ones to get on the plane,' says Hakeem. 'When I entered I saw the cabin crew, they recognised me. We went and sat down in an exit row of seats. There was just two seats there, so it was perfect. Just us and lots of room for our legs. Evan gave me his phone and I called Nani again to tell her I was almost ready to leave. We talked for a few minutes. I asked her about all the people who had supported me, and what they have done to bring me back. She asked me to call her as soon as we landed and I agreed. They told me to turn off the electronics then so I said goodbye. But I was happy then, I thought finally that I was really safe.' After hanging up the phone, he turned the map on the video screen and watched it until the plane took off.

Evan recounts their journey home together: 'I took a selfie of us while we were still sitting on the tarmac and tweeted it. Later I saw that Scott Morrison had re-tweeted my photo, but only after cutting me out of the shot!'[1] He laughs. 'Once we took off, we just both talked about how ridiculous the day had been for the first three hours. Then we talked about Bahrain, we talked about him growing up . . . about how nice the water is in Bahrain and how he used to go swimming from Bahrain to some islands off the coast. We talked about

Pascoe Vale . . . we talked about our families, about the court case . . . it was really just a hodgepodge of everything. We just bantered non-stop for a few hours.

'He got up to go to the bathroom maybe halfway through and then I gave him a signed Pascoe Vale shirt when he came back, which he was pretty stoked with. He had a genuine heartfelt smile on his face. Mark from the Australian embassy had given it to me at the airport for him. Ironically, it had only just arrived at the embassy that morning, sent by his teammates down in Melbourne in the nick of time. We spoke about how much he loves Australia, oh and finally . . . because we never really could do it in the prison properly because the telephone's terrible and it's difficult to communicate sometimes, I showed him a picture of me and my friend standing together, the friend that had initially contacted me about Hakeem being in the immigration detention centre, and he was like, "Oh," you could see the penny drop, he was like, "Yes, yes, yes, I remember him now." So then we talked about him a bit and talked about Syria and Palestine, different things.

'The whole time we had the flight map tracking, so we could see where we were . . . the further he was getting away from Thailand, I think the happier he was . . . Once we were over Indonesia we had a little high-five action happening and then once we got over Australia, again, we had a little high-five, pat-on-the-back moment so that was pretty special.

'We also talked about what it would be like when we landed in Melbourne. I told him there would be heaps of media, everyone's really interested, everyone wants to talk to you, everyone wants to hear from you, and I said, "But it's neither here nor there. You don't owe them anything, if you want to go straight home that's totally fine, if you want to go out the back way I'm sure we can find a back way out. The human rights guys I've been talking to will have a plan for this if you need it."

'There were a few other passengers on the flight who you could see when they were walking past to go to the bathroom, or whatnot, had a glance down and you could see them being, "Oh is that Hakeem?" I also heard behind me people speaking in Thai saying, "Hakeem, that's the kid" . . . and then when we were preparing to land the air hostess . . . she was bantering about her flight schedule and whatever, but then Hakeem went to the bathroom she was like, "Oh, he looks like such a nice guy, looks so friendly, I'm really happy for him," and yeah she had a couple of nice words, she seemed really quite genuinely happy about it.'

The moment the plane landed, Hakeem phoned Nani to let her know that he'd landed safely. She hadn't come to meet him at the airport for security reasons, but would be waiting for him when he arrived home.

•

The world was stunned. The speed at which it happened was just so incredible. SBS arranged to come over to my house to do an interview and break the story. It was going to be streamed live to Reuters for international wires.

I needed to get down to Melbourne for the morning, and it was already mid-evening. We booked the last flight, and

Tim and Alex from Amnesty were on it as well. After we made sure Hakeem was safe and sound, it would be one heck of a celebration. SBS were setting up the cameras in my living room when I received a message from a contact at the Australian embassy.

'The wheels are up,' it said. Emotion was flooding over us. My brain was almost too overwhelmed to take it in.

I thought of Nani, who'd been so strong; Hakeem, how must he feel? The interview was one of the most difficult I've ever done. By now, with the job suddenly completed, I simply felt drained, as though the well had run dry. I felt it was important to do it though, because the media had been critically important throughout the campaign. I wanted them to participate in the celebrations, although I felt guilty to be the only person speaking at that moment. As you see in this book, there were many extraordinary people who had contributed to Hakeem being on that plane.

My first words on camera were that I wished everyone involved could be here to speak. I wished that I could line them all up, in front. Show the world who they were. I was so, so proud of them all.

Bob Icevski recalls the night was a mix of sober emotion and joy. 'I was basically flying through red lights, so that I could take Craig straight from the SBS interview to make his flight at the airport. Lara and I had to quickly pack him up so he was ready. When we got the news that the plane had taken off, Lara and Fozz were very teary. We all were. But there were no high fives or anything. It was one of the most sombre moments. I could tell that Craig wouldn't be entirely happy until Hakeem landed and had his feet on the ground in Melbourne. After the interview, we jumped in the car and rushed off. There was only about two minutes of the entire car ride where he wasn't on the phone. And in those two minutes, I said, "Good on you," but that was it. We sat in absolute silence. Complete reflection, without music or anything. Knowing him, he would have been thinking about what everyone else did, how he was going to thank them, give them credit. And about next steps, how to use this case to do bigger things. That's what he's like.'

Before I took off, I tweeted:

@Craig_Foster Flying to Melb to see everyone close to Hakeem, welcome him tomorrow. This is significant win for humanity, people everywhere standing up for good, pushing back against regimes who flout international law, for human rights. Gives us hope to help others, everywhere #Hakeemhome

I was already thinking about doing this again, helping those who'd reached out during the campaign, and there were many. We arrived in Melbourne after midnight and John picked us up. Tired, but we could have stayed awake forever.

Our main concern was Hakeem's security on arrival. Could anyone just turn up at the airport? How was Bahrain reacting? Were there risks, for anyone? We didn't know what condition Hakeem was in physically and mentally, or whether he wanted to speak with the media or rush to his waiting wife. We had coordinated closely with Evan, who would speak with him on the flight and let us know exactly what he wanted to do as soon as they arrived. But for now, we had to just plan for every scenario. We knew there was going to be an unprecedented level of media coverage.

Fortunately, John and the PFA had some useful contacts with the Airport Authority via their work with the Socceroos and Matildas, and they arranged for a small group of us to meet Hakeem and Evan in a room behind security within the airport.

Tim from Amnesty had proven himself adept at managing the media at the protests, and together we mapped out the most likely scenario if Hakeem did choose to make a statement. How we'd walk out, where he'd speak, how we'd get him through the crowd.

Nani would not be coming to the airport, in order to keep her identity protected and Yahya and Fatima from GIDHR had made arrangements for a car to collect Hakeem from the terminal and take him straight home to her. We kept saying, 'He's out, we won, we did it.' It was so unbelievable, it happened so fast, it all felt unreal.

TUESDAY, 12 FEBRUARY 2019

That morning started with the media treadmill at ABC, Melbourne. My main focus was ensuring that everyone who had been involved in the campaign got the credit they deserved. There was a huge coalition here, I kept telling the media. A tremendous team performance.

To the airport, then. What we hadn't anticipated was that, while the airport had security, all they were really concerned about was what happened inside the building. It wasn't really their role to manage anything happening outside, so we were left with a situation that needed a fair bit of security and management, without the means to do it. A large crowd had swelled outside the arrival doors where it was expected Hakeem would come out and security managed to at least cordon off a boundary arc with cones to create some space. Hundreds of people had showed up to welcome Hakeem home, including friends from the Bahraini community, Amnesty supporters, union groups and individuals who had just passionately followed the case.

Thankfully, Tim was there to help direct and manage the media crews, who were doing their best to jostle for positions close to the doors. We moved to the private room and waited, nervously, for them to arrive. Evan messaged as soon as they landed and I explained where we were. How is Hakeem? Is he okay? See you soon.

Hakeem recalls: 'We didn't really know what the plan was but Craig called Evan and said, "You're coming to the VIP room, you can have a shower if you need to or whatever." I had told Evan, maybe an hour before the plane landed, that I wanted to say something to the media. Even if it was just a few words to say thank you to all the Australian people for supporting me. So we got off the plane, and there was some woman from customs or Melbourne airport there.

'When we got to the immigration area the woman took us straight to the front of the line. We had a man, maybe he was 40, at the desk . . . I'm not sure if he recognised me, but I remember he just grabbed my passport, looked down at it and said, "All right, Mr al-Araibi, welcome back, mate, all right have a good day." It was really short, but really welcoming. To me it was so good, after everything. To have such nice warm welcome back like that. There was some other people who saw me on the way and just said things like, "G'day mate, welcome back." Little comments like that as we were walked to meet Craig . . . it was really nice.'

And then the door opened, and in strolled Hakeem. It was unforgettable. He walked straight over and we hugged. He was just incredibly elated, beaming. He was saying, 'I can't believe it, thank you to everyone, I'm so happy to be back in Australia, I'm so happy to be back on the ground here.' He gave me another hug and he said, 'Last night Nani explained to me how you'd fought for me, how you went to FIFA and everything. I just want to say thank you.'

John reflects on the emotion of the moment, 'I've got to say it was probably the most incredible experience of my life. I was sitting in the room with Craig, Hakeem walks through the door and he's there to be greeted by Fozz and they embraced and for me to be able to stand there and watch that, is something that I will never forget.'

John introduced himself and then shortly after, Fatima and Yahya arrived and it was hugs all round. We had a chat for a few minutes about how he was feeling, and I expected him to say, 'Well, it was a horrible time and I'm not great' . . . but he kept repeating, 'I'm just so happy, I'm just happy to be home and I can't wait to see my wife.' So the effect on him from being in jail, in the sense of psychological damage, wasn't evident. It wasn't the image we had feared.

It was the same kid I saw in jail, with the fear replaced by absolute jubilation.

We asked Hakeem what he wanted to do and gave him all the options. He said he wanted to say something to the Australian people and then he would leave to see his wife. We gave him time to freshen up and prepared to walk the 40 metres or so down the hallway and out together into the media scrum. The shock of it still hit me when we walked out those doors. The cameras started clicking, people screaming and crying, singing, shouting, it was utter chaos. The media was an impermeable mass in front of us. All we could see was a sea of cameras. Okay, buddy, are you ready? I'm with you, we'll just walk together and get it done, let's go.

Soon after we walked out, a group of people broke from the crowd, rushed up and started hugging Hakeem, crying and wailing. I was on high alert, and my instinctive reaction was to start trying to shield him from them. I didn't know who they were and we had very real security concerns. Things felt out of control for a moment or two, and then Tim started yelling loudly at the media and directing the crowd slightly off to the left. Turned out they were known to Hakeem, part of the Melbourne Bahraini community, but we couldn't know.

Hakeem recalls the moment: 'When I was coming out, the first people I saw were my team from Pascoe Vale. I was very happy to see them. I saw all the cameras facing the door waiting for me to go out. I was so excited but at the same time I felt I could not talk or speak. Because what I saw was beyond my expectation or imagination. At that moment I felt less toward the Bahrain Government. They had a bad treatment of me, but when I saw the people in the airport, they don't even know me but they care about me. I felt safe. I knew this is my home. They are taking care of me more than Bahrain. I felt overwhelmed.'

We managed to herd everyone over to the microphones and Hakeem addressed the nation, live. 'I want to thank Australia. It is amazing to see all the people here, all the Australian people, all the media and, everyone who supported me . . . Australia is my home.' The Amnesty crew and John formed a ring around him and pushed through the crowd to where Fatima waited in the car. Within a few minutes he was on his way. To Nani.

Hakeem recalls, 'She waited for me downstairs and gave me some flowers and some gifts. It was a happy and important moment in my life. She was weak when I left her in Thailand . . . she was not eating well and feeling very sad because seeing news about me made her health condition go bad. Now she beamed. Nothing could make me lose the moment, it was the best moment in my life. I felt like I was going back from death to life . . . going back to *Alsaadah*, which means in Arabic, "great happiness". A colourful life.'

•

Despite the fact Hakeem was now safely back in Australia, I was still feeling nervous, especially about Bahrain's response to Hakeem's release. They had issued a public statement that said they'd taken note of the 'halt in legal proceedings' against Hakeem, but stated that 'The guilty verdict against

Mr. Al Araibi remains in place and Mr. Al Araibi holds the right to appeal this court verdict at Bahrain's Court of Appeal. The Kingdom of Bahrain reaffirms its right to pursue all necessary legal actions against Mr. Al Araibi.'

The news also reported that Australia's Ambassador to Bahrain and Saudi Arabia, Ridwaan Jadwat, had been 'hauled in' to Bahrain's foreign minister's office to discuss the international arrest warrant. The Australian Government had also issued a joint statement that morning from Scott Morrison and Marise Payne, announcing that Hakeem was home. That statement, as well as a tweet from Scott Morrison, acknowledged the efforts of Bahrain to help resolve the issue and emphasised that 'Australia and Bahrain share an important and longstanding relationship which we will continue to build upon'.

I sent a text message to Marise requesting clarification about what exactly this all meant. I told her that I wanted to know if Australia had made any kind of deal with Bahrain and if there was any possibility at all that Hakeem could be extradited from Australia. Her response was that, as far as Australia is concerned, Hakeem is a protected refugee and under no circumstances is he in any danger of being extradited to Bahrain.

I turned my mind to the task ahead. During the campaign I had refrained from making any public commentary about Australia's broader refugee policies, and also resisted responding to criticisms directed at myself and the football community throughout, saying that we only cared about

Hakeem because he was a footballer and there were count-less other deserving refugees who needed similar advocacy. I completely agreed with them and, now that he was safely home, it was time to deal with those issues.

Before I go there though, let's take stock of what actually happened to get Hakeem out of Klong Prem prison the previous day.

Unless the King of Thailand himself ever says it publicly, there will never be any hard evidence about the extent of his involvement in Hakeem's eventual release. Some very well-placed sources in Thailand claim that one of Thailand's princesses, in response to the outcry after the footage of Hakeem at the court case, called the king up and said, 'Enough is enough,' which then led him to intervene. Others claim that it was the letter from the cave rescue divers that finally engaged him, as the king was such a strong, quiet supporter of the rescue operation to save the young footballers the previous year. In my mind, the letter was absolutely critical and came at the perfect moment; it was brilliantly handled.

Unfortunately, the likelihood is that, like most things related to the royal families in all these countries, we'll never have any hard proof of who said what exactly, when and to whom. We can, however, infer that Thailand's new king was involved in the final decision.

Firstly, Thailand's foreign minister was given an audience with both Bahrain's Prime Minister Khalifa bin Salman Al Khalifa and Crown Prince Salman bin Hamad Al Khalifa.

It is unlikely that an audience like this would be granted at short notice without the knowledge or involvement of Thailand's king, who we've previously established has close financial and personal ties with Bahrain's royal family. The fact that the Thai prime minister also made a phone call to his counterpart in support of the foreign minister's visit,[2] also reveals that Thailand's most senior government officials considered this issue to be incredibly significant and highly sensitive.

The lightning speed with which the case was eventually resolved also points to potential royal involvement. As former Thai diplomat turned professor Pavin Chachavalpongpun pointed out, for diplomats in Thailand, 'the number one priority is not about maintaining good relationships. The number one priority is about making sure you serve the royal family ... Fifty per cent of our operation [in the Foreign Ministry] is about the monarchy, we have to serve the monarchy before anything else ... If you know that the palace wants [something], you have to serve it.'[3]

What is certain, though, is that the Australian Government and embassy played a decisive role. And having read this saga, you will now understand that public pressure ultimately forced every organ to act. As people raised their voices to a crescendo, there was simply nowhere to hide. The elections in both Australia and Thailand, and the coronation, were ideally timed and Hakeem became too much of a public liability for those trying to steal him away.

By 12 February, Twitter informed me that the #SaveHakeem hashtag had been tweeted more than 1.7 million times across six continents,[4] trending in 81 countries and this only goes a small way towards capturing the media stories published, meetings held, petitions signed, banners hung and actions taken. That's an extraordinary achievement.

In the end, you won the day. People power.

Chapter 13

DEAR SCOTT AND BILL

The design of Parliament House says everything about why we got you out, mate, I told Hakeem. They built it into the side of the hill here so that the people can walk over the top. I pointed towards the inviting lush grass that surrounds the main face of the building. It means that the government can never forget it's here to serve the people, and not the other way around. The contrast with the privilege and disregard for the rule of law that we'd just witnessed couldn't have been more stark. And welcome.

We were up very early, on a crisp but sunny morning in Canberra on 14 February as our small group strolled up the slope towards Capital Hill. It was not lost on any of us that it was 14 February. Exactly eight years ago to this day, the mass pro-democracy uprising had kicked off at the Lulu roundabout in Bahrain. The monument itself had long been turned into dust, but now, here was Hakeem, a symbol of hope and freedom, casually ambling up the footpath towards Australia's Parliament House.

'It was an important place for the traditional owners of this land too,' I explained. 'After the match, you'll have to walk back with Nani to see the beautiful Aboriginal mosaic there on the forecourt.' We were on our way to the Senate Oval on the right-hand side of the building, where a celebratory football match was to be played with Senators and MPs.

Before travelling, Hakeem asked me for advice about whether he should come to Canberra or not. I had given it some thought and decided it would be a good thing for us to meet the prime minister, shake his hand, do the media rounds and give due credit to everyone involved. Despite Australia's horrible record on the treatment of asylum seekers, one key reason why we succeeded was because we were fair, gave credit to all who did the right thing, and had no political agendas. It was an opportunity to have the Australian prime minister shake the hand of a refugee whom he, and all of us, had fought for. The only way we're going to move this country forward is by being fair-minded. By the end, Scott had undertaken his responsibilities well, as had Marise, and I wanted to see them receive due credit for it.

It was a powerful statement for Hakeem, a young male Muslim refugee, to stand in the halls of Parliament House and remind everyone what a strong and courageous country we can be for people who seek our protection. You will want this photo when you're older too, I told him, to demonstrate what people are capable of in the world and to use in your own community to tell the story of social cooperation between all. Personal connections change the world, Hakeem had proven that. When a name and cause has a face, when we meet them, understand that they are just like us, we see positive change happen. Who knows? Perhaps getting to meet Hakeem and others like him might change some personal views within Parliament House, of all political persuasions?

As we walked together towards the oval, Hakeem was virtually unrecognisable. Gone was the fearful, gaunt kid who had appeared barefoot and in shackles just one week before. Beside me now was a strong, confident young man with a sharp haircut and an unfading grin. The real Hakeem. Alex had given him her #SaveHakeem t-shirt, and its black and yellow design perfectly matched the colour scheme of his fitted tracksuit top.

When we arrived at the oval, Nani stood back with Alex out of camera shot and the rest of us walked down to where the huddle of MPs and media waited in bright yellow and blue #SaveHakeem shirts. Former Matildas captain, now PFA Deputy CEO, Kate Gill had come along to show her support, and a number of Canberra United women's players were there. I joined them in my kit and we played the friendly match while Hakeem, who would take weeks and months to be ready to kick a ball again, chatted with Marise Payne and watched. 'I was so happy, this was such a magical moment,' reflects Hakeem. 'Marise Payne and everyone fought so hard for me and I was grateful to them.'

After the match, we all headed up into Parliament House. Amnesty had been flat out fielding calls from MPs. Everyone was dying to meet the guy who'd just survived the wrath of two royal families and he had a jam-packed schedule lined up until early afternoon.

First stop was Marise Payne's office. She had kindly offered her rooms for Hakeem to freshen up and relax in before his meetings kicked off. Hakeem says, 'She was so kind and I had a good feeling with her . . . we had coffee and breakfast in her office and I will never forget the moment when she cleared things off the table after we had finished . . . and then,' he waves his hands excitedly, 'she went and brought some cups of water and served it to people in the room. I was very shocked . . . the politician would never do this in Bahrain . . . and I said to myself, this is a reason to love this country because they don't have any differentiation between the people. I saw there is no discrimination and it made me feel very safe and very proud.

'Craig and I then went to meet the prime minister. On the way I was very nervous. Craig said to me that I'm like a younger brother to him now and that he's here to help me, to give me whatever help and advice I need. He said I didn't need to worry about meeting the prime minister, because he is just a guy from Sutherland, south of Sydney . . . he's just the same as you and me, and there's no difference. One day I could be in his position. He said, let's just go and shake his hand, and enjoy ourselves. I felt very honoured to meet Scott Morrison. I got a signed football and we took a selfie together. This memory and this feeling, I will keep it forever in my heart.'

After several more meetings, including with then Leader of the Opposition, Bill Shorten, and members of the Standing

Committee on Indigenous Affairs, a friendly MP hosted us all for lunch in the parliamentary dining room. It is an all-you-can-eat buffet in one of Australia's most formal settings. 'I was laughing with Alex because only four days ago I was eating wet rice in the prison and now we were eating soft-shelled crab and delicious baked potatoes,' remembers Hakeem.

I watched him eat, with Nani next to him, ever smiling and it was difficult for us all to absorb what we were witnessing.

'It was all so strange, and when we walked around Parliament that day I was very pleased to see normal people are seeing and watching what's happening there, they are speaking freely and there is nothing to hide . . . we went into the green room and saw the people there, working together to build this country with our own eyes . . . in Bahrain you cannot even go across the Parliament or see what's happening . . . you cannot go to Parliament or attend.'

By the end of the day we were all even more exhausted than before, if that were even possible, but it was worth it. To not only have Hakeem safely home, but also have him stand in Parliament House, shake the prime minister's hand and have parliamentarians of all political persuasions, including many who opposed more humane treatment of asylum seekers, taking celebratory selfies with a young Muslim refugee – job done, I thought.

•

About a week after our trip to Canberra, I fulfilled the promise I'd made to Guy Ryder in Geneva weeks before. The day after Hakeem's emotional homecoming match at

Pascoe Vale, I published an open letter in the *Sydney Morning Herald* to Scott Morrison and then Leader of the Opposition Bill Shorten.[1] I had worked on it for some weeks, but it represented the years of sorrow and despair I'd felt, watching Australia's policies towards people seeking refuge spiral dangerously away from our country's core values and become utterly inhumane, demonising and unjustifiable.

I am proud of the Australian people and I was honoured to be involved in this remarkable campaign to save a young man's future, which I felt was executed according to our most important values and qualities, but I also believed it demonstrated something much bigger. That Australians were ready to confront ourselves in the mirror and finally end the heinous refugee policies that have shattered our international image and made a mockery of the values we have historically claimed to possess as a people.

I hoped that this letter would solidify the legacy of the campaign and that our leaders, having welcomed us so generously the week before in Canberra, would be inspired to continue showing such courage in the area of refugee policy and other areas of social justice, for all that need a helping hand. I hope that they both received my message, along with their many colleagues, who are tasked with the solemn and difficult role of representing people from all corners of this great country. They have the power to change things that are done in our name and if they don't, it will continue to be our job to demand that they do.

•

Melbourne's Federation Square was packed and the air was electric with excitement. More than 200 people from 44 countries were crammed in the glass-walled Edge theatre, there to become Australian citizens. A crowd of us, including Pascoe Vale members and John from the PFA, had all come to support Hakeem. He had on a light-pink jacket, white tank top and gelled hair; a stylish, confident young man. It reminded me that we would have to get to know him; there's a very interesting character under there. He'd scored 100 per cent on his citizenship test the week prior, and now his face beamed as he held up the citizenship certificate the foreign minister had just presented him with. As with a key moment in Bangkok, the Queen of England was there too . . . well, at least her portrait was.

It was a poignant moment as I stared at her oversized portrait which sat beside the national flag on the stage. Ironically, the very reason that we got Hakeem out, I reflected, was because we refused to treat anyone like royalty. The egalitarian nature of our society is that all are equal, and we see the person, not the title, nor the crown. That's part of what made this country special and something that we need to keep alive.

Even if a king is acting improperly, an Australian is duty-bound to let them know. That's who we are. We treated the Bahrainis, Thais, FIFA, Salman, everyone fairly, nothing personal. And in the same way we'd treat anyone else and as we expect to be treated. The queen, Thai king or Bahrain royals could play all the anthems they like, I thought, remembering the fateful Bangkok function that seemed eons ago. We do not snap to attention for anyone.

It also occurred to me that I needed to get in touch with the Republic movement after all these years. I'd had enough of royals for a lifetime.

Marise Payne addressed the crowd of new Australians. Her speech was both moving and promising. 'There was an enormous public outpouring of support for Mr al-Araibi . . . from complete strangers across the Australian community who were concerned for his welfare . . . the public support for Hakeem played an enormous part in ensuring he was returned to Australia, and as foreign minister, I was proud to witness that campaign. It embodied some of the best elements of Australia: looking after one another, mateship, a fair go,' she said.

'Finally, I felt safe,' Hakeem says. 'I will never go back to Bahrain. I owe this country everything and I will be so strong for Australia. My hopes and dreams for the future? I would like to continue in my field as a professional, to become a stronger player and move forward. Maybe one day I will be a coach or in a position in future where I can help other athletes, especially refugees.'

•

Life slowly began to return to normal for Hakeem and Nani, down in Melbourne, although I suspect they won't truly know the full meaning of that word for a long time to come. Pascoe Vale staged a wonderful celebratory return match to which thousands turned up. There were speeches, wonderful Muslim singers, awards and DJs. Hakeem had Nani, but also an incredible football family, and they too played a huge role in his return. Lou and Athena, particularly, were unbelievable throughout the entire ordeal. They and the club should be given an award as a model of advocacy. We almost had Barnesy playing live at that match. Unfortunately, he couldn't come in the end, but I appreciated his offer.

John and the PFA agreed to fly Hakeem's mother and sister out from Bahrain as a surprise. How I wish I could have seen that reunion, but the visas took too long and they arrived a week later. We can only imagine the hugs. The players paid for their flights. I happened to be in town for an event and caught up with Hakeem, his mother and sister. It was beautiful to see them all together again. FIFPro agreed to an emergency funding grant and the PFA ended up spending around $130,000 on the entire campaign, of which $44,000 was generously donated by members of the public. Incredible on both fronts, and a model for any athlete union anywhere in the world. A real credit to Brendan, John, Francis, their executive of current players and all of their members. I hope the next generation take up the mantle of these three, and all the fabulous PFA staff members who invested so much energy and belief into their work.

Hakeem and Nani finally went on their long-awaited honeymoon. You'll be pleased to know they only travelled as far north as Hamilton Island this time. Hakeem also started working with Football Victoria as their Community and Human Rights Advocate, a part-time role where he'll be engaging with Victoria's multicultural football community and inspiring them with his own personal story.

Despite loud protestations from Hakeem, Brendan and myself as well as the PFA, the football community and human rights organisations globally, the ASEAN Football Federation, which includes Australia, announced its unanimous support for Sheikh Salman to remain as the AFC President for another term.[2] He was re-elected to the post on 6 April 2019 and Gianni Infantino hailed the appointment, as did the FFA. 'It was a real slap in the face to everyone who had worked so hard on the campaign,' says Brendan. 'It shows just how far we still have to go.'

Later, in July, the FIFA HRAB released its periodic report in which it published the set of recommendations that FIFA had largely failed to comply with back in January. The seventh recommendation, that all electoral candidates, including in the AFC Presidential election of April, be vetted in relation to how they would comply with Article 3 of the FIFA Statutes should they be elected, was completely disregarded. Global football did what it always does. The minimum necessary, then moved on with no accountability. Not one question has been asked by the global governing body as to the silence of Salman and the AFC for two months while a player's life was in jeopardy.

FIFPro, too, need reform. During the AFC election, FIFPro should have been ensuring that a full investigation was undertaken into Salman's conduct and past. At the very least the HRAB recommendation had to be emphasised. That no comment was made, then or at the time of writing, shows that both the governance of the game itself, and the players, needs to improve. As a former international and chairman of the Australian PFA, I believe that FIFPro must be willing to hold the game to the very highest standards. The game will be so much stronger when the players and their representative body accept their responsibility to provide oversight of the governance of their game. We need more legendary players to involve themselves and to assert their power as the true custodians of the game.

On this note, very late in the case, FIFA had offered financial support for Hakeem's legal fees to FIFPro, which I strongly opposed as Hakeem needed their support, advocacy and determination to uphold their and their delegates' human rights obligations from 27 November 2018. These cannot be purchased retrospectively. In future, with a global body properly committed to their obligations, the next 'Hakeem' should have access to a global legal and advocacy fund shared between the two bodies and de-politicised through an independent chamber. Otherwise the trading of interests will occur again, as it did here.

While the campaign shone a spotlight on the events of 2011 in Bahrain, we face an ongoing battle to rid our game and international sport more generally from people like this. We will not stop fighting until a thorough investigation is conducted into the events of 2011 in Bahrain and until the perpetrators of violence against athletes and others are held to account.

In March 2019, just weeks after Hakeem's release, the Grand Prix was also held without so much as a hitch in

Bahrain. This was despite Formula One being well aware of, and supposedly 'concerned', about the ongoing imprisonment of Najah Yusuf, a young woman who was beaten, sexually abused and jailed for protesting against the Bahrain Grand Prix. Najah was imprisoned in 2017 after a series of Facebook posts that were critical of the race and the government.[3] Where were the drivers, the managers and the fans in the public calls for Formula One to take action? I realised then the real value of people power, and what football had actually achieved.

At the time of writing, the issue of asylum seekers and their treatment under Australia's care remains as vexed as ever. I hope that as a country we can accept that while security is always an important factor, everyone has a right to seek refuge and to be treated humanely in so doing. And that we will not continue with a policy that forces people into dire hopelessness. While I know that it is not only hope that we need, we must believe in the goodness of Australians and people everywhere and one major motive for writing this book is to keep the conversation going as to what Australia is, what we want to be and how we are prepared to conduct ourselves regarding vulnerable people being left behind, or aside by society.

On reflection it is clear that Hakeem was lucky in many ways. He had a range of forces converge at the very moment he needed them most. He's fortunate that he sought refuge in a sports-mad country with a very strong athlete union framework and a football players' union which is among the best in the world. That 2019 was both an election year in

Australia and a coronation year in Thailand, that the movement of human rights in sport had reached a point where accountability mechanisms could be road-tested. And that one of the best human rights lawyers in Thailand planned to be on holidays in December and was therefore available to pick up his case at a moment's notice. He is lucky that, in July 2018, two Australian divers had been involved in the rescue of 12 young footballers and their coach from a cave in northern Thailand, that a senior and highly experienced diplomat was appointed to the Bangkok post just one month before his detention, and that a number of incredibly capable and brave Australians had worked their way into positions of global influence in sport. We made the most of all of these factors.

But while the sport and human rights movement has come a long way, the system did not save Hakeem. The people did. Football still needed to be forced to act and this is the next step in the mission to ensure that the next 'Hakeem' does not need a global campaign.

The central tenet of this story, though, is that no one involved would compromise on their fundamental beliefs in equality and justice. I have had an opportunity since to speak about the campaign alongside Hakeem in many fora, and when asked how we all did it, I simply say, because we truly tried to. What does that mean? Not only that everyone stepped forward but more importantly they refused to sell Hakeem out for personal gain. By being so forceful, we placed many organisations, particularly in football, in situations of intense discomfort and there is a price to pay for this. We didn't have to; no one would ever have known if we had let a few off the hook. No, we said we'd fight for him, and we went all the way. There is too much self-interest in the world, too much politics overriding fundamental protections that every human being should be able to rely on. The lesson is that we can change anything if we want it enough. We just have to truly try. This is the challenge that *Fighting for Hakeem* poses to us all.

Are we prepared to step up and fight for our vision for the game, and for sport, as a powerful tool for realising human potential and equality? Are we prepared to work hard for a world where the rights of everyone are respected, to fight for what we believe in across every field of social and political life?

The coming years provide an opportunity, like never before, for us to finish building this vision for sport as an enabler of a more just world. *Fighting for Hakeem* provides us with the perfect blueprint for how we'll get there.

ACKNOWLEDGEMENTS

There are too many people who contributed to this incredible movement for me to be able to adequately thank them all. But there are certainly some specific groups and individuals that I need to acknowledge, who either contributed to the campaign itself, or to the recording of this important story.

To the global football community, you were incredible. The fans and participants above all, who took up the cause. To the footballers, Olympians and athletes, in Australia and around the world, who used their profile to amplify Hakeem's story – your support was both invaluable and inspirational. To the many Australian and world political leaders, who came together in a spirit of shared compassion and used Hakeem's case to talk about what unites us, not what divides us – thank you for stepping up when you were called upon.

To all of you who joined forces to challenge the power of two monarchies, a military junta, and the world's largest sporting institutions, FIFA and the AFC – your support gave us the power to create action and real change. Not just for one young man, but hopefully for future generations of players, fans, officials, sports journalists – the billions of people connected to sport around the world.

While I strongly disagree with laws that imprison citizens for speaking up in opposition to authority, whether governmental or monarchical, and believe that no person is above international law, there is a great deal of affection and respect between Thailand and Australia and nothing in this book should be interpreted otherwise. Thank you to our Thai friends for your support of Hakeem at a crucial time.

The Bahraini people are some of the most impressive and courageous that I've ever known. When the Bahrain Government and rulers implement democracy, freedom of speech and let your passionate people extend their human capabilities and have a voice in the administration of their country, not only will you prosper, but I'll be the first to congratulate you.

To everyone who worked on the case, from Schwabby; Orsat; JD, his executive, membership and incredible staff; Fran; Alex, Tim and Graham at Amnesty; Evan and Nat; Elaine, Minky and Phil from Human Rights Watch; Fatima and Yahya; Sayed; Lou and Athena; Bob; Peter; Marise; Allan, Paul and Mark – you are all amazing, beyond words. This book was written so that the world knows the contribution you all made.

To our Twitter team . . . what you did is one of the most extraordinary things I've ever seen, or been involved in. You didn't know Hakeem, or me, but you stepped up and gave it everything you had. Your time, energy, and a large part of your life during that period. You are the true embodiment of people power.

To our publishers at Hachette, and to Alex again, for a mountain of research and her commitment to telling this story about the value of fighting for just one person's rights, as a proxy for us all. And to SBS management, CEO James Taylor, Head of Sport Ken Shipp and Head of News and Current Affairs Jim Carroll, for their understanding and support.

To my parents, my wife Lara, and our children. You were with me on the journey and suffered throughout. Thank you for giving Hakeem and Nani a chance at a future together.

Finally, this story is a celebration of the very human qualities of devotion, friendship and loyalty. Of a wife's boundless love. Of a group of people who have known each other for decades through football in Australia, who believe in similar values, trust each other implicitly and are proudly Australian. They are some of my oldest and dearest friends with whom I would trust my life. Hakeem never knew it, but he was fortunate that the fight for his life had been entrusted to them. They didn't let him down.

TIMELINE

Date	Event	Relevant to Red Notice
2004	Hakeem starts playing football for Club al-Shabab at 10 years old; his favourite school teacher, Sadiq, saw him playing and recommended him.	
2009	Hakeem joins the national youth team at 15 years old; signs of civil unrest start to show in Bahrain.	
2010	Police come to Hakeem's house looking for his half-brother, Emad, in October. Hakeem is arrested by police and kept in prison without charge until February 2011.	
2011	On 14 February, Valentine's Day, Arab Spring pro-democracy peaceful protests kick off in Bahrain at the Lulu roundabout. Many athletes join their fellow Bahrainis, including Hakeem. Participating athletes are later publicly targeted by authorities. Many are imprisoned and tortured.	
2012	On 7 November 2012, Hakeem is arrested and tortured for alleged involvement in an attack on Al Khamis police station on 3 November. On 8 November Hakeem tells the public prosecutor he has an alibi. He was playing a live football match that evening with his club al-Shabab. He is detained until 6 February 2013.	

Date	Event	Relevant to Red Notice
2013	Hakeem is released on bail 6 February 2013. On 14 February, the anniversary of the Lulu roundabout protests, a 16-year-old boy is shot by police at point-blank range and killed. Hakeem returns to play for his local team and is made captain. He continues playing for the national squad and travels internationally for tournaments. In late 2013 Hakeem is called up for the senior national team. In November 2013 he travels with them to Qatar for the 2014 West Asian Football Federation Championship.	
2014	On 6 January Hakeem's friend calls and tells him he's been convicted in absentia to 10 years in prison. Hakeem panics and then escapes to Iran, a majority Shia country. He then travels to Iraq, Malaysia and Australia. He arrives in Melbourne in May 2014 to play football. He applies for asylum within two months and is granted a bridging visa in June 2014.	
2015	Bahrain national team travels to Australia to play in the Asian Cup in Melbourne. Hakeem stays with them and asks the President of the Bahrain football club if he might be safe to go home to Bahrain.	
2016	Sheikh Salman bin Ibrahim al Khalifa runs for FIFA presidency. Hakeem critiques Salman's human rights record publicly; he was President of the Bahrain Football Association at the time athletes were tortured for participating in Arab Spring protests. Salman does not win the presidency.	
	Nani and Hakeem met on instagram in 2012 and have been in regular contact ever since. Nani travels to Australia in December 2016.	
2017 **Feb**	Nani and Hakeem are married in a small ceremony on 25 February 2017. They can't go overseas as Hakeem is only on a bridging visa, so they delay their honeymoon. Hakeem suggests Thailand because he's travelled there before and loved it.	
May	FIFA launches Human Rights Policy.	
Nov	Hakeem's refugee protection visa, which he applied for on 2 June 2014, is granted by Australia on 30 November 2017.[1]	
2018 **Sept**	Hakeem buys plane tickets to Thailand.	
Oct 12	Bahrain elected to UN Human Rights Council.	

Date		Event	Relevant to Red Notice
2018	**Nov (early)**	Hakeem contacts DFAT. Receives generic advice that there are no restrictions on his travel to Thailand, as per his visa status. Their policy is not to provide case-specific travel advice.	
		Hakeem applies for a Thai visa. He has to return to the embassy twice before his visa is processed. He is asked to provide details of his flight to Bangkok.	✓
	Nov 7	Hakeem's three-month tourist visa is granted from Thailand – valid from 7 November (his birthday) until 6 February 2019.	
	Nov 8	Interpol issues red notice from Bahrain (dated 8 November 2018).	✓
	Nov 9	AFP sends red notice to ABF. At this time, neither the AFP nor the Australian Interpol NCB are aware of Hakeem's visa status.	
	Nov 22	ABF 'assesses' red notice and runs details across Home Affairs systems. Fails to send 'true match' notification manual email to the AFP NCB, as per usual process. This 'true match' notification email would have included Hakeem's visa type.	✓
	Nov 27	Bahrain formally requests extradition from Thailand.	
		Hakeem arrives at Melbourne International airport 1208 AEDT. SmartGate machine doesn't work so he is asked to go to a counter. The officer calls the AFP NCB at 12.08 and informs them of the Interpol red notice. At 12.18, the AFP NCB advises that no domestic warrant exists, and clears Hakeem to travel. Hakeem remains unaware of the red notice. At 2.15 pm AFP NCB notifies Thailand and Bahrain that he is travelling.	✓
	Nov 27	Hakeem is arrested walking off the plane in Bangkok's Suvarnabhumi Airport at 8.50 pm.	
	Nov 28	Bahrain has raised allegations with Interpol that Hakeem is travelling on a suspected fake travel document. The Home Affairs Department notifies AFP of Hakeem's protection visa status and validity of travel document. AFP employee had gone home by time reply came with advice re: protection visa. **NB: this was the first time AFP was notified of his visa status.**	✓

Date		Event	Relevant to Red Notice
2018	**Nov 29**	AFP obtains permission from Home Affairs to share Hakeem's visa status with Interpol's Office of Legal Affairs.	✓
		Hakeem told to book flight back to Australia. He and Nani book flights leaving at 9 pm on 1 December.	
	Nov 30	Interpol rescinds notice on 30 Nov in Lyon, France **NB: Red notice is rescinded 1 Dec in Australia and Thailand (Canberra is 10 hours ahead and Bangkok is 6 hours ahead of France).**	✓
		Hakeem is stopped from boarding his flight and moved to the Immigration Detention Centre Suan Plu in Bangkok.	
	Dec 3	Embassy of Bahrain submits the relevant documents required for the provisional arrest warrant to Thailand's Ministry of Foreign Affairs. This is forwarded to the Office of the Attorney-General, in line with procedure stipulated in Thailand's Extradition Act B.E. 2551 (2008).	
		Hakeem is taken to court and served with a 12-day detention order.	
	Dec 4	Thailand's Immigration chief Surachate Hakparn publicly confirms the lifting of the red notice and the 12 further days of detention.	✓
		Protest outside the Thai Consulate in Victoria, Australia, takes place. Bahraini activists, GIDHR and Amnesty International call on the Thai authorities to free Hakeem.	
	Dec 5	Bahrain sends legal documents to Foreign Affairs in Thailand that need to be forwarded to Thai Immigration before case can begin.	
	Dec 6	News reports Hakparn's statement that 'The Bahraini government knew that [Hakeem] would be arriving in Thailand [on the 27th of November], so they coordinated with Thailand's permanent secretary of foreign affairs to detain him, pending documents sent from Bahrain.'	✓

Date		Event	Relevant to Red Notice
2018	**Dec 7**	Thai Office of Attorney-General endorses Bahrain's arrest warrant and files an application for the issuance of a provisional arrest warrant with the court, which approves it that same day.	
	Dec 8	Thai Government issues a press release presenting an account of the circumstances leading to Hakeem's detention, his status and 'the course of action required under Thai laws'.[2]	
	Dec 9	Marise Payne issues a media statement expressing concern regarding Hakeem's ongoing detention and calling for his immediate return to Australia.[3]	
	Dec 11	Hakeem goes to court, is informed about provisional arrest warrant and notified that the Thai attorney-general has 60 days to file an application with the court for his extradition. He is taken to prison straight from the court hearing.	
	Dec 22	First press conference at PFA office in Melbourne with PFA, Football Victoria, Craig Foster, A-League Champion Rodrigo Vargas, GIDHR and Amnesty.	
	Dec 31	Bahrain's Court of Cassation upholds five-year prison sentence of human rights defender and prisoner of conscience Nabeel Rajab.	
2019	**Jan 1–5**	2019 AFC Asia Cup held in the United Arab Emirates from 5 January to 1 February 2019.	
	Jan 5	Rahaf Mohammed Al-Qunun lands in Bangkok.	
	Jan 9–11	Australia's Foreign Minister Marise Payne visits Thailand en route back to Australia and directly advocates for Hakeem's release.	
	Jan 10	First Sydney Opera House press conference – gains international coverage in Thailand's *The Nation*.	
		AFC Asian Cup Bahrain versus Thailand football match.	
	Jan 17	Thailand signals more tolerant refugee policy after the case of Rahaf Al-Qunun and Immigration chief Hakparn announces Thailand will not force any refugees to return home 'involuntarily'.[4]	

Date		Event	Relevant to Red Notice
2019	**Jan 18**	Bahrain Government states that Hakeem's life is not in danger and he will face a fair court trial if he returns to Bahrain.[5]	
	Jan 20	Calls for inquiry into Interpol red notice and Australia's role start to gain traction in Australia, including Federal Parliament.	✓
	Jan 22	Craig visits Hakeem in Bangkok remand prison for the first time and takes a written message from Nani with him.	
	Jan 25	Craig speaks at Foreign Correspondents' Club and attends Australia Day function in Bangkok. Craig finds out that Bahrain has filed the extradition paperwork. It must still be approved by Thailand's Attorney-General.	
	Jan 26	Craig travels to Zurich, Switzerland.	
	Jan 27	Thai Football Clubs, including local FA Cup champions Chiang Rai United FC, publicly call for their supporters to call on the Thai Government to meet its international legal and human rights obligations.[6]	
	Jan 28	Craig and Brendan Schwab meet Fatma Samoura at FIFA House.	
	Jan 29	Hakeem's wife Nani pleads for his release.	
	Jan 29	Craig attends FIFPro board meeting in Amsterdam with Andrew Orsatti.	
	Jan 30	Craig goes to Geneva to meet Guy Ryder from the International Labour Organization (ILO).	
	Jan 31	*The New York Times* publishes an article, escalating the audience for the campaign significantly.[7]	
	Feb 1	Second major public demonstration at Sydney Opera House (a separate one also occurs in Melbourne); Asian Cup Final in UAE.	
		Bahrain's extradition request approved by Thai Attorney-General.	

Date		Event	Relevant to Red Notice
2019	**Feb 2**	Thai football fans display #SaveHakeem banners at Thailand Champions Cup 2019 match between Buriram United and Singha Chiangrai United – kick off at 7 pm on 2 February 2019 at Royal Thai Army Stadium, Bangkok.[8]	
	Feb 3	Craig travels back to Thailand.	
	Feb 4	Hakeem appears in shackles at court in response to Bahrain's extradition request. Many foreign embassies attend and the Australian Ambassador to Thailand delivers statement on steps outside courthouse regarding the detention of Hakeem Al-Araibi.[9]	
		Thailand's prosecutor publicly confirms that Thailand's Extradition Act allows for executive discretion in such cases.	
		'#BoycottThailand' hashtag ramps up on Twitter.	
	Feb 5	Minister Payne issues media statement calling for Hakeem's release.[10]	
		Thai foreign minister issues press release urging Australia and Bahrain to talk to each other and 'find a mutually agreeable solution' and says Thailand would not have become involved in the issue 'had we not received the red notice alert from the Australian Interpol'.[11]	
		Morrison writes a second time to Thai PM after 'shackles moment'.[12]	
	Feb 7	Strong response from Australian Government to Thai statement.	
		Thai princess Ubolratana Mahidol announces intentions to run in Thailand's elections.	
	Feb 8	Hakeem's family speak out in press: https://www.sbs.com.au/news/release-him-immediately-hakeem-al-araibi-s-family-speak-out-as-bail-option-raised	
		Craig's planned meeting with Thai Ambassador to Australia called off 'due to unforeseen circumstances'.	
		Originally the final date for Bahrain to submit the extradition papers.	

Date		Event	Relevant to Red Notice
2019	**Feb 9**	Craig gets call from Australia's ambassador in Thailand indicating there could be a deal on the table soon.	
	Feb 10	Thailand foreign minister meets with Crown Prince Salman bin Hamad Al Khalifa; state-run Bahrain News Agency reports that PM Khalifa bin Salman Al Khalifa had a phone call with Thai PM Prayut Chan-o-cha, but offered no specifics.	
	Feb 11	Thailand attorney-general requests the case for Mr al-Araibi's extradition to Bahrain be dropped.	
		Bahrain responds with ambassador meeting and on Twitter.[13]	
	Feb 12	Hakeem returns to Australia! Lands at Melbourne airport around 1 pm.	
	Feb 14	Eighth anniversary of the mass protests in Bahrain during the 2011 Arab Spring uprisings.	
		Hakeem travels to Canberra and meets with Prime Minister Scott Morrison, Foreign Minister Marise Payne and many other Australian parliamentarians.	
	Feb 18	Hakeem attends first 'training session' at Pascoe Vale Football Club, Melbourne.[14]	
		Hakeem's case and issues concerning the Interpol red notice are addressed in detail during Senate Estimates sessions in the Australian Parliament.	
	Feb 22	Homecoming match at Pascoe Vale Football Club.	
	Feb 27	Hakeem publishes article in *The Guardian* thanking Australia and calling on international sporting bodies to step up and protect human rights.[15]	
	Mar 12	Hakeem becomes an Australian citizen at a citizenship ceremony in Melbourne. Foreign Minister Marise Payne attends and speaks.	
	Mar 14	Letter urging @FIFAcom to publish reasons deeming @theafcdotcom President Sheikh Salman eligible for election given litany of issues since (at least) 2011, specifically serious concerns regarding purported recusal day after submission of Al-Araibi extradition paperwork by Bahrain Government, 25 Jan.	

Date		Event	Relevant to Red Notice
2019	**Mar 17**	AFF reports that Australia joined unanimous support for candidacy of Sheikh Salman[16] to remain as AFC President for another term.[17]	
	Mar 28	Formula One races begin in Bahrain and human rights groups urge F1 management and champions like Lewis Hamilton to act over jailed Bahraini activist Najah Yusuf, who was imprisoned in 2018 after posting criticism of the Grand Prix and regime on Facebook.[18]	

ACRONYMS

AAA	Australian Athletes' Alliance
AAFC	Association of Australian Football Clubs
ACTU	Australian Council of Trade Unions
AFC	Asian Football Confederation
AFF	ASEAN Football Federation
AFP	Australian Federal Police
AOC	Australian Olympic Committee
APRRN	Asia Pacific Refugee Rights Network
BFA	Bahrain Football Association
BIRD	Bahrain Institute for Rights and Democracy
CSHR	Centre for Sport and Human Rights
DFAT	Department of Foreign Affairs and Trade
EPL	English Premier League
FFA	Football Federation Australia
FIFA	Fédération Internationale de Football Association (International Federation of Association Football)

FIFPro	Fédération Internationale des Associations de Footballeurs Professionnels (International Federation of Professional Footballers)
FV	Football Victoria
GIDHR	Gulf Institute for Democracy and Human Rights
HRAB	Human Rights Advisory Board
HRW	Human Rights Watch
IDC	Immigration Detention Centre
ILO	International Labour Organization
INTERPOL	The International Criminal Police Organization
IOC	International Olympic Committee
NCB	National Central Bureau (Australian INTERPOL contact point)
PFA	Professional Footballers Australia
PVFC	Pascoe Vale Football Club
SBS	Special Broadcasting Service
SRA	Sport and Rights Alliance
TFA	Thai Football Association
UAE	United Arab Emirates
UEFA	Union of European Football Associations
UNHCR	United Nations High Commissioner for Refugees
WPU	World Players United

GLOBAL FOOTBALL UNIONS AND HUMAN RIGHTS STRUCTURE

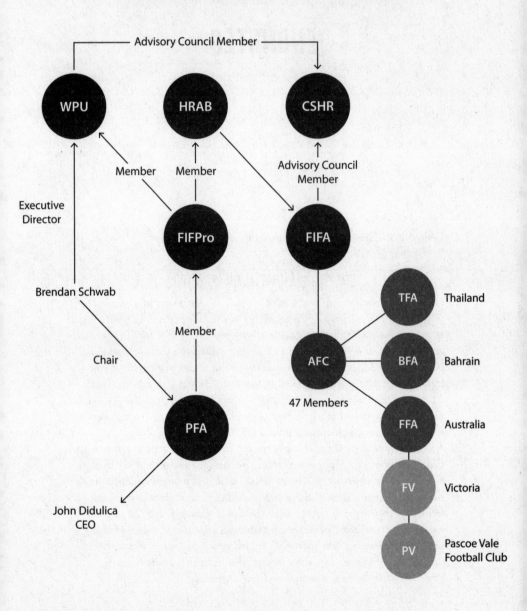

ENDNOTES

EPIGRAPHS

1 From theworldgame.sbs.com.au/some-of-the-best-of-les-murray
2 Translation by As'ad Abu Khalil

CHAPTER 1: A HONEYMOON ARRESTED

1 Hakeem was on Bridging Visa A (BVA), which is a temporary visa. According
to Australia's Department of Home Affairs website (https://archive.homeaffairs.
gov.au/trav/visi/visi/bridging-visas): 'It allows you to stay in Australia after your
current substantive visa ceases and while your substantive visa application is
being processed . . . A BVA does not allow you to return to Australia if you
leave.' Home Affairs typically finalises humanitarian visa applications within
12–18 months; however, their website notes that due to the current high numbers
of applications and a limited number of Special Humanitarian Programme places
it may take several years for applications to be decided.
2 A United Nations (UN) travel document is given to people seeking refuge when
they are officially recognised as a refugee by Australia under the 1951 Refugee
Convention. It acts as a replacement passport, so that refugees no longer have
to use the passport of the country that is seeking to harm them and are able
to exercise their right to travel freely. The words 'Convention of 28 July 1951'
are written on the front of Hakeem's document, and refer to the specific date
of the UN conference that approved the landmark Convention, which remains
the key legal document of today's international refugee protection regime.
https://www.passports.gov.au/travel-related-documents

3   An Interpol red notice is similar to an international arrest warrant. The international police organisation circulates red notices to its member countries listing people who are wanted for extradition by those same countries. The date Hakeem's red notice was issued by Interpol at Bahrain's request is visible on the red notice document, and was also confirmed by Australian Federal Police Commissioner Andrew Colvin in an Australian Parliament Senate Estimates Committee session on 18 February 2019: https://parlinfo.aph.gov.au/parlInfo/search/display/display.w3p;db=COMMITTEES;id=committees%2Festimate%2F3240c844-7e08-4975-85c1-34afe52a21d0%2F0002;query=Id%3A%22committees%2Festimate%2F3240c844-7e08-4975-85c1-34afe52a21d0%2F0000%22

4   There's little doubt that Les Murray has been one of the most influential contributors to the establishment of football in Australia as we know it today. Les came to Australia by boat with his family in 1957, when he was just 11 years old. His family was seeking refuge from a brutally oppressive communist regime in Hungary. He later changed his name from László Ürge to Les Murray, as many migrants do, to make it easier for his fellow Australians to pronounce. Not much was known about Les's childhood or refugee background until it was covered in the mainstream media back in 2017; *Dateline* and SBS captured his experience returning to Hungary in 2011, to track down the man who helped his family escape the communist country: https://www.sbs.com.au/news/dateline/my-refugee-journey-les-murray

CHAPTER 2: HAKEEM'S STORY

1   'The family of a Bahraini activist will remain in jail after their sentences were upheld', SBS News, 25 February 2019, https://www.sbs.com.au/news/the-family-of-a-bahraini-activist-will-remain-in-jail-after-their-sentences-were-upheld

2   Tony Thompson, 'Britain Silent on "Butcher of Bahrain"', *The Guardian*, 30 June 2002, https://www.theguardian.com/politics/2002/jun/30/uk.world

3   Human Rights Watch, 'World Report 1997 – Bahrain', 1 January 1997, https://www.refworld.org/docid/3ae6a8b414.html

4   Human Rights Watch, 'Routine Abuse, Routine Denial', June 1997, https://www.hrw.org/reports/1997/bahrain/

5   Simon Chadwick, 'Sport-washing, soft power and scrubbing the stains', APPS Policy forum, 24 August 2018, https://www.policyforum.net/sport-washing-soft-power-and-scrubbing-the-stains/

6   Cesar Jimenez-Martinez and Michael Skey, 'How repressive states and governments use "sportswashing" to remove stains on their reputation', *The Conversation*, 26 July 2018, https://theconversation.com/how-repressive-states-and-governments-use-sportswashing-to-remove-stains-on-their-reputation-100395

7   Gregor Brown, 'Bahrain-Merida: "The idea is to have a mega team in three years, like BMC or Sky"', *Cycling Weekly*, 7 January 2017, https://www.cyclingweekly.com/news/latest-news/bahrain-idea-mega-team-three-years-like-bmc-sky-305800

8   Karim Zidan, 'Sports diplomacy: Bahrain's martial arts venture
    distracts from human rights abuses', *Open Democracy*, 23 September
    2016, https://www.opendemocracy.net/en/north-africa-west-asia/
    fight-sports-diplomacy-bahrain-s-mma-venture-distracts-from-tension-human/

9   Ali Rabea, 'Sport and politics in Bahrain: A case study of the royal
    family Al-Khalifa's control of sports media', Master of Arts – Research
    thesis, School of the Arts, English and Media, University of Wollongong,
    2015. http://ro.uow.edu.au/theses/4834; David Conn, 'How Bahrain uses
    sport to whitewash a legacy of torture and human rights abuses', *The
    Guardian*, 17 July 2017, https://www.theguardian.com/sport/2017/jul/17/
    bahrain-accused-sport-whitewash-history-torture-human-rights-abuses

10 Ben Quinn, 'Royal Windsor Horse Show condemned for Bahraini sponsorship',
    The Guardian, 5 December 2018, https://www.theguardian.com/uk-news/2018/
    dec/04/royal-windsor-horse-show-condemned-for-bahrain-sponsorship-human-
    rights-abuses-complaint

11 Husain Abdulla, 'Bahrain's intolerant prince is now poster boy for regime
    whitewashing', *Middle East Eye*, 12 September 2018, https://www.middleeasteye.
    net/opinion/bahrains-intolerant-prince-now-poster-boy-regime-whitewashing;
    A photo of Prince Nasser attending the London Olympic Games in Summer
    2012, Source: Donny Mahoney, 'Bahraini Prince Who Allegedly Tortured His
    Country's Athletes DOES have Olympics Tickets', BALLS.ie, 31 July 2012,
    https://www.balls.ie/athletics/bahraini-prince-who-allegedly-tortured-his-countrys-
    athletes-does-have-olympics-tickets-55539

12 In October 2018, Bahrain was elected to the United Nation's Human Rights
    Council, despite human rights organisations globally highlighting extensive
    human rights abuses were being perpetuated by Bahrain's government:
    https://www.amnesty.org/download/Documents/MDE1100162019ENGLISH.pdf

13 UNESCO 1992–2019, 'Pearling, Testimony of an Island Economy', viewed 12
    July 2019: https://whc.unesco.org/en/list/1364

14 Karolak, M. (2017) 'Social Media and the Arab Spring in Bahrain: From
    Mobilization to Confrontation', in: Çakmak, C. (ed.) *The Arab Spring, Civil
    Society, and Innovative Activism*, Palgrave Macmillan, New YorK, 10 December
    2016, https://doi.org/10.1057/978–1-137–57177–9_5; Howard, Philip N. and
    Duffy, Aiden and Freelon, Deen and Hussain, M.M. and Mari, Will and Maziad,
    Marwa, 'Opening Closed Regimes: What Was the Role of Social Media During
    the Arab Spring?' 2011, https://ssrn.com/abstract=2595096

15 Ethan Bronner and Michael Slackman, 'Saudi Troops Enter Bahrain to Help
    Put Down Unrest', *The New York Times*, 14 March 2011, https://www.nytimes.
    com/2011/03/15/world/middleeast/15bahrain.html; BBC reporting at the time
    also included footage of the demonstrations and clashes between civilians and
    police: BBC Middle East, 'Gulf states send forces to Bahrain following protests',
    14 March 2011, https://www.bbc.com/news/world-middle-east-12729786

16 *Bahrain: Shouting in the Dark*, Al Jazeera, first aired 4 August 2011,
    https://www.youtube.com/watch?v=xaTKDMYOBOU

17 Bahrain Independent Commission of Inquiry, 'Report of the Independent
    Commission of Inquiry', presented in Manama, Bahrain on 23 November 2011,
    http://www.bici.org.bh/BICIreportEN.pdf

18 *The Times*, 'Bahrain's soccer stars tortured in custody', *The Australian*, 12 July
    2011, https://www.theaustralian.com.au/news/world/bahrains-soccer-stars-tortured-
    in-custody/news-story/874113e3e700b8cf161641ace767d0ae

19 Bahrain's state broadcaster Bahrain TV (BTV) broadcast footage of the
    pro-democracy demonstrations, publicly identifying and denouncing athletes
    that had participated in the events. Athletes' faces are circled and named,
    and the broadcasters discuss them as troublemakers and traitors. At the
    time of publication, clips from these programmes were still accessible online:
    https://www.youtube.com/watch?v=HXd6UQ5MAds; https://www.youtube.com/
    watch?v=F-SH9oqgl84

20 Bahrain Ministry of Information, 'Sheikh Nasser Issues Decision to Set Up
    Official Investigation Committee for Breaches of Some Belonging to Sports
    Movement', *Bahrain News Agency (BNA)*, 11 April 2011, http://www.bna.bh/
    portal/news/452380?date=2011–04–15

21 'Bahrain: Sheikh Nasser Appointed to top security post despite
    evidence of torture', Americans for Democracy and Human Rights
    in Bahrain, 4 October 2017, https://www.adhrb.org/2017/10/
    bahrain-sheikh-nasser-appointed-to-top-security-post-despite-evidence-of-torture/
    In April 2011 the Government of Bahrain published information about the
    committee, including its membership and stated goals:
    Bahrain News Agency , 15 April 2011, *BNA*, http://www.bna.bh/portal/
    news/452380?date=2011–04–15. See also http://www.bahrainrights.org/
    en/node/4374 and – https://www.theguardian.com/football/2015/oct/26/
    sheikh-salman-headed-committee-bahrain-protests?CMP=Share_iOSApp_Other

22 On 2 January 2014, the Bahrain Institute for Rights and Democracy (BIRD)
    submitted a letter to the Chair of the FIFA Ethics Committee, detailing gross
    human rights abuses against Bahraini footballers and the role of the Committee
    in targeting and punishing more than 150 athletes. On 3 November 2015,
    BIRD and Americans for Democracy and Human Rights in Bahrain (ADHRB)
    also jointly submitted a formal complaint to FIFA's Ethics, Electoral and Reform
    Committees regarding the candidature of Sheikh Salman for FIFA President,
    asking them to disqualify his candidacy on the grounds of breaching FIFA's
    Code of Ethics. These letters provide detailed evidence of the events in 2011
    and the actions taken by Bahrain's government officials under the leadership of
    Prince Nasser and Sheikh Salman. See: BIRD & ADHRB, 'Complaint Regarding
    Candidature of Sheikh Salman Bin Ebrahim Al Khalifa for President of the
    Fédération Internationale de Football Association (FIFA)', 3 November 2015.

23   Bahrain Ministry of Information, Bahrain News Agency, 20 April 2011, 'The Bahrain Football Association Downgrades Al Malkiyah and Al Shabab to Second Division and Issues Punishments to Suspended Clubs', viewed in – BIRD & ADHRB, 'Complaint Regarding Candidature of Sheikh Salman Bin Ebrahim Al Khalifa for President of the Fédération Internationale de Football Association (FIFA)', 3 November 2015.

24   BBC News, 'Prince Nasser of Bahrain torture ruling quashed', BBC News UK, October 2014: https://www.bbc.com/news/uk-29521420

25   'Hundreds of British Protest against King Hamad's attendance at Royal Windsor Horse Show', *Bahrain Mirror*, 14 May 2018, http://www.bahrainmirror.com/en/news/47064.html

26   'Athletes of Bahrain', *ESPN*, Reporter Jeremy Schaap, 8 November 2011: https://www.youtube.com/watch?v=wfhPWwhWlJU

27   James Montague, 'As F1 returns to Bahrain, footballers languish in jail', CNN, 6 June 2011, http://edition.cnn.com/2011/SPORT/football/06/05/football.bahrain.arrests.F1/

28   Nabeel Rajab, 'Don't Profit From Abuses by Bahrain', *The New York Times*, 17 May 2017, https://www.nytimes.com/2017/05/17/opinion/bahrain-human-rights-abuses-weapons.html; 'Bahrain: Five-year prison sentence over tweets upheld for Nabeel Rajab', Amnesty International, 31 December 2018, https://www.amnesty.org/en/latest/news/2018/12/bahrain-five-year-prison-sentence-over-tweets-upheld-for-nabeel-rajab/

29   Recorded footage of game against Busaiteen Club, including the live commentary and Bahrain national television branding, was uploaded online by the Bahrain Institute for Rights and Democracy (BIRD) on 12 December 2018. It clearly shows Hakeem played in the match and the game clock confirms the match lasted over 90 minutes. The footage was still viewable at the time of publication: https://www.youtube.com/watch?v=vXwLpHnou7s

30   An image of the official match sheet clearly shows Hakeem's name and identify number.

31   'Al Mahafdha: Member of the Board of Directors of BCHR under constant harassment by security measures at Bahrain Airport', Bahrain Center for Human Rights, 8 October 2011, http://www.bahrainrights.org/en/node/4744; 'Bahraini Human Rights Activist Arrested: Sayed Yousif Almuhafdah', Amnesty International, 5 November 2012 https://www.amnesty.org/en/documents/mde11/063/2012/en/

32   Nexis Uni news database https://www.lexisnexis.com/en-us/support/nexis-uni/default.page which compiles both online and print news sources from the Bahraini and international press – including the official Bahrain News Agency, produces no report of such an incident on that date. Likewise, the University of Maryland's Global Terrorism Database https://www.start.umd.edu/gtd/, which seeks to be comprehensive and accepts reports in the official press as sufficient

for inclusion in its dataset, includes no record of any violent incidents in Bahrain on that date.

33 A letter from Hakeem's club – al-Shabab – was provided to the authorities as further evidence that Hakeem could not have been physically present at the times indicated on the police reports and court documentation to commit the alleged offences.

34 https://www.theguardian.com/football/2015/oct/16/ sheikh-salman-al-khalifa-fifa-president-bahrain-human-rights

CHAPTER 3: EARLY DAYS

1 'Refugee footballer in Thailand denied flight back to Australia', SBS News, 1 December 2018 – last updated 3 December 2018, https://www.sbs.com.au/news/ refugee-footballer-in-thailand-denied-flight-back-to-australia

2 On 30 November 2018, Bahrain's embassy in Thailand sent two tweets from its official Twitter account stating: 'Referring to what has been circulated through social media about the detention of a Bahraini citizen in #Thailand' 'The Embassy states that the suspect is wanted for security cases with the Embassy is aware of. It adds that it is following up with relevant security authorities in this regard.' Phil Robertson from Human Rights Watch replied directly to this tweet on 1 December: 'Interpol Red Notices do NOT apply to recognized #refugees like Hakeem al-Araibi. @MFAThai should coordinate with @dfat & @Refugees to ensure that he is not forced back to #Bahrain to face imprisonment, & torture': Twitter, https://twitter.com/BahrainEmbTH/ status/1068765155096322048

3 Jasmine China, 'Detention Centres stuck in past century', *Bangkok Post*, 18 Feb 2018, https://www.bangkokpost.com/news/special-reports/1414047/ detention-centres-stuck-in-past-century

4 AAP, News Corp Australia Network, 'Aussie refugee soccer star Hakeem al-Araibi remains detained in Thailand', *Adelaide Advertiser*, 5 December 2018, https://www.adelaidenow.com.au/sport/football/aussie-refugee-soccer-star-hakeem-alaraibi-remains-detained-in-thailand/news-story/12f5551d3ad652d2673258270 4b9c281

5 Habeas corpus is a court order demanding that a public official deliver an imprisoned individual to the court and show a valid reason for that person's detention.

6 Ministry of Foreign Affairs of the Kingdom of Thailand, 'Press Release: the Case of Mr. Hakeem Ali Al Oraibi, a Bahraini national', 8 December 2018, http://www.mfa.go.th/main/en/news3/6886/97217

7 https://www.uniglobalunion.org/sites/default/files/imce/world_players_ udpr_1-page_0.pdf

8 Report 'Between a rock and a hard place', Amnesty International, 2017, https://www.amnesty.org/download/Documents/ASA3970312017ENGLISH.PDF

9   https://twitter.com/MinkysHighjinks/status/1070845631156109313;
     https://www.nytimes.com/2018/12/06/world/asia/bahrain-thailand-asylum-fifa.
     html; https://www.sbs.com.au/news/fifa-joins-fight-to-free-australian-refugee-
     footballer-held-in-thailand; https://www.abc.net.au/news/2018-12-07/
     thailand-process-extradition-request-for-refugee-soccer-player/10595828
10   http://www.ffa.com.au/news/support-mr-hakeem-al-araibis-safe-return-australia/

CHAPTER 4: A DEAFENING SILENCE

1   A full transcript of Brendan Schwab's address to the third annual
     Sporting Chance Forum can be found at: 'Centre for Uniglobal
     Union', 12 December 2018, https://www.uniglobalunion.org/news/
     centre-sport-and-human-rights-can-empower-people-affected-sport
2   FBI case of USA v Lai, 2017 investigated allegations of corruption, and
     specifically examined the support for Salman's candidacy for the AFC
     Presidency by Kuwaiti sport officials, who bribed President of the Guam
     Football Association, Richard Lai, and others in what the FBI described
     as a 'scheme to gain control of the AFC and influence FIFA': United States
     Attorney's Office Eastern District of New York, 'Fifa Audit And Compliance
     Committee Member Pleads Guilty To Corruption Charges – Defendant
     Accepted and Facilitated Bribes Within the Asian Football Confederation',
     27 April 2017, https://www.justice.gov/usao-edny/pr/fifa-audit-and-
     compliance-committee-member-pleads-guilty-corruption-charges; Graham
     Dunbar, 'FIFA audit official admits bribery in US federal probe', AP News,
     29 April 2017, https://apnews.com/fb9300df08f84aeaa7ea0156a2f46fad;
     see also https://www.sportsintegrityinitiative.com/
     renewed-allegations-put-pressure-on-sheikh-salman/
     https://www.sportsintegrityinitiative.com/
     interview-damian-collins-mp-sports-new-reformer/
     https://www.aljazeera.com/programmes/2011/08/201184144547798162.html
3   Excerpts from letter sent by Theo van Seggelen on 13 December 2018 and reply
     from Dato' Windsor John on 19 December 2018.
4   https://www.bna.bh/en/BFApresidentbacksShaikhSalmanbinIbrahimsreelectionbid.
     aspx?cms=q8FmFJgiscL2fwIzON1%2BDrvtJd23CNEabDxsZtsgjnc%3D
5   Letter from Fair Trials to Australian Minister for Home Affairs Peter Dutton, 12
     December 2018, https://www.fairtrials.org/sites/default/files/publication_pdf/Fair-
     Trials-Letter-Peter-Dutton-Hakeem-Al-Araibi.pdf
6   'Radha Stirling, British barristers & human rights groups call for Interpol
     safeguards to protect refugees like Hakeem Alaraibi', *My News Desk,* Press
     release, 23 January 2019, http://www.mynewsdesk.com/uk/stirling-och-partners/
     pressreleases/radha-stirling-british-barristers-and-human-rights-groups-call-for-
     interpol-safeguards-to-protect-refugees-like-hakeem-alaraibi-2827801

7   https://www.theguardian.com/world/2018/dec/06/bahrain-requested-arrest-of-refugee-before-he-arrived-in-thailand

CHAPTER 6: THE ASIAN CUP OF HUMAN RIGHTS

1   '"I was sure I'd die": UK football fan detained in UAE feared for his life', *The Guardian*, 16 February 2019, https://www.theguardian.com/world/2019/feb/15/i-was-sure-i-would-die-ali-issa-ahmad-uk-football-fan-detained-in-uae-feared-for-his-life

2   Sophie McBain, 'Social media, not the UN, saved Saudi woman Rahaf al-Qunun's life', *New Statesman America*, 9 January 2019, https://www.newstatesman.com/world/middle-east/2019/01/social-media-not-un-saved-saudi-woman-rahaf-al-qunun-s-life

3   David Conn, 'Bahrain-Merida cycling team being used to "sportswash", campaigners say', *The Guardian*, 3 July 2019, https://www.theguardian.com/sport/2019/jul/03/bahrain-merida-cycling-team-being-used-to-sportswash-campaigners-say

4   Excerpt from FIFPro's statement on 16 January 2019 that publicly supported the #SaveHakeem campaign and called on FIFA's Human Rights Advisory Board to investigate if FIFA's policies had been breached: Accessed 02/09/2019 https://fifpro.org/news/savehakeem/en/

5   The WPA, FIFPro and PFA provided a detailed submission on Hakeem's case to FIFA's Human Rights Advisory Board entitled 'Urgent Request for Special Procedure Into The Severe Violation of The Human Rights of Football Player Hakeem Mohamed Ali Al-Araibi'. The submission provided detailed background information and evidence in support of Hakeem's case, analysed FIFA's responsibilities under its own statutes and human rights policies, and requested that the Advisory Board become a key player in helping to bring about Hakeem's safe return to Australia. The undersigned organisations explicitly called on FIFA to: 1. **review** the conduct (or lack thereof) of FIFA, confederations, member associations, bodies, officials and other relevant parties in terms of the advancement of the essential outcome; 2. **assess** that conduct (or lack thereof) considering FIFA's regulatory obligations and human rights commitments; 3. **define** the most effective strategy to realise the essential outcome including by reference to FIFA's regulatory obligations and human rights commitments; and 4. **monitor and report** publicly on these steps.

6   Excerpt from FIFA's Human Rights Advisory Board (HRAB) letter dated 20 January 2019 to FIFA that included seven key recommendations. These outlined the need for FIFA to step up the actions it was taking in order to meet its human rights responsibilities given Hakeem's status as a professional player operating within the system and governance framework overseen by FIFA, and his case's linkages to several of FIFA's member associations, as well as the Asian Football Confederation. The recommendations were published in May 2019 within The Third Report by the FIFA Human Rights Advisory Board Oct 2018 – April 2019: Accessed

02/09/2019 https://www.business-humanrights.org/sites/default/files/FIFA%20
Human%20Rights%20Advisory%20Board%20Third-report_June%202019.pdf

CHAPTER 7: BANGKOK

1   Post from Chiang Rai United FC coach Miti Tiyapairat on the club's official
    Facebook page, including a photo of the team with a #SaveHakeem banner:
    https://www.facebook.com/MitiTiyapairat/posts/savehakeem/2100148356749172/

2   Amnesty International Thailand Twitter Feed, '#SaveHakeem campaign
    at Thailand Champion Cup 2019 by Football fans and players from
    Chiangrai United during the match between Buriram United vs Singha Chiangrai
    United. Kick-off at 19.00 on 2 February 2019 at Royal Thai Army
    Stadium, Bangkok', 2 February 2019: https://twitter.com/AmnestyThailand/
    status/1091674398526910464

3   Dubravka Voloder, 'Privileged, unpredictable and "a bit of a Don Juan" – who
    is the new Thai king?', SBS News, 6 May 2019, https://www.sbs.com.au/news/
    privileged-unpredictable-and-a-bit-of-a-don-juan-who-is-the-new-thai-king

4   See *Penn State Journal of Law & International Affairs*, April 2012,
    https://elibrary.law.psu.edu/cgi/viewcontent.cgi?article=1009&context=jlia; *TIME*
    article, http://content.time.com/time/world/article/0,8599,1969920,00.html

5   Paul Sanderson, 'Stuck between two kings: a possible explanation for Hakeem
    al-Araibi's detention', *Sydney Morning Herald*, 4 May 2019, https://www.smh.
    com.au/world/asia/two-kings-a-billion-euros-and-an-australian-trapped-in-
    thailand-20190314-p5146l.html

6   In Australian Parliament Senate Estimates Committee session on 18 February
    2019, Deputy AFP Commissioner Ramzi Jabbour confirmed that 'It is highly
    unlikely that [Interpol] would have issued the red notice . . . 'had they been
    in possession of all of the facts, which include that Mr al-Araibi had been
    accepted as a refugee by Australia on the basis of persecution in Bahrain' –
    https://parlinfo.aph.gov.au/parlInfo/search/display/display.w3p;db=COMMI
    TTEES;id=committees%2Festimate%2F3240c844–7e08–4975–85c1–34afe5
    2a21d0%2F0002;query=Id%3A%22committees%2Festimate%2F3240c84
    4–7e08–4975–85c1–34afe52a21d0%2F0000%22

7   Document obtained via Freedom of Information Request, *Email to IP Bangkok,
    IP Bahrain, Advise of Travel Movements (Log No.11)*, sent Tuesday 27
    November 2018 2:15 PM from Interpol Canberra: 'INTERPOL Canberra
    takes this opportunity to attend its compliments to INTERPOL Bangkok and
    INTERPOL Bahrain. Please be informed the above mentioned subject is due to
    depart Australia at 3.05pm today, 27 November 2018.'

8   Helen Davidson, 'Bahrain requested arrest of refugee before he arrived in Thailand',
    The Guardian, 6 December 2018, https://www.theguardian.com/world/2018/
    dec/06/bahrain-requested-arrest-of-refugee-before-he-arrived-in-thailand

9 Document obtained via Freedom of Information Request, *Email from INTERPOL Canberra to Office of Legal Affairs – INTERPOL General Secretariat*, 30 November 2018 8:17 AM: 'Please be advised that our Bureau is currently conducting urgent enquiries with the relevant Australian authorities to confirm the refugee status of MR ALARAIBI.'

10 Document obtained via Freedom of Information Request, *Email from INTERPOL Canberra to Office of Legal Affairs – INTERPOL General Secretariat*, 30 November 2018 3:03 PM, 'the Australia Department of Home Affairs has confirmed Mr ALARAIBI was granted an Australian permanent protection [redaction] visa [redaction] and remains the holder of that visa.'

CHAPTER 8: FIFA HOUSE

1 https://www.scmp.com/sport/football/article/2183905/save-hakeem-afc-inept-and-naive-think-conflict-interest-absolves-al

2 The statement was sent to journalists and then tweeted online: Henry Belot, ABC Federal Politics reporter – https://twitter.com/Henry_Belot/status/1090179540129730560

3 AFC's statement, 29 January 2019, http://www.the-afc.com/afc/documents/PdfFiles/he-pm-of-thailand-hakeem-al-araibi; FIFA's statement, 29 January, https://www.fifa.com/about-fifa/who-we-are/news/fifa-holds-meeting-on-situation-of-player-al-araibi-and-calls-for-urgent-solution

CHAPTER 9: AMSTERDAM – GENEVA – SYDNEY

1 Dan Andrews Twitter message, 31 January 2019: 'I sent this note to Hakeem, to let him know that all Victorians are standing with him. Stay strong, mate. We will get you home. And we'll look forward to seeing you out on the field again very soon,' https://twitter.com/DanielAndrewsMP/status/1090863060829462528

CHAPTER 10: PEOPLE POWER

1 The main campaign Hashtags used included: #savehakeem #hakeemalaraibi #freehakeem #thailand #boycottthailand

2 Tweet https://twitter.com/Jo_Soucek/status/1093359933075017728

3 'Amnesty International calls for Thailand to release Australian refugee footballer wanted in Bahrain', ABC News, 5 December 2018, https://www.abc.net.au/news/2018-12-04/amnesty-international-calls-for-release-australian-refugee/10582628

4 Valeria Paulet, 'Evidentiary challenges in universal jurisdiction cases', Universal Jurisdiction Annual Review 2019, *Trial International*, https://reliefweb.int/sites/reliefweb.int/files/resources/TrialInternational_UJAR5_FINAL_DIGITAL.pdf

5 'Paul Pogba train selfie story helps to spread word on Hakeem al-Araibi with jailed refugee footballer "losing hope"', *South China Morning Post*, 23 January

2019, https://today.line.me/id/pc/article/Paul+Pogba+train+selfie+story+helps+to+spread+word+on+Hakeem+al+Araibi+with+jailed+refugee+footballer+losing+hope-qQzJ7x

6 A troll farm is an entity set up by organisations and even governments, whose employees or members attempt to create conflict and disruption in an online community by posting deliberately inflammatory or provocative comments. The entity acts as an organised group e.g. Twitter users, and is commonly used to push a particular political or social agenda and/or disrupt the effectiveness of another online campaign or agenda.

7 Peter Beaumont, 'The truth about Twitter, Facebook and the uprisings in the Arab World', *The Guardian*, 25 February 2011, https://www.theguardian.com/world/2011/feb/25/twitter-facebook-uprisings-arab-libya; Carol Huang, 'Facebook and Twitter key to Arab Spring uprisings: report' *The National*, 6 June 2011, https://www.thenational.ae/uae/facebook-and-twitter-key-to-arab-spring-uprisings-report-1.428773

8 Suchit Leesa-Nguansuk, 'Thailand makes top 10 in social media use', *Bangkok Post*, 1 March 2018, https://www.bangkokpost.com/tech/local-news/1420086/thailand-makes-top-10-in-social-media-use

9 'Number of Twitter users in Thailand from 2014 to 2019', Statista, https://www.statista.com/statistics/490584/twitter-users-thailand/

10 Wasamon Audjarint, 'A mum keeps the faith in a democratic Thailand', *The Nation Thailand*, 24 February 2018, http://www.nationmultimedia.com/detail/politics/30339617

CHAPTER 11: SHACKLES

1 Twitter campaign heatmaps show the size and scale of the campaign: https://twitter.com/TwitterSportsAU/status/1095082597267300352 https://twitter.com/TwitterSportsAU/status/1093334862071656449

2 Tweet https://twitter.com/NuttaaBow/status/1092667058523758593

3 Ben Lucky, 'Thai Airways reports huge 2018 losses', One Mile at a Time, 3 March 2019, https://onemileatatime.com/thai-airways-losing-money/Chayut Setboonsarng; Panu Wongcha-um, 'Headwinds before takeoff for new Thai Airways team', *Reuters*, 18 September 2018, https://www.reuters.com/article/us-thai-airways-strategy-focus/headwinds-before-takeoff-for-new-thai-airways-team-idUSKCN1LY0C2

4 https://www.bangkokpost.com/thailand/general/1624102/araibi-has-new-ally-in-twitter

5 'HRH Crown Prince receives the Minister of Foreign Affairs of Thailand', Bahrain News Agency, 10 February 2019, https://www.bna.bh/en/HRHCrownPrincereceivestheMinisterofForeignAffairsofThailand.aspx?cms=q8FmFJgiscL2fwIzON1%2BDhf6xYXQdCgooLiFEXsJFdg%3D; 'Bahrain values Thai ties, says FM', *Bangkok Post*, 13 February

2019, https://www.bangkokpost.com/news/general/1628178/
bahrain-values-thai-ties-says-fm

CHAPTER 12: FREEDOM

1 Tweet https://twitter.com/ScottMorrisonMP/status/1095080444922449920
2 'Bahrain drops extradition request for "terrified" refugee soccer player Hakeem
   al-Araibi', CBS News, 11 February 2019, https://www.cbsnews.com/news/
   bahrain-hakeem-al-araibi-extradition-soccer-refugee-free-thailand-australia/
3 Paul Sanderson, 'Stuck between two kings: a possible explanation for Hakeem
   al-Araibi's detention', *Sydney Morning Herald*, 4 May 2019, https://www.smh.
   com.au/world/asia/two-kings-a-billion-euros-and-an-australian-trapped-in-thai-
   land-20190314-p5146l.html.
4 Refer earlier note – Twitter heatmap – https://twitter.com/TwitterSportsAU/
   status/1095082597267300352

CHAPTER 13: DEAR SCOTT AND BILL

1 Craig Foster, 'Dear Scott and Bill, we've strayed from our values: a Socceroo's
   plea', *Sydney Morning Herald*, 22 February 2019, https://www.smh.com.au/
   national/dear-scott-and-bill-we-ve-strayed-from-our-values-a-socceroo-s-plea-
   20190221-p50zbm.html
2 https://twitter.com/AFFPresse/status/1107168828436283392
3 Sean Ingle, 'F1 finally admits concern over woman jailed for Bahrain Grand
   Prix protests', *The Guardian*, 15 November 2018, https://www.theguardian.
   com/sport/2018/nov/14/f1-woman-jailed-bahrain-grand-prix-protests; Paul
   Scriven, 'Bahrain Grand Prix: The shocking imprisonment of Najah Yusuf shows
   why F1 has a huge role to play in fighting human rights abuses', *Independent*,
   29 March 2019, https://www.independent.co.uk/sport/motor-racing/formula1/
   bahrain-grand-prix-2019-who-is-najah-yusuf-imprisoned-f1-protests-human-
   rights-abuses-a8845151.html

TIMELINE

1 Australia Government, Department of Immigration and Border Protection,
   'Notification of grant of a Protection (subclass 866) visa', Letter to Hakeem Ali
   Mohamed Ali ALARAIBI, 1 December 2019.
2 Ministry of Foreign Affairs Thailand, 'Press Release: The Case of Mr. Hakeem
   Ali Mohamed Ali Al Oraibi, a Bahraini national', 8 December 2018 16:29:37
   / Updated 8 December, 2018 19:26:10 http://www.mfa.go.th/main/en/
   news3/6886/97217
3 Minister for Foreign Affairs the Hon. Marise Payne, Media Release, 'Detention
   of Hakeem Ali Alaraibi in Thailand,' 9 December 2018, https://foreignminister.
   gov.au/releases/Pages/2018/mp_mr_181209.aspx

4   'Thailand signals more tolerant refugee policy after Saudi case', *The Nation Thailand*, 17 January 2019, https://www.nationthailand.com/breakingnews/30362429

5   Helen Davidson, 'Hakeem al-Araibi: Bahrain says refugee footballer's life is not in danger', *The Guardian*, 18 January 2019, https://www.theguardian.com/world/2019/jan/18/hakeem-al-araibi-bahrain-says-refugee-footballers-life-is-not-in-danger

6   Post from Chiang Rai United FC coach Miti Tiyapairat on the club's official Facebook page, including a photo of the team with a #SaveHakeem banner: https://www.facebook.com/MitiTiyapairat/posts/savehakeem/2100148356749172/; 'Thai football team urges Hakeem Al-Araibi's release', SBS News, 28 January 2019, https://www.sbs.com.au/news/thai-football-team-urges-hakeem-al-araibi-s-release

7   Hannah Beech, 'Soccer Player's Detention Poses "Historic Test" for Global Sports', *The New York Times*, 31 January 2019, https://www.nytimes.com/2019/01/31/world/asia/bahrain-soccer-thailand-fifa.html

8   Amnesty International Thailand Twitter Feed, '#SaveHakeem campaign at Thailand Champion Cup 2019 by Football fans and players from Chiangrai United during the match between Buriram United vs Singha Chiangrai United. Kick-off at 19.00 on 2 February 2019 at Royal Thai Army Stadium, Bangkok.' 2 February 2019, https://twitter.com/AmnestyThailand/status/1091674398526910464

9   'Australian Ambassador to Thailand Statement Regarding the Detention of Hakeem Al-Araibi', 4 February 2019, https://thailand.embassy.gov.au/bkok/Australian_Ambassador_to_Thailand_Statement_Regarding_the_Detention_of_Hakeem_Al-Araibi.html

10 Minister for Foreign Affairs the Hon Marise Payne, Media release, 'Hakeem Alaraibi', 5 February 2019, https://foreignminister.gov.au/releases/Pages/2019/mp_mr_190205.aspx?w=E6pq%2FUhzOs%2BE7V9FFYi1xQ%3D%3D

11 Ministry Foreign Affairs Thailand, 'Press Release: Ministry of Foreign Affairs, Statement on the Australian-Bahraini Issue concerning Mr. Hakeem Al Araibi', 5 February 2019 23:56:15, Updated 6 February 2019 13:23:30, http://www.mfa.go.th/main/en/news3/6886/99433

12 Helen Davidson, 'Morrison writes to Thai PM after "disturbed" to see Hakeem al-Araibi in shackles', *The Guardian*, 6 February 2019, https://www.theguardian.com/sport/2019/feb/05/australia-urges-thailand-to-use-its-powers-to-free-hakeem-al-araibi

13 http://bahrainmirror.com/en/news/53230.html?utm_source=dlvr.it&utm_medium=twitter

14 https://twitter.com/SBSNews/status/1097428006006472704

15 Hakeem al-Araibi, 'Hakeem al-Araibi: thank you Australia for bringing me home – but my fight is not over', *The Guardian*, 27 February 2019,